Documenting Results

RESEARCH ON PROBLEM-SOLVING JUSTICE

EDITED BY GREG BERMAN, MICHAEL REMPEL, AND ROBERT V. WOLF

CENTER FOR COURT INNOVATION
NEW YORK, NEW YORK

Published by the Center for Court Innovation. Printed in the United States of America

First Edition

Library of Congress Control Number: 2006937520

ISBN: 0-9759505-1-7

Contents

Acknowledgements

The Center for Court Innovation is the product of a unique public-private partnership between the New York State Unified Court System and the Fund for the City of New York. This partnership would not be possible without the vision, leadership and ongoing support of New York State Chief Judge Judith S. Kaye, New York State Chief Administrative Judge Jonathan Lippman, and Fund for the City of New York President Mary McCormick. Nor would it be possible without the vision of the Center for Court Innovation's founding director, John Feinblatt.

The essays contained in this collection were underwritten by a range of funding sources including the Bureau of Justice Assistance of the Office of Justice Programs at the U.S. Department of Justice (Chapters 1, 2, 3, 4, 7, 9 and 12), the Office on Violence Against Women of the Office of Justice Programs at the U.S. Department of Justice (Chapter 5), the National Institute of Justice at the U.S. Department of Justice (Chapter 6), the New York State Unified Court System (Chapters 8 and 10), the New York State Office of Mental Health (Chapter 11), and the California Administrative Office of the Courts (Chapter 13).

Thanks to both past and present research staff at the Center for Court Innovation for their many insights and contributions. Special thanks to Amanda Cissner and Carolyn Turgeon for their keen-eyed proofreading.

The publication of this book was underwritten by the New York State Office of Court Administration and the Bureau of

Justice Assistance, Office of Justice Programs, U.S. Department of Justice. Special thanks to the U.S. Congress and the members of the New York delegation for their support of the Center for Court Innovation.

Opinions expressed in this book reflect those of the authors and not necessarily those of funders.

Introduction

GREG BERMAN

The Center for Court Innovation has spent more than a decade creating demonstration projects that test new solutions to difficult problems like drug addiction, mental illness and neighborhood disorder. Developed and implemented with the active support of the New York State court system, these demonstration projects range from large-scale reform efforts like the Red Hook Community Justice Center that handle thousands of cases each year to smaller experiments like the Brooklyn Mental Health Court that work intensively with less than a hundred offenders at a time.

Just testing new ideas is not enough, of course. At the Center, we are committed not just to innovation but to reflection as well. We use rigorous research to measure the effectiveness of new programs—both our own experiments and the experiments of others. Researchers at the Center for Court Innovation are responsible for taking a close look at reform efforts, asking what works, what doesn't, and why.

Does linking addicted offenders to substance abuse treatment instead of incarceration reduce recidivism? Do batterer programs reduce re-offending? What do defendants think about how they are treated in criminal court? Does treatment coupled with judicial monitoring make a difference in the lives of mentally-ill offenders? Is it possible to improve perceptions of public safety in crime-plagued neighborhoods?

The answers to these questions, and more, can be found here in *Documenting Results.* We had two goals in mind as we began putting this book together. First, by compiling some of the "greatest hits" of the Center for Court Innovation's research department in a single volume, we've sought to document a remarkable era of judicial innovation in New York State. Under the leadership of Chief Judge Judith S. Kaye and Chief Administrative Judge Jonathan Lippman, New York has defined the cutting edge of court reform—both nationally and internationally. New York was the first state to pioneer community courts, which attempt to improve the judicial response to low-level, quality-of-life crime. New York was also among the first states to commit to the wide scale replication of specialized drug courts that attempt to halt the revolving doors of drugs, crime and jail. More recently, New York has attempted to spread the idea of "problem-solving justice"—the idea that courts should seek to improve the results they achieve for litigants, victims and neighborhoods rather than simply processing cases—to every corner of a geographically and politically diverse state.

This book offers testimony to both the successes and challenges of these efforts. In the process, *Documenting Results* tells the story of a court system grappling with serious problems in a thoughtful, creative fashion. By telling this story through research findings, we implicitly seek to highlight the value of empirical data, as well as the New York court system's ongoing commitment to rigorous self-analysis.

Indeed, problem-solving justice is, by its very nature, reflective. Research and evaluation are an intrinsic part of the problem-solving model. New York's problem-solving courts seek to give judges more information with which to make decisions in individual cases. The goal is to identify the problem, learn its causes and effects, act to alleviate the problem, and then determine whether the solution worked. In other words, New York's commitment to problem-solving justice and research and evaluation go hand in hand.

Our second goal in publishing this book is to help bridge the gap that often exists between researchers and practitioners/policymakers. Our experience has been that there is a great hunger on both sides of the fence for better dialogue. It would be difficult to count how many conversations among criminal justice officials end with the cry, "I wish we had better data." It is probably roughly equal to the number of conversations among researchers that end with someone saying, "Why won't policymakers listen to us?"

Creating meaningful connections among researchers, practitioners and policymakers is part of what we do at the Center for Court Innovation. In performing this work, we've learned a few lessons. It is worth taking a moment to draw out these lessons here, since they inform much of the writing contained in this book.

The Importance of Modesty

Sociologist Peter Rossi once wrote: "The expected value for any measured effect of a social program is zero." Those of us who work to implement criminal justice innovations need to remember this rule. Nothing poisons the relationship between researchers and practitioners quite like programs that disseminate inflated, self-reported numbers. We've all seen them: the recidivism statistics that are simply too good to be true, the cost-savings numbers that don't add up, the retention rates that are based on misleading information or faulty assumptions.

The reality is that criminal offenders are not an easy population to change. They bring lots of problems with them in addition to criminal behavior: drug addiction, homelessness, mental illness, and joblessness, to name just a few. Anyone who works directly with offenders to try to change their behavior will tell you that one of the overriding characteristics of their work is failure. Even drug courts, which are arguably one of the most successful criminal justice interventions of the past generation, fail nearly as often as they succeed: the evidence suggests that close to half of drug court participants won't make it to graduation let alone experience positive post-program impacts.

Of course, innovation doesn't happen in a vacuum and it usually doesn't happen without seed money either. The pressure to over-promise and over-sell—to funders, to elected officials, to the media—in order to generate the political momentum necessary to launch any new initiative is enormous. Innovators must resist this temptation, and to do so they need the help of researchers, who can help make the case that achievements—seemingly small but statistically significant improvements in recidivism, marginal reductions in street crime, etc.—that may seem modest to the general public are, in fact, meaningful. By cataloging a broad range of program impacts beyond simply looking at crime rates, *Documenting Results* is a small step in this direction.

The Standard Can't Always Be Gold

One of the enduring frustrations of policymakers is the difficulty of measuring much of what happens in the world of criminal justice. The recent reduction in crime in New York City is one of the most important criminal justice achievements of the past generation. How did it happen? Was it COMPSTAT, the New York Police Department's computer information system? Or was it the decision to double the size of the police force in the early 1990s? Or maybe it was the city's decision, under both Mayor Rudy Giuliani and Mayor Michael Bloomberg, to crack down on quality-of-life offending? Or the increased use of incarceration which left many would-be offenders incapacitated? Or perhaps the booming economy that improved the fortunes of so many New Yorkers? Or some combination of all of the above?

It is nearly impossible to get a clear answer from the academic community. One reason for this, of course, is that criminal justice initiatives do not tend to take place in controlled environments. Randomized trials (the so-called gold standard of research) are few and far between in the world of criminal justice. There is an organization called the Coalition for Evidence-Based Policy working to correct this problem, and researchers and practitioners should come together to promote the use of (and funding for) scientifically rigorous evidence whenever feasible.

But even as we attempt to encourage more experimental studies, we should acknowledge that there are often good reasons (including ethical and legal ones) not to conduct randomized trials. And we should also acknowledge that randomized trials are not the only kinds of studies that have value. We can learn a lot from other types of research (most notably, from quasi-experimental studies) as long as it is conducted in a rigorous way by talented investigators.

Documenting Results contains findings from a randomized trial. It also contains findings from quasi-experiments, process evaluations, focus groups, structured interviews, court observations, and neighborhood surveys. In the process, we hope to offer evidence that there are many legitimate and valuable forms of information gathering.

When Do We Know Enough?

Caveats and conditional judgements are occupational hazards for many researchers—very few make the kind of simple, categorical statements that policymakers, who typically only want to know if something works or not, crave.

Policymakers must learn to forgive researchers for this. They must accept that often there is no silver bullet and that in many cases it may not be possible to isolate the cause of a change in public safety or offender behavior, for better or for worse. And they must understand that "we don't know" doesn't mean "it doesn't work."

On the other side, if they hope to have any voice at all in policy decisions, researchers must be more willing to be reductive and to venture educated guesses, even in the absence of rigorously drawn control groups. When do we know enough about the success of a model to say that a larger public investment is worth making? This question is particularly important when times are tight and budgets are shrinking. Often, policymakers are faced with the need to choose among two or more innovations. Which should be supported and which should be shut down? Without data, it is difficult for policymakers to make informed decisions. Researchers can help guide government officials by articulating interim measures and preliminary indicators of positive outcomes.

Failure Must Be Celebrated (Or At Least Publicly Discussed)

It is impossible to have trial without error—not every new idea is a good one.

Unfortunately, it is human nature to shout about our successes while discussing our failures in hushed whispers—if at all. In order to encourage innovative thinking, we need to create a climate where failure is openly discussed and dissected. While there is plenty of discussion, particularly in the media, about errors of corruption and gross incompetence, precious little attention is paid to situations where smart, decent, well-intentioned people try to achieve something difficult and fall short of their objectives for whatever reason.

While no non-profit group or government agency can survive for long on a steady diet of failure, it is also true that every organization has had projects that have fizzled or failed to meet expectations. It is also true that failure is rarely complete. We need to learn from our partial failures (and our partial successes), examining whether an initiative works for some groups but not for others, or figuring out what was wrong with the underlying assumptions that led us to try that approach.

For example, supported work for ex-offenders was seen as an initiative that didn't work for years—until a re-analysis showed that employment programs reduced recidivism for older offenders (those who were ready to work to change their lives) but not for younger ones. This kind of learning process isn't possible without a broad dissemination of research findings, particularly from process evaluations like the ones found in *Documenting Results*, which can help encourage a more honest conversation about criminal justice reform and its challenges.

Context Matters

Two contexts are particularly important when it comes to evaluating criminal justice innovations. The first is the reality of how our criminal justice system actually works. For example, overwhelming caseloads, masses of defendants with complicated social problems (e.g., addiction, mental illness, homelessness), a reliance on plea-bargaining just to get through the daily calendar: this is the reality for many criminal courts, particularly in urban areas. In assessing court reform efforts, it is crucial to look at the context from which they have emerged rather than some idealized notion of how courts operate. The relevant question is not just "What has the innovation in question achieved?" but "How does that record compare to business as usual?"

The second context to remember is the general consensus, in the years following the publication of Robert Martinson's seminal article about prison rehabilitation programs in *The Public Interest* in 1974, that "nothing works." While Martinson's conclusions have subsequently been amended and debunked by a number of scholars, the reality is that there are indeed plenty of criminal justice initiatives that can muster precious little evidence of effectiveness. These include boot camps, midnight basketball, scared straight programs, and initiatives to prosecute children as adults.

Thankfully, this book offers compelling evidence to refute the notion that nothing works. While it is by no means all sunshine and daisies—included in this volume, for example, are reports of domestic violence offenders who continue to abuse their partners and ex-offenders who have trouble staying sober and out of trouble—*Documenting Results* does make the case that it is possible to change the behavior of offenders, improve procedural fairness, enhance public trust in justice, reduce levels of neighborhood fear, and eliminate gaps in communication among criminal justice agencies. These are truly results worth documenting.

The research in this book is organized into four sections. The first looks at drug courts, the oldest and most widely implemented form of problem-solving justice. We begin by summarizing the current drug court literature, framing a set of questions that still need to be answered about even these well-documented innovations. We go on to compare the perceptions of drug court staff and participants, and explain the basics of "action research" before taking a closer look at a drug court in Staten Island that has shown success in reducing substance abuse among participants.

The second section of *Documenting Results* focuses on domestic violence, including a comparative analysis of domestic violence courts in New York City, a process evaluation of an experimental effort to combat teen dating violence, and the findings from an experimental study in the Bronx that examined the impact of judicial monitoring and batterer programs on the behavior of domestic violence offenders.

The third section of this book is devoted to community courts. In addition to a literature review that documents the current state of the research in the field, we include a look at how one neighborhood perceives its community courts as well as new research that examines defendant perceptions of fairness at the Red Hook Community Justice Center.

We conclude *Documenting Results* by looking at other problem-solving experiments, including a mental health court in Brooklyn and a reentry court in Harlem. We also take note of efforts to uncouple problem solving from court specialization, asking what kinds of principles and practices can be transferred from problem-solving pilot projects to the rest of state courts.

Drug Courts

Since the first one opened in 1989, drug courts have flourished, approaching 1,600 programs nationwide as of September 2006. Drug courts began with modest ambitions, embracing goals concerned primarily with improved case processing and better predisposition monitoring of the country's escalating number of drug defendants. To achieve these goals, it made practical sense to route defendants charged with drug-related crimes to a single specialized docket, rather than have them spread throughout the courthouse. By the mid-1990s, drug courts adopted a far more expansive agenda focused on rehabilitating lives shattered by addiction and increasing public safety by achieving meaningful reductions in recidivism.

Many believe that treatment is the key innovation behind drug courts, but it isn't. After all, criminal courts do have a fairly long tradition of mandating defendants to substance abuse treatment of one form or another. More unique is everything else about drug courts, the judicial element in particular—frequent status hearings before a judge trained in the pharmacology of addiction; direct conversational interaction between judge and defendant; intermediate sanctions and rewards in response to behavior (replacing the typical practice of sentencing defendants to jail upon a first or second violation); and active involvement by a team of case managers responsible for drug testing and linking defendants to appropriate treatment programs.

Does the approach work? Of the several dozen evaluations of drug courts completed in the 1990s, most reported positive effects on recidivism. Yet, many of these evaluations were criticized for failing to compare drug court participants with a matched comparison group of similar defendants and for measuring recidivism over extremely short time frames, usually one or two years after the initial arrest.

Then in the early 2000s, the research outlook changed dramatically as a series of rigorous studies emerged, nearly all of which reported significant recidivism reductions. Among these studies was a statewide evaluation of New York's drug courts, completed by the Center for Court Innovation in 2003. It demonstrated significant recidivism reductions in each of six drug court sites, extending to three years after the initial arrest. Another particularly influential study was a randomized trial of the Baltimore City Treatment Court. It also demonstrated significant recidivism reductions over a three-year measurement period. Indicating the emergence of a new consensus, a number of literature reviews and commentaries published in the early 2000s agreed that drug courts generally produce significant reductions in recidivism.

The foregoing discussion sets the stage for the chapters that follow. Amanda B. Cissner and Michael Rempel provide a review of the drug court literature, written for researchers and practitioners alike. The review begins by detailing the impact of drug courts on recidivism, drug use, cost savings, and other outcomes. This chapter goes on to consider a series of second-generation research questions focused less on whether drug courts work and more on how, why, and for whom. In particular, Cissner and Rempel examine which of the many elements of the drug court model are truly critical to success, which may be less important, and which elements need to be investigated in future research.

Continuing to look beyond bottom-line program impacts, in Chapter Two Donald J. Farole Jr. and Amanda B. Cissner explore drug court participant and staff perspectives, reporting the results of separate focus groups conducted in three New York State drug courts. The groups were designed to tease out how participants perceive various aspects of the drug court experience, especially the role of the judge. Practitioners will be particularly interested to learn which factors motivate participants to comply and to what extent participants and staff see eye to eye.

In Chapter Three, Kelly O'Keefe and Michael Rempel evaluate the Staten Island Treatment Court, a program in the least populous borough of New York City. The evaluation examines how the program evolved, from planning to implementation, and reports on a series of performance measures, including drug test results, intermediate sanctions, and program retention rates. The evaluation also includes a quasi-experimental impact study of the court's effects on recidivism.

Chapter Four is the only one in this volume not grounded in a substantive research project. In it, Michael Rempel describes the action research model, a way for drug court practitioners to engage in ongoing performance monitoring, even without the benefits of technical evaluation expertise. The chapter describes in lay terms the philosophy of action research, elementary data collection principles, and five critical types of performance indicators for monitoring adult drug courts.

CHAPTER ONE

The State of Drug Court Research: Moving Beyond 'Do They Work?'

AMANDA B. CISSNER AND MICHAEL REMPEL

When the Miami Drug Court opened its doors in Florida in 1989, it launched a dramatic shift in how courts respond to the criminal behavior of drug-addicted defendants. By combining treatment with close judicial supervision, the drug court model offered a new alternative to the unproductive and costly cycle of addiction, crime, and incarceration. Unlike conventional courts, the success of drug courts is measured not by how quickly they process cases, how many convictions they produce, or how much jail time defendants receive; but by the achievement of tangible impacts—less drug use and crime, gains in employment and education, improved mental and physical health among participants, and cost savings from diverting offenders away from jail and prison. Their vast potential has led to a stunning national expansion—over 1,500 drug courts in early 2006, just over 15 years after the Miami program enrolled its first defendant (Office of Justice Programs 2006).

To test their performance, early drug court evaluations primarily focused on the bottom line: did they work? Most evaluations found that drug courts, while not a cure-all, produce meaningful

---

This chapter was published in slightly different form in 2005 by the Center for Court Innovation as a white paper under the same title. Its publication was supported by the Bureau of Justice Assistance, Office of Justice Programs, U.S. Department of Justice. Opinions and interpretations are those of the authors and do not necessarily represent the official position or policies of the U.S. Department of Justice.

reductions in re-offending compared with conventional prosecution (Aos, Phipps, Barnoski, and Lieb 2001; Government Accountability Office 2005; Roman and DeStefano 2004; Wilson, Mitchell, and MacKenzie 2003). The combination of favorable results and ongoing efforts to open new drug courts nationwide has now spawned an urgent set of second-generation questions focusing less on whether drug courts work and more on how and for whom, along with how they might work better. Among the topics that drug court researchers are currently investigating are:

Target Population Which categories of participants (e.g., based on drug use and treatment history, criminal history, charges, socioeconomic variables, mental health, or other factors) are especially likely to benefit from drug court? Are today's programs reaching and enrolling the ideal target population?

Program Components How important is each component of the drug court model (e.g., team approach, treatment, case management, judicial supervision, rewards, and sanctions)? How is each component best administered?

Quality of Treatment Which treatment modalities are most appropriate for different categories of participants, and are such modalities widely available? How can drug courts better monitor the quality of the treatment services on which they depend?

Drug Court Retention and Graduation How long should drug court participants be retained in the program in order to benefit from the intervention? What steps can be taken to improve retention? How important is drug court retention and graduation in achieving positive long-term outcomes?

The answers to these questions can be used by drug court practitioners to refine their practices and apply resources more wisely. States engaged in large-scale institutionalization efforts can incorporate known best practices into statewide drug court protocols. Indeed, "action research" (see Chapter 4 for a discussion of how local drug courts can start their own action research program by using simple and easy-to-collect data to answer practical questions about their volume, participant characteristics, and performance) may be critical to the long-term sustainability of drug courts. Without understanding which of the key drug court components have the greatest impact, and which categories of participants will benefit most, newer drug courts coping with fewer resources and lacking the charismatic leadership of early pioneering judges may not know which parts of the model must be preserved intact—and which can be tinkered with.

Although the early 2000s have seen the completion of many valuable studies, some of the most interesting results have yet to be widely disseminated. This paper synthesizes some of the more revealing national findings and highlights areas where we need to know more.

The Drug Court Model: What Are We Evaluating?

What do drug court evaluations typically report? In most examples to date, the evaluation found that drug court participants (including both graduates and failures) had lower recidivism rates than similar defendants prosecuted with conventional methods. Some evaluations have considered other outcomes, such as drug use, employment, health care, time spent in jail and prison, or cost savings; but most have examined effects on recidivism alone—mainly because the availability of official criminal justice records makes recidivism analyses the easiest and least costly to implement.

As important as it is to know that drug courts reduce recidivism, this is not nearly enough. The figure on the next page illustrates how little we learn merely from knowing that a drug court, in its totality, reduced re-offending. More helpful at this point would be research telling us which specific drug court components made the greatest difference in producing successful outcomes, and which, if any, made no difference. Perhaps a drug court receiving a positive evaluation would have been equally effective with a model excluding rewards and sanctions, or excluding case management, or excluding treatment while relying only on court-based judicial supervision. Or perhaps the drug court would have produced even better results if certain policies were administered differently, for example if in-court interactions with the judge were longer or more probing, or if more effective treatment modalities were used, or if drug testing was more frequent. Consider just a few of the specific components that are *believed* by many practitioners to underlie drug court success (see the third column in the figure):

Early Identification Participants are believed to be most receptive to change at the crisis moment of the arrest (or outset of the case); hence potential participants should be identified, assessed, and placed in treatment as rapidly as possible.

Community-Based Treatment Effective substance abuse treatment modalities are believed to exist that can promote sobriety; hence drug courts should match participants to appropriate community-based residential or outpatient treatment programs. However, the science of treatment-matching is not very well developed; there is little evidence

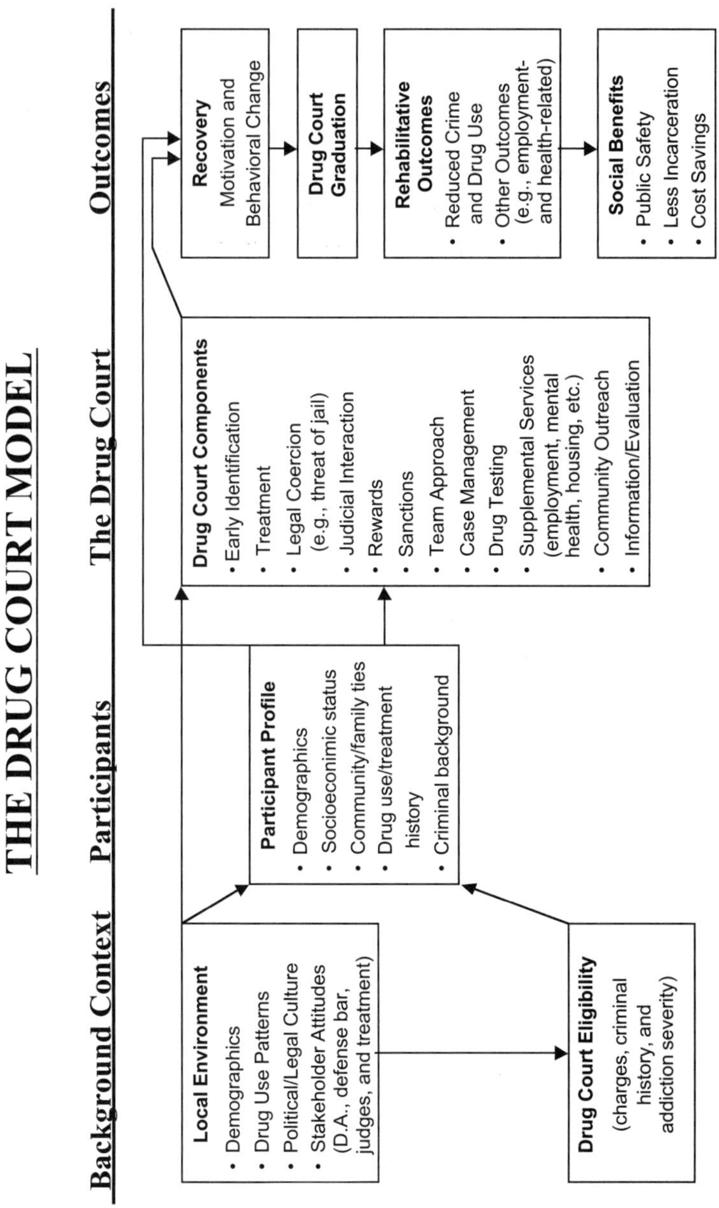
THE DRUG COURT MODEL
Background Context
Participants
The Drug Court
Outcomes
Local Environment
• Demographics
• Drug Use Patterns
• Political/Legal Culture
• Stakeholder Attitudes (D.A., defense bar, judges, and treatment)
Drug Court Eligibility
(charges, criminal history, and addiction severity)
Participant Profile
• Demographics
• Socioecinimic status
• Community/family ties
• Drug use/treatment history
• Criminal background
Drug Court Components
• Early Identification
• Treatment
• Legal Coercion (e.g., threat of jail)
• Judicial Interaction
• Rewards
• Sanctions
• Team Approach
• Case Management
• Drug Testing
• Supplemental Services (employment, mental health, housing, etc.)
• Community Outreach
• Information/Evaluation
Recovery
Motivation and Behavioral Change
Drug Court Graduation
Rehabilitative Outcomes
• Reduced Crime and Drug Use
• Other Outcomes (e.g., employment- and health-related)
Social Benefits
• Public Safety
• Less Incarceration
• Cost Savings

indicating which treatment interventions work best and with which populations.

Legal Coercion Drug court participants are believed to be retained in treatment at higher rates than those entering voluntarily because drug courts offer concrete legal incentives to do well—namely, the prospects of a charge reduction or case dismissal in the event of graduating and jail or prison in the event of failing.

Judicial Supervision Through regular status hearings before the drug court judge, in which the judge engages in direct conversation with the participant about progress and setbacks, the judge is thought to play an instrumental role in promoting sobriety.

Rewards and Sanctions Drug courts are believed to encourage progress by applying a continuum of intermediate sanctions and rewards; sanctions are thought to be most effective when applying principles of *certainty* (each infraction receives a sanction), *celerity* (sanctions are imposed as soon as possible after the infraction occurs), and *severity* (sanctions rise in severity in response to repeat infractions and consider the severity of the behavior).

Team Approach Drug courts are believed to be more effective when the parties (e.g., judge, lawyers, and clinical staff) work together to figure out what will best promote the recovery of each participant.

Official drug court publications and everyday practitioners hold all of these components to be important, but are any backed by evidence? This paper considers what we know now concerning: (1) whether drug courts work, (2) how they work, and (3) for whom. The first question, while the most researched, is covered only briefly, given this paper's focus on probing deeper to what lies behind the more widely known findings. Nearly all results presented here pertain exclusively to adult drug courts, since research is only beginning to emerge on the family and juvenile drug court models.

Do Drug Courts Work?

Before tackling the more challenging questions of how and for whom drug courts work, what does the literature show concerning their overall success? It is worth noting here that much of the literature to date has been plagued by methodological issues necessitating the careful interpretation of many drug court studies. For instance, in a review of the literature, Steven Belenko (2001) points to a lack of precision in defining data sources, time frames, and measures as well as data quality issues and missing data in many studies. Additionally, several studies have relied on inappropriate comparison groups (e.g., drug court graduates compared to drug court failures; drug court participants compared to those who were found ineligible for the program) or have used no comparison group. Nevertheless, it is now possible to draw solid conclusions about several important indicators of success:

Treatment Retention *Drug court retention rates far exceed those for the general treatment population.*

Retention is a key measure of program success. A one-year retention rate, for example, indicates the percentage of participants who, exactly one year after entering drug court, had either graduated or remained active in the drug court program. Earlier research finds that longer retention not only indicates success in treatment but also predicts continued future success in the form of lower *post-treatment* drug use and criminal offending (Anglin, Brecht, and Maddahian 1989; DeLeon 1988; Peters and Murrin 1998; Taxman 1998; Taxman, Kubu, and DeStefano 1999).

Drug courts have been consistently found to produce higher retention rates than community-based treatment programs accepting a combination of voluntary and court-mandated treatment participants (Condelli and DeLeon 1993; Lewis and Ross 1994). This is believed to be due in part to the legal pressure entailed by the threat of incarceration drug court participants face in the event of failure; several studies confirm that legal coercion is a sizable force improving both short-term and long-term treatment outcomes (Anglin et al. 1989; DeLeon 1988; Hiller, Knight, and Simpson 1998; Young and Belenko 2002).

As for hard numbers, one review estimates that drug courts nationwide have an average one-year retention rate of 60 percent (Belenko 1998). A study of 11 New York State drug courts found a slightly higher median one-year retention rate of 66 percent, and estimated graduation rates exceeded 50 percent in eight of 11 sites (Rempel *et al.* 2003). On the other hand, a study of four "mentor" drug courts in other states reported an average graduation rate of only about one-third (Anspach, Collom, and Ferguson 2003).

Nevertheless, every one of these estimates improves considerably upon those obtained at community-based treatment programs, where many participants enter voluntarily—*without the pressure of a court mandate.* Nationwide, approximately half of those enrolling in outpatient treatment are retained for less than three months (Simpson, Joe, and Brown 1997). Since attrition always increases over time, one-year retention rates across these same programs would presumably drop much lower. Indeed, focusing on therapeutic communities (involving residential treatment), one study reports one-year rates ranging from just 10-30 percent, lower than even the very worst performing drug courts (Lewis and Ross 1994).[1] So drug courts have clearly achieved success in keeping addicted persons in treatment for longer than other treatment models.

Recidivism *Adult drug courts significantly reduce recidivism, although the level of impact varies over time and by court.*

In their comprehensive review, David Wilson and colleagues reported that 37 of 42 studies found lower recidivism rates among drug court participants than comparison groups composed of similar but non-participating defendants. Most of the studies defined recidivism as re-arrests, some as re-convictions. The average effect size was approximately 13 percentage points (Wilson et al. 2003). Other literature reviews that considered fewer total drug court evaluations, mainly by eliminating ones with particularly weak methodologies, still reported lower recidivism rates among drug court participants than comparison group defendants in nearly all sites (e.g., Aos et al. 2001; Belenko 2001; Government Accountability Office 2005; Roman and DeStefano 2004).

An important caveat to these results is that most studies only examined recidivism over a brief time frame, usually coinciding with the *in-program* period of active drug court participation. Only a handful extended the measurement period beyond two years after program intake. For example, a study of the Baltimore City Treatment Court, which used a strong research design where defendants were randomly assigned either to the drug court or conventional case processing, tracked defendants over a third year and found sustained differences, with a recidivism rate that was 10 percent lower for drug court participants than the comparison group (Gottfredson, Kearley, Najaka, and Rocha 2003).

Several studies have been able to isolate recidivism over a *post-program* period after drug court participation has ended (i.e., after the date of graduation or failure/release from incarceration). A study of six New York State drug courts, for example, reported consistent recidivism reductions over a one-year period after graduation or failure—an average 31 percent reduction in relation to the comparison group during a comparable one-year post-disposition period.[2] When focusing on graduates alone, the impact is truly staggering—an average 71 percent reduction across the same six sites. On the other hand, drug court failures were as or more likely as comparison group defendants to re-offend (Rempel et al. 2003). This means the benefits of the drug court accrue primarily to those who successfully complete; therefore, to have a substantial net impact when averaged across *all* participants, graduating a significant percentage may be extremely important.

Overall, qualifications concerning methodology and measurement periods notwithstanding, results to date offer strong support for drug courts. Indeed, the U.S. Government Accountability Office (2005) concluded definitively that adult drug courts succeed in reducing recidivism.

Drug Use *Studies show varying levels of continued drug use among drug court participants. Many comparison groups are not tested for drug use.*

Few studies directly measure reductions in drug use, primarily due to the inherent difficulties in locating both drug court participants and comparison group members for follow-up interviews and urinalysis testing. In one study, participants in Maricopa County, Arizona, were found less likely than defendants randomly assigned to a regular probation group to test positive for heroin or cocaine one year after program entry; however participants were found *more* likely to test positive for marijuana (Deschenes, Turner, and Greenwood 1995). Two other studies found that drug court participants were significantly less likely than comparison group defendants to use several illegal substances after a short follow-up period (Gottfredson, Najaka, and Kearley 2003; Harrell,

Roman, and Sack 2001). The Government Accountability Office aptly concluded that results are limited and mixed when it comes to effects on drug use.

Other Rehabilitative Outcomes *Virtually no studies measure other outcomes such as employment, welfare dependence, and mental or physical health. Some evidence suggests that drug courts may produce modest gains in these areas.*

Studies of the Baltimore City and Brooklyn drug courts detected few significant social and economic impacts, such as reductions in family, psychiatric, medical, or employment problems. However, where differences were evident, the tendency was for drug court participants to show modest relative improvement on these types of measures (see Gottfredson et al. 2003; Harrell et al. 2001). Clearly, more research is needed here.

Cost Savings *While few studies measure cost impacts, nearly all of the available evidence demonstrates that drug courts save money over the long term.*

Most studies considering cost savings have focused on savings to the criminal justice system (e.g., courts, corrections, probation, or prosecutors). These savings are the easiest to quantify but not necessarily the largest, as compared with others, such as reduced taxpayer-funded health care costs and emergency room visits, reduced dependence on public assistance, and savings to the community through reduced victimization costs.

According to two recent reviews of the literature, nearly all completed cost studies show significant net savings (Roman and DeStefano 2004). Of the completed studies, the most noteworthy are two statewide evaluations of drug courts in Washington and California. The Washington State study found savings of $3,892 per drug court participant, or savings of about $1.74 for every dollar invested (Aos et al. 2001). The California study was a comprehensive analysis of the investments and costs of drug courts in each of nine sites. Eight of the nine sites produced net savings per participant over a four-year tracking period; the median (fifth) site produced net savings of almost $9,500 per participant, and the three best-performing sites exceeded $15,000 per participant (Carey, Crumpton, Finigan, and Waller 2005).

Particularly valuable about the California study is its distinguishing the investments and savings that were specific to each of several key agencies: the courts, prosecutors, public defenders, probation, police, corrections, treatment. While corrections saw the largest and most consistent savings, all of the other agencies also saw net savings in more sites than not, with the exception of treatment and probation. Since many of the savings stem from reductions in recidivism (the savings arise because justice system agencies do not have to deal with future cases), drug courts that achieve larger reductions in recidivism will naturally produce larger cost savings.

Although recidivism-related savings accrue in the long term, one should acknowledge that the immediate up-front costs to the court system of running a drug court generally exceed those of conventional case processing. Other justice system agencies, such as the District Attorney's Office, the defense bar, or corrections, may see more immediate cost efficiencies, particularly in those drug courts managing to reduce incarceration time on the initial drug court case. Still, drug courts do not always produce a short-term budgetary payoff and should be viewed instead as an investment in the future.

Reduced Use of Incarceration *As an alternative to incarceration, drug courts typically aspire to reduce the time that defendants spend in jail or prison on their current case. Limited data indicates that this happens to some degree, but not always.*

Some drug court critics argue that, due to the lengthy jail or prison sentences commonly imposed on drug court failures, when considering all drug court participants together, they face more severe criminal justice sanctions on average than conventional prosecution (Nolan 2001). Indeed, the study of the Baltimore drug court found that while participants spent fewer days than the comparison group in jail due to their sentence, they spent substantially more time in jail due to intermediate sanctions for noncompliant behavior. Therefore, when all time was considered, the total number of days that drug court participants spent incarcerated was only slightly lower than for the comparison group (Gottfredson et al. 2003). In the New York State study, drug court participants in three of six sites averaged significantly fewer days incarcerated than the comparison group on the initial case, but participants in one court spent significantly more time incarcerated and, in the final two sites, there was not a significant difference in either direction (Rempel et al. 2003). (Of course, since drug courts reduce recidivism, it is likely that if including incarceration time served as a result of new offenses, more drug courts would ultimately achieve reductions in net jail or prison time.)

Further breaking down the results in the New York study, it bears emphasizing that drug court graduates were never incarcerated as part of their final sentence; therefore, graduates gained the full benefit of the alternative to incarceration opportunity. On the other hand, in four of six New York sites, drug court failures averaged significantly longer sentences than the comparison group. This again underscores the critical role of drug court graduation determining whether or not participants will benefit from the intervention.

How Do Drug Courts Work?

Here the evidence is more limited. The third column of the figure included above identifies 12 drug court components, of which notable evidence exists bearing on seven.

Early Identification *Those drug court participants who are identified and begin treatment quickly are more successful than those whose entry into a community-based treatment program is delayed.*
A growing body of research suggests that immediate engagement is critical. Participants engaged early in the drug court process, often measured by whether a participant actually begins attending treatment within the first 30 days after formally agreeing to enter a drug court, are more likely to be retained and to have successful long-term outcomes (Rempel and DeStefano 2001; Rempel et al. 2003; and for additional research demonstrating the importance of immediate treatment engagement, see Leigh, Ogborne, and Cleveland 1984; Maddux 1983; and Mundell 1994).

Implication: Drug courts should strive to implement formal, streamlined intake procedures that can move potential participants rapidly from screening and assessment to formalization of participant status to placement in a suitable community-based treatment program. Where treatment slots are difficult to locate, or systematic delays in case processing cannot be overcome, this may hinder a drug court's effectiveness. To compensate, strategies such as holding pre-placement groups on-site at the drug court may help to keep participants engaged while they wait for a community-based treatment slot to become available.

Treatment *Some contend that treatment* per se *does not explain the overall effectiveness of drug courts and that, instead, judicial supervision makes the greatest difference. Contrary to this position, evidence indicates that treatment can make a difference, but little is known about the relative impact of different treatment modalities or about which modalities are most appropriate for different categories of participants.*

Researcher Mark Kleiman (2001) has advanced the argument that the limited scope and duration of the drug court coupled with up-front costs associated with treatment ultimately restrict the potential impact of this intervention. Kleiman argues that the drug court model could be replaced with a bare-bones approach requiring substance abstinence reinforced through drug screening and guaranteed sanctions for noncompliant behavior—but excluding a requirement of attendance in community-based treatment.

Others respond that treatment itself is essential. Many studies (though not specifically of drug court participants) confirm that more time in treatment leads to more positive post-treatment outcomes on measures such as drug use, criminal activity, and employment (Anglin et al. 1989; DeLeon 1988; Peters and Murrin 2000; Simpson et al. 1997; Sirotnik and Roffe 1977; Taxman 1998; Taxman et al. 1999). The Baltimore drug court study confirms that participants who completed more total days in treatment reported less illegal drug use than others three years after program entry (Gottfredson et al. 2003).

While the literature confirms that treatment is important, it is unclear whether drug courts use the most effective treatment modalities and programs. What is known is that practices vary widely. For example, across 11 New York State drug courts, the percentage of participants initially referred to a residential treatment program ranged from 1 percent to 53 percent (Rempel et al. 2003). In part, this variation reflects the desire of some drug courts to keep participants in their own neighborhood, rather than sending them to a residential facility. In addition, rural or semi-rural areas often lack residential substance abuse treatment programs; and even where residential programs are available, there are often fewer treatment slots and hence lengthier delays in placement than with outpatient programs.[3]

Not only do practices among courts vary, but information concerning best practices is limited. For example:

- Which modality is most appropriate for different categories of participants (e.g., severely addicted heroin users, young marijuana users, or addicted women with children)?
- How much treatment is ideal—and do drug courts that require treatment stays well in excess of one year encounter a point of diminishing returns? (In recent years, several drug court researchers, including one of this chapter's coauthors, have proposed that it may be counterproductive to keep participants enrolled for too long before allowing them to graduate.)
- Within each basic type of modality (e.g., residential, short-term rehabilitation, or outpatient), are quality treatment services available? Are treatment providers using methods found to be therapeutically effective? How can drug court staff assess the quality of available treatment?
- Do variations in treatment program quality tangibly affect participant outcomes?

From a comprehensive review of the treatment literature, Faye Taxman (1999) synthesizes existing treatment knowledge and recommends certain specific practices (e.g., cognitive behavioral approaches, matching defendants to appropriate programs, and clinical assessments) as crucial to successful outcomes. At the same time, Taxman laments that treatment programs serving drug court participants tend to spend relatively little time—less than 20 percent in one study—addressing clinical issues with an approach known to be effective (Taxman and Bouffard 2003). Several other researchers participating in a round table discussion echoed concerns that programs available to drug courts do not generally use the most effective of available modalities (Fox 2004). And drug court participants themselves criticized the quality of their treatment in several recent focus groups (Farole and Cissner 2005, and Chapter 2). While it is debatable how much control drug courts can actually exert over treatment administered in community-based programs, these findings at least raise concerns about whether drug court effectiveness might be greater if the average quality of treatment was improved.

Legal Coercion *Legal coercion can increase the incentive for drug court participants to succeed.*

As discussed previously, part of the success of drug courts in retaining participants is believed to stem from the legal coercion entailed by the threat of incarceration for failing. Further, some evidence indicates that added amounts of legal coercion within drug courts can produce incrementally better outcomes. For instance, presumably because of the added leverage that results when participants are required to plead guilty in advance of participation, drug courts using "post-plea" as opposed to "pre-plea" models may be more effective. One study of a court-mandated treatment program (not a drug court per se but similar to one) confirmed that the program's one-year retention rate rose by 10 percent (64 percent to 74 percent) after switching from a pre-plea to post-plea model (Sung 1999). Also, comparing different post-plea situations, a study of the Brooklyn Treatment Court found that participants facing a progressively longer jail or prison sentence in the event of failing were increasingly likely to become engaged in treatment (Rempel and DeStefano 2001).

A study of the Las Vegas drug court similarly found that clients entering the drug court post plea performed worse than pre-plea clients, but the authors believed this may be due to a higher risk clientele entering the court post plea (Goldkamp,

White, and Robinson 2001). However, the recent statewide study in New York found less strongly supportive evidence for this relationship across a range of drug courts, and the Baltimore study did not confirm this relationship at all (Kearley and Gottfredson 2003; Rempel et al. 2003). While the coercive aspects common to all drug courts are effective when compared with voluntary treatment, further research is needed to clarify under what conditions extra levels of coercion produce added value in terms of improved participant outcomes.

In this regard, the work of Doug Young and Steven Belenko is highly suggestive. In one study (Young and Belenko 2002), they found that treatment retention rates varied as a direct result of variation on four distinct legal coercion dimensions: (1) information (degree to which program rules and consequences of noncompliance were clearly communicated to participants); (2) monitoring (degree to which compliance was closely monitored through regular progress reports to the court and other means); (3) enforcement (degree to which noncompliant participants could expect to be rapidly caught, brought back to court, and face consistent consequences); and (4) severity (length of the resulting jail or prison sentence or other consequence). Further, this research suggests that legal coercion becomes more effective when coupled with clear communications by justice system authorities that reinforce participants' impressions that failure will elicit adverse consequences. This reinforcement creates a perception of coercion, which in turn mediates the relationship between the court's objective mandate on one hand and the resulting compliance outcomes on the other. For example, the dimension of "severity" is not measured merely by the objective facts of what will happen if participants fail but by participant *perceptions* of how much jail or prison time or what other consequence they will face.

Implication: Drug courts should convey clearly, frequently, and specifically to participants exactly what will happen if they graduate (case dismissal or other legal benefit) and what will happen if they fail (how much jail time they will have to serve), and should convey the nature of the court's monitoring and enforcement efforts to detect and address noncompliance.

Judicial Supervision *Ongoing judicial supervision by the drug court judge works with "high-risk" drug court participants.*
Research suggests that judicial status hearings—especially ones that include positive feedback from the judge and that focus on "high-risk" participants—can be effective. A series of randomized trials found that drug court participants diagnosed as having antisocial personality disorder and/or having previously failed a drug treatment program did significantly better when required to appear biweekly before the drug court judge rather than "as needed" (only when a problem arose). On the other hand, "low-risk" participants who did not have these characteristics did either similarly or worse across different drug court sites when monitored biweekly (Marlowe, Festinger, and Lee 2004).

Since participants who do attend status hearings often develop a relationship with the judge, some research has found that it can be damaging when one judge replaces another. A study of the Portland drug court reported declining treatment attendance after it switched from a single, dedicated judge to a judicial rotation system involving frequent changes in the presiding judge. Likewise, the study found that participants appearing before a single judge were less likely to be terminated unfavorably from the drug court program than participants appearing before multiple judges in the course of their participation (Goldkamp et al. 2001).

Concerning the content of effective status hearings, a Broward County, Florida, study found that in general, supportive comments by judges resulted in fewer subsequent positive drug screens, while adverse comments had the opposite effect (Senjo and Leip 2001). Further confirming the importance of positive feedback, interviews with participants in two different drug courts using the same scales both found that participants rated "praise from the judge" and "direct interaction with the judge" as among the most useful drug court components (Porter 2000, 2001). Similarly, participants offering feedback in two separate focus group studies spanning nine drug court sites consistently underlined the motivating role of praise and approval from the judge (see Chapter 2; and see Goldkamp, White, and Robinson 2002). By contrast, the overriding prevalence of negative and stigmatizing judicial feedback was held largely responsible for the negative evaluation results (higher rates of re-offending among participants than the comparison group) in one study of the Las Vegas drug court (Miethe, Lu, and Reese 2000).

Implication: Scarce judicial supervision resources are best targeted to "high risk" participants.

Rewards *Rewards appear effective when they are tangible and applied frequently throughout the drug court participation process; but the literature is limited.*

As noted above, several studies cite the importance of positive judicial feedback. Whether more tangible rewards such as tokens, journals, or gift certificates are effective is, however, a different question. Classic behavioral modification techniques recommend the liberal use of rewards. Yet, only one study has tested the impact of rewards in drug courts with a rigorous research design. For this reason, caution is still advised before drawing conclusions about the degree to which rewards make a difference. In the one completed study, Doug Marlowe and his colleagues randomly assigned participants in one drug court to one of three rewards schedules:

Standard rewards: hat or candle after three months of compliance; reduced community service after six months; reduced drug testing after seven; reduced treatment requirements after eight; reduced judicial status hearings after 10; and reduced homework assignments after 11.

Enhanced graduated rewards: gift certificates after each additional month of compliance (i.e., 12 total certificates) that begin at $5 after month one and grow to $60 after month 12.

Enhanced thinning rewards: gift certificates of $30 after months one, two, and three of compliance; $50 after month five; $75 after month nine; and $125 after month 12.

Within one year, the graduation rate and Phase Four completion rate (the drug court used four phases) were significantly higher for participants on the two "enhanced" schedules than for participants on the "standard" schedule. In particular, 55 percent and 60 percent respectively of participants on the two enhanced schedules had at least completed Phase Four by the one-year mark, but only 26 percent of those on the standard schedule had done so (Marlowe 2004). As this is the only study of its kind, results should be interpreted with substantial caution.

Implication: Based on this study, rewards may be effective, but not in the way they are traditionally implemented in drug courts; instead, participants may respond better when the rewards have tangible value, are administered more frequently throughout participation, and are administered in escalating quantities. Further research is needed on these issues.

Sanctions *Drug court sanctions appear effective when applied consistently and fairly, but the literature is limited.*
Following classic behavior modification principles, sanctions and rewards have always been core components of the drug court model. In one study of the Washington, D.C. Judicial Sanctions Program, defendants assigned to receive sanctions in response to noncompliance were less likely to be re-arrested than a second group of defendants assigned to receive regular drug testing but without judicial monitoring or sanctions (Harrell, Cavanagh, and Roman 1998). Unfortunately, little is known about precisely why or how sanctions work—which specific types of sanctions are most effective, under what circumstances, and how much of a difference they truly make in a drug court setting. It is possible that intermediate sanctions are less important in drug courts than other aspects of judicial supervision, such as probing and positive judicial interactions with participants and the overarching incentive created by the threat of jail or prison for failing. And because some research has shown that negative, stigmatizing in-court interactions can adversely affect subsequent performance, intermediate sanctions must be administered with care. Where similar sanctions are consistently applied in response to similar behaviors, and where the judge clearly articulates the reasons for imposing each sanction, participants may become more likely to respond positively. In general, research shows that where defendants believe justice system authorities have treated them fairly and with respect, they are more likely to comply with court orders (Tyler 1990).

Implication: Drug courts need to cultivate a sense that their sanctioning process is fair. Developing and consistently implementing a formal graduated sanctions schedule may be helpful in this regard.

Team Approach *The impact of the team approach has not been rigorously tested, but drug courts appear to function better when a non-adversarial team model is present.*

Most drug courts hold regular case conferencing meetings that include the judge, attorneys, treatment providers, and other affiliated staff. In these meetings, disparate goals (e.g., of opposing attorneys) are supposed to be put aside to promote the recovery of each participant. While it is difficult to quantify the impact of a team model, a couple of studies suggest it may be important. In one involving focus groups with judges from drug courts and other problem-solving courts (e.g., domestic violence courts, mental health courts, community courts), judges repeatedly cited the team approach as among the most critical ingredients for their programs to be effective (Farole, Puffett, Rempel, and Byrne 2005). Also, a recent process evaluation of the Staten Island, New York, drug court found that the strong personal and working relationships established among team members—the judge, prosecutors, and assigned defense counsel especially—enabled the court to successfully address multiple implementation challenges during the planning stages and first year and a half of operations (see Chapter 3). Still, these studies by no means involved rigorous, carefully designed tests of the team model. More research is needed here as well.

Other Drug Court Components *There is little or no evidence on the impact of case management, drug testing, community outreach, and supplemental services in areas such as employment, housing, or mental health.*

Concerning case management in particular, today's drug courts exhibit considerable diversity of practice. Different drug courts range from employing their own on-site case management team (the most costly option), to collaborating with local departments of probation to perform case management, to eliminating case management services altogether and folding their functions under substance abuse counselors at assigned treatment programs (Rempel et al. 2003). Yet it is entirely unclear which, if any, of these approaches is more or less effective than any other.

Graduation *Participants who reach graduation are more likely to have continued success thereafter.*

What role does drug court graduation play in producing long-term rehabilitative outcomes? Can those who fail drug court nonetheless gain from the experience? Several studies suggest that they cannot—that graduation is a pivotal milestone and that without it continued progress is unlikely (Peters, Haas, and Murrin 1999; Peters and Murrin 2000; Rempel et al. 2003). For example, the New York study found that across six drug courts, there was consistently no additional benefit gained from completing more time in the drug court program only to fail in the end. Among those who failed, more time enrolled in the drug court or attending treatment prior to failure had no impact on future re-offending rates.

Implication: Graduation may be necessary to achieve successful long-term outcomes; drug courts should seek to graduate a meaningful percentage of their participants.

For Whom Do Drug Courts Work?

Are some components—or the drug court model overall—more effective with some categories of participants than others? If policymakers knew who benefits the most, they could adjust their target populations appropriately. By contrast, consider how a drug court's target population is typically defined now. Local community values and the specific attitudes of powerful stakeholders (e.g., the prosecutor, defense bar, and judiciary) inevitably influence a drug court's eligibility criteria: e.g., whether it will admit defendants charged with felonies or misdemeanors only, whether drug sales charges are eligible, and what type of prior criminal history is acceptable. The drug court population also reflects the character of the local population (e.g., the racial makeup or income distribution; the nature of the local drug problem).

In addition to these real-life factors, in the ideal the target population for a drug court would be defined at least in part based on hard evidence concerning which categories of participants (e.g., based on drug use, treatment, or criminal history, sex, age, race, socioeconomic background, or other factors) are most likely to benefit from the intervention.

A number of studies indicate that "high-risk" offenders are especially likely to benefit from the drug court model. As noted above, biweekly judicial status hearings had a positive impact on drug court participants with previous failed treatment episodes and/or anti-social personality disorders, while biweekly status hearings made no difference or even a negative difference for other categories of participants (Marlowe et al. 2004). Also, a study of the Los Angeles drug court found that while the drug court did not produce significantly different re-arrest rates from the comparison group among "low-risk" defendants, it did generate considerably lower re-arrest rates among both "medium" and "high-risk" defendants. In this study, high-risk defendants had more serious criminal records and weaker community ties (Fielding et al. 2002).

Complementing this research is the finding cited above that participants perform better if they face greater legal exposure (more jail or prison time in the event of failing). In short, this means that defendants arrested on more serious charges and possessing a longer rap sheet, both characteristics that generally increase legal exposure, should perform better than other categories of defendants.

Finally, a study of one drug court found that it produced a relatively greater reduction in recidivism for defendants entering on drug than on non-drug charges, such as property offenses or prostitution (Rempel et al. 2003). Perhaps drug courts work better at reducing crime related to drug use and addiction but relatively less well with crime driven by other criminal impulses or motivations. And while many property offenders may be seeking to support an addiction, it is possible that, on average, crimes committed by property offenders are less often driven by an addiction and more often by other criminal propensities. This relationship should be interpreted with extreme caution until additional research replicates the finding.

Implication: Drug courts produce better outcomes if they expand their eligibility criteria to defendants with a prior criminal record, felony level criminal charges, previous failed treatment, and other risk factors; conversely, limiting the drug court opportunity to less serious types of offenders (as many jurisdictions have chosen to do) will reduce program efficacy. In general, drug courts accepting participants over whom they can exercise more legal coercion stand to produce better outcomes.

Conclusion

The past several years have seen a remarkable convergence of support throughout the research community around the effectiveness of drug courts. Recent opinion pieces by John Goldkamp, Adele Harrell, and Doug Marlowe, three of the most prominent researchers in the field, all conclude that adult drug courts have been proven effective, a conclusion further echoed in an early 2005 report by the Government Accountability Office (Goldkamp 2003; Harrell 2003; Marlowe 2003). Marlowe adds for emphasis, “We know that drug courts outperform virtually all other strategies that have been attempted for drug-involved offenders” (2003: 2).

Alongside this bold endorsement, however, Marlowe offers an equally important caution, “Some components [of the model] may be indispensable, others may not be worth the cost, and still others may have negative side effects" (2003: 3). Indeed, the future of drug courts may well depend not on producing additional studies demonstrating their effectiveness overall but on increasing our understanding of which components are critical, which are not, and for which categories of participants the intervention works best.

Information concerning the essential ingredients of drug courts becomes all the more important in light of recent efforts by many states to go to scale, expanding the reach of drug courts to far greater numbers of defendants. These efforts appear to fall under two possible paths. One involves increasing the number of drug courts as well as attempting to boost the volume of defendants served by each one. Many states, including California, Florida, Louisiana, Missouri, and New York, have already begun proceeding in this manner through statewide coordination and expansion efforts (Fox and Wolf 2004). The second possible path involves applying problem-solving practices (i.e., the set of practices common to drug courts and other specialized courts) outside the specialized court setting—throughout conventional courts (Farole et al. 2005 and Chapter 13). While this second path has not been undertaken systematically by any state, interest in this area is growing.

Both paths of expansion stem in no small part from the results achieved by adult drug courts. Yet, it is unclear whether broader institutionalization can produce equally positive results. It is possible that a drug court approach will not work as well if institutionalized in greater numbers of courtrooms, targeting a wider range of defendants, and requiring the collaboration of far more judges, attorneys, and other stakeholders who may not all possess the dedication or skill of the movement's pioneers.

This paper has sought to inform the future of the drug court movement by summarizing what we know so far about successful drug court implementation and where future research has a critical role to play. While the research to date cannot give policymakers a blueprint for how to go to scale with drug court, it does offer a number of helpful lessons that will hopefully spark new thinking about how to ensure that these courts are making a difference in the lives of addicted offenders.

CHAPTER TWO

Seeing Eye to Eye: Participant and Staff Perspectives on Drug Court

DONALD J. FAROLE JR. AND AMANDA B. CISSNER

Over the past several years, a broad consensus has emerged that adult drug courts fulfill their promise of increasing treatment retention and reducing recidivism among drug-involved offenders. While findings vary across courts, the question of whether adult drug courts work has been answered largely in the affirmative (see Chapter 1). There is less certainty about why drug courts are effective, although several critical elements of the intervention have been suggested, including legal coercion (Rempel and DeStefano 2001; Young and Belenko 2002); the role of the judge in monitoring compliance (Goldkamp et al. 2001; Marlowe, Feitinger, and Lee 2004,); and the use of intermediate sanctions (Harrell, Cavanagh, and Roman 1998).

This chapter focuses not on the effectiveness of drug courts, but rather on the perspectives of the key drug court players themselves, both participants and staff. The goal is to explore whether the attitudes, opinions, and experiences of participants in drug courts correspond to those operating the courts—in other words, do they see eye to eye? Motivating the research is a recognition

---

This chapter is adapted from a research report originally published in 2005 by the Center for Court Innovation under the same title. Its publication was supported by the Bureau of Justice Assistance, Office of Justice Programs, U.S. Department of Justice. Opinions and interpretations in this chapter are those of the authors or, where attributed, the focus group participants and do not necessarily represent the official position or policies of the U.S. Department of Justice.

that drug courts, like any intervention designed to change behavior, are likely to be most effective when those operating the programs are fully cognizant of the attitudes and experiences of the participants. Staff and participants will, of course, have their areas of agreement and disagreement. But it is crucial for staff to be aware of how their perceptions and attitudes might differ from participants' so that they can most effectively manage those differences, deliver the drug court intervention, and identify areas for continuous improvement.

To get a better sense of staff and participant attitudes, we conducted focus groups at three New York State drug courts. The research was designed to provide feedback about court operations and to assist programs by examining commonly held assumptions about drug courts. Participants and court staff offered their views about many aspects of the drug court experience. Many of the key issues and themes raised during our discussions with drug court participants were also heard in subsequent staff sessions, leading us to conclude that participants and staff in these drug courts do indeed see eye to eye on most matters.

Research Methodology

This research relies primarily on the focus group method, an informal group interview technique that has proven an effective means of obtaining information about the drug court experience (e.g., Goldkamp et al. 2001). Focus groups allow research subjects—participants and staff—to shape the discussion and incorporate the comments of others to elaborate on their own ideas. This reveals insights and nuances that other methods, such as individual interviews, cannot. However, these advantages are accompanied by limitations. Focus groups are not based on a random sample, therefore, unlike with surveys, the findings cannot be generalized to broader populations. Additionally, because focus groups require in-depth conversation, the number of questions or topics addressed must be kept small. Focus groups provide depth rather than a breadth of information.

During spring and summer 2004, focus groups were conducted with participants and staff in three New York State drug courts. To ensure confidentiality for all research participants, particularly staff whose responses might be more easily identifiable, the participating courts are not identified. The courts are diverse in terms of geographic location—urban, suburban, semi-rural. The courts also differ in terms of their policies. For example, two programs accept only participants arrested on felony charges, while the third accepts those charged with both felonies and misdemeanors. Graduates of two programs have their cases dismissed or charges reduced (depending on the case); those at the third are assigned to felony probation. Note that in all three courts, defendants must enter a guilty plea prior to entering the drug court.

A total of seven focus groups were conducted.[1] The size of the focus groups ranged from five to 15 participants and most sessions lasted between 75 and 120 minutes. Individual interviews, averaging one hour in length, were conducted with the judge at two courts, on the reasoning that including the judge in the staff focus group might inhibit other staff from speaking candidly about some issues. At the third, staff requested that the judge participate in the focus group, and the judge agreed to do so.

As noted, a key objective of this study is to examine the extent to which drug court participants and staff hold comparable views about various aspects of the drug court experience. Accordingly, at each site, focus groups were conducted first among drug court participants and then among court staff. To generate discussion and provide feedback to court staff, findings from the participant sessions were at times introduced during the staff sessions.

Participant Focus Groups

In recruiting for the participant focus groups, court staff introduced the research team to potential participants, and then left the room while researchers met participants to explain the project and inform them that participation was voluntary and confidential. At two sites, participants were offered an honorarium of $25, paid at the end of the session.[2]

Overall, the focus groups included a diverse mix of drug court participants in terms of racial and ethnic background, history of drug use/dependence, and status in the program. The make-up of the groups did, however, vary considerably across courts. All participants at one site had either recently graduated from the drug court or were about to do so; thus these participants were clearly biased in attitudes favorable to the program. The age, race, ethnicity, and socioeconomic status of participants also varied across courts. In light of these differences, we exercise considerable caution in comparing and contrasting findings across drug courts.

Staff Focus Groups

The project coordinator at each drug court recruited participants for the staff focus groups. In addition to the project coordinator, participants in staff sessions included clinical staff, case managers, probation officers, mental health staff, and in one instance the judge. Note that court attorneys did not participate in any of the sessions. Like the participants, drug court staff members participating in the focus groups were briefed on the purpose of the research, the confidential and voluntary nature of their participation, and the recording of the session. Findings from the participant group, which preceded the staff group at each site, were at times used to inform the staff discussion, as staff reacted to feedback from participants.

Emergent Themes and Findings

Following are the principal findings, organized according to the focus group protocol's broad topic areas: entering the drug court, perceptions about the program and its staff, what does and does not work about drug court, and suggestions for improvement.

Entering Drug Court

Drug court participants identified a variety of factors influencing their decision to enter the drug court, including being tired of an addicted lifestyle, sickness from addiction, "needing help" to fight addiction, being unable to afford bail, and wanting to reestablish or improve family relations. However, participants in all drug courts agreed that the primary factor behind the decision to enter drug court was to avoid incarceration. This conversation was typical:

> Moderator: *Why did you enter the treatment court program?*
> Participant 1: *To stay out of prison.*
> Participant 2: *To avoid prison.*
> Participant 3: *It's pretty simple.*
> Participant 4: *Yeah, it's plain to me.*

Most also felt that this decision is not completely voluntary. Drug court versus prison presents little real choice to most participants, with one commenting that "it was this [drug court] or jail so we just picked this." Some expressed the belief that the program "was forced" on them.

A few participants did, however, suggest that their arrest and opportunity to enter treatment court occurred at the "right time" when they "wanted to enter a program":

> *I was facing a lot of time [in prison] upstate, and I knew I had a problem, so this seemed like a reasonable way of taking care of both things at once.*

> *I was facing jail time ... but also I thought it would be a good idea because of all the [treatment] programs I had been to, they weren't working.*

> *I always inevitably wound up in front of another judge. And I was just tired of it, you know, I was beaten ... I was beaten down emotionally, mentally, physically.*

Some participants who said they initially entered treatment court solely to avoid prison acknowledged that their motivation changed after being in the program for some time, and they became more concerned about completing treatment, staying clean, and improving their lives. The treatment court experience appears to have been positive for these participants, enhancing their motivation to change.

Drug court staff were not surprised to learn that most participants initially entered drug court to avoid incarceration. One staff member felt that this motivation was "absolutely valid" and commented that, at entry, a participant's "state of mind [is] 'I gotta do what I gotta do. I gotta stay out of jail.'" Another agreed:

> *Not wanting to go to jail is a valid reason to stop using drugs; not wanting to lose your family, not wanting to lose your job ... not wanting to go to jail is a good way to start.*

Many drug court staff also agreed that participation in drug court—although nominally voluntary—is effectively coerced for most. One conceded, "I guess the goal is to coerce the person into taking a plea so they can stay out of jail." Others disagreed, maintaining that although participants may not feel they were given a choice, in fact they were. One case manager opined:

> *[Defendants] say... "You're giving me no choice. Now I just have to go to jail." No. The choice is either to do this or go to jail.*

Expectations When Entering the Program

The decision to enter drug court is typically made in a relatively short period.[3] Since participants are using drugs and may not be thinking clearly, they might not fully understand the commitment they are making by agreeing to enter drug court. In fact, many participants complained that staff did not explain the full scope of the commitment when they entered the program:

> *[The rules] should be explained to you before you sign [the drug court contract].*

> *Nobody sits down to get down and talk to you and explain these things to you, and, if you have any questions, let you ask the questions so they can answer them. None of that happens. A lot of people are kind of misled, as far as I can see; it's like a lack of information.*

Others reported that program requirements were explained to them by attorneys and drug court staff, but it was not until they attended a program orientation or began treatment that they fully comprehended what they were getting into.

Drug court staff agreed that participants "normally opt for treatment [court] not even realizing what the treatment will entail":

> *Invariably, a lot of them say to me, "I wasn't really paying attention in the beginning, I really had no clue. I know you guys were telling me, but I really didn't get it until later."*

> *When [the defendant is] up there, they get a brief synopsis of [drug court] when they're signing the contract and I really don't think they're paying attention other than, "Am I getting out today?"*

Court staff also said they make every attempt to ensure that all potential participants are aware of what they would be agreeing to by entering drug court "because we know very clearly that we're asking them to sign up for a lot and for a very long period of time of supervision by a whole bunch of people." Courts use a variety of techniques for informing participants, including orientation sessions, meetings with case managers, participant handbooks outlining program rules, and attorneys and clinical staff informing potential participants of the commitment required by the program.

Perceptions About Drug Court Program and Staff

Participants spoke at length about drug court staff members and, in general, had very positive impressions. Participants praised staff for genuinely caring and wanting what is best for them, and many said they could turn to staff if they had a problem.

> *I think that everyone who works here takes a personal interest in every individual here.*

> *It's not over when you get out of this [i.e., graduate the program]... If you needed help or something, or... lost your job and you needed help doing a resume or you needed help finding*

employment, you can come back here in this door here and they're going to do anything they can to help you out.

They also acknowledged staff members' dedication:

[Staff] are true to the program, that's one thing. I don't trust a lot of people, and I can honestly say, the people I've dealt with through the drug court... they work hard, and they're true about it.

They go beyond their job. You know, it's not just a job to them.

In addition to general remarks, participants also offered many comments about specific drug court staff—the judge, case managers, defense attorneys.

The Judge

In general, drug court participants spoke positively about the judge in their court. Most felt the judge knew what was going on in their lives and took this information into consideration when assigning sanctions and incentives, making treatment decisions, and talking to participants in court. When asked what they liked about the judge, several attributes were commonly cited across courts—fair, sympathetic, caring, concerned, and understanding.

That said, participants in all courts were well aware that the judge could be tough when necessary.

He's very strict and he doesn't bend at all, you know, to anybody. But if you're doing good, he treats you like a human being.

He's a very reasonable guy, if you're doing the right thing. Otherwise, he's really rough.

Very reasonable guy. I used to hate him, because he kept locking me up all the time, you know. But once you're doing the right thing, it's a different world over there.

Drug court staff also reported hearing similar participant praise of the judge:

The other thing [participants] say too, all the time, is how much the judge cares, that they can tell that the judge really cares about them, that they are people, that they're not just faces, they're not people that no one cares about.

For their part, court staff also hold their judge in high esteem. They appreciate working with a judge who is caring and compassionate but also enforces the rules and is strict with participants when necessary.

A lot of them are not just faces to him or not just bodies. He knows who they are.

I think what's really important is that you know he cares and some decisions he makes we may not agree with but he truly cares. He takes his time when he sentences someone. He'll ask them, "What are you doing? Do you want to do this any longer?"

If there needs to be a sanction, she'll do the sanction. If it needs to be a severe sanction, she'll do the sanction, but she doesn't do it just as a blatant thing cause she can because she's the judge.

In addition, court staff spoke positively about the judge's willingness to learn about addiction as a disease and to rely on other members of the court's clinical team.

> *One of the things that struck me about [the judge] right away was that even though he didn't know a heck of a lot about addiction, he always sat here and said, "Teach me, tell me." ... All of us as a team are really respected for our individual knowledge and areas of expertise.*

> *When [the judge] started this, he didn't know anything at all about alcoholism as a disease or drug addiction... But he made an attempt. He asks everybody questions. That's how he finds out.*

> *[The judge] waits to hear what we have to say and is open to all suggestions, especially for strange interventions.*

By contrast, discussion among participants in one drug court was rather critical of the judge. Participants felt the judge did not give them the opportunity to explain themselves and felt the judge could be arbitrary, with one telling researchers that the judge "makes his own rules." Staff at this court, although generally positive in their comments, did concede that the judge could be impatient in court. One noted that "he doesn't always listen and he jumps to conclusions... It's frustrating for us and for the defendants." Staff also felt that—despite making advances in understanding addiction—this judge still does not always recognize the power of the disease.[4]

All three judges reported having great respect for the clinical staff working with the court. The judges said they work closely with the entire team, and rely on them for clinical knowledge and recommendations.

Case Managers

In general, case managers were viewed positively by participants.[5] Case managers were described as helpful and encouraging, with one participant referring to his probation officer as a "good guy." Case managers were praised for their dedication to both participants and to the drug court program. In two courts, participants appreciated that case managers made themselves available—coming to work early and staying late to accommodate participants' schedules. Participants in one court also noted that case managers were present in the community and had a sense of what was going on in participants' lives. This, some felt, helped to encourage participants to follow court orders.

Several participants at one court complained about limited access to their case managers—with most attributing this problem to that court's high caseload. Participants in this court were also concerned that their case managers relied heavily on written reports from treatment providers, which they worried were not always accurate.

Some participants felt they could talk to their case manager if they were having problems with treatment, sobriety, or personal issues. Many staff members, upon hearing these reports, were skeptical that participants are actually quite so forthcoming, pointing out that participants are aware that their case manager is an employee of the court.

> *I think sometimes they're reluctant to verbalize some stuff in this room because of what we still represent. They know that we're workers of the court and depending on what they say, sometimes, disclosure [to the court] has to follow.*

While there may be some reluctance, staff admit that drug court participants "get invested in each of their case managers at a very deep level." One case manager, in fact, suggested clients may be too willing to share information with her and noted that "I've had very few clients who were reluctant to come and tell me anything."

Case managers generally agreed that they have close relationships with participants. One told us that most program graduates characterize their relationship with case managers as "tremendously important." Probation officers noted that some of their expectations as a case manager (e.g., advising clients and helping them to succeed in treatment) can at times conflict with their responsibility to protect public safety—and that "the number one priority for us is protection of the community always."

Defense Attorneys

Many participants complained about their defense attorneys' lack of involvement in their cases. For example, one reported that his attorney "didn't deal with me at all." Another was unaware that he even had an appointed counsel until a fellow participant brought it to his attention that "that woman" was his attorney. At the same time, however, many participants conceded that it was their attorney who first told them about drug court and encouraged them to enter the program. But clearly, participants did not believe the defense attorney was an important part of their drug court experience.

Drug court staff were aware that this was a common complaint among participants and generally agreed that defense attorneys played little role after participants entered drug court—with one staff member commenting "attorneys are basically a non-factor." Staff acknowledged, however, that defense attorneys play a key role in getting defendants to consider drug court.

> *A big part that the attorneys play is when they do realize that their clients are in a lose/lose situation here and that's when*

> *they really push hard to coerce their clients to enter treatment court.*

> *Attorneys play a pretty big role in explaining to them the reality that most of these cases ... stand an excellent chance of being convicted, and going to jail for a very long time, and [drug court] is a way out of that. I'm sure this is how the attorneys present it to them, not, "We both know you've got a problem and you've got to start to deal with it." They're totally selling them on "If you want to avoid going to jail, you do the program. It's that simple."*

In one court, staff told us that defense attorneys play a key role even after their clients enter the program. However, it is a behind-the-scenes role—much of the drug court team's decision making takes place at staff meetings prior to court appearances—so participants may be unaware of the work attorneys do in that setting:

> *We always have to reassure them in orientation... and let them know that their defense attorneys are advocating for them, if they're facing a sanction that week. They're advocating for them in the team meeting, not necessarily up in court in front of the judge.*[6]

Drug Court Rules and Procedures

While participants' comments about drug court tended to focus on the judge and court staff, the researchers did attempt to engage participants in a more general discussion of the rules and procedures of drug court, in light of considerable evidence that litigants' satisfaction with the justice system, and willingness to cooperate with its decisions, is influenced by the perceived fairness of the process (Tyler 1997, 1990; Casper, Tyler, and Fisher 1988).

Most participants reported that the rules of drug court are fair and felt that they are treated fairly by the treatment court team. For example, one participant commented that any time he received a sanction "there was a reason for it. [I] may have been mad at the time, but afterwards I understood." Many drug court participants spoke favorably about the way the judge and other staff account for participants' personal histories when making decisions such as phase advancement and sanctioning. These individualized responses were generally viewed as evidence that participants are treated fairly by the court. The opportunity to appear before the judge and explain themselves, particularly when given an infraction, also enhanced participants' perceptions of procedural justice.

The comments equating "personalized" court responses with fair treatment appear at first to be at odds with research suggesting that individualized responses may actually enhance the perception that procedures are unfair. For example, Paternoster, Brame, Bachman, and Sherman (1997) argue that people expect consistency from authorities—to be treated similarly to others and to have the same rules applied to them at different times—for a response to be fair. Individualized responses, or the tailoring of responses to circumstances, may thus be perceived as inconsistent and unfair.

These apparent conflicts may be reconciled, however, by the fact that drug court staff are often available to explain apparently differential treatment. Several participants conceded that, while sitting in drug court, they have been surprised to see similar infractions result in different sanctions, but that court staff have later discussed with them reasons for the different treatment (e.g., due to a participant's criminal or addiction history, or living situation). In one court, participants are invited to attend a post-court discussion with clinical staff to talk about what they saw in court that day. In another, case managers reported discussing such matters during individual meetings with participants. It appears that individualized responses might actually enhance some participants' perception that treatment is fair, provided they have the opportunity to discuss with court staff the reason for apparently disparate treatment (and presumably, that the justification is convincing).

Despite generally positive comments from participants, several participants in one drug court said they did not feel free to explain themselves to the judge, felt decisions were sometime arbitrary and that the judge "makes his own rules."[7] Other participants, however, disagreed with this criticism. One placed the burden on participants, saying, "Rules are rules—it's just a matter of how well you can adapt."

Drug court staff, while pleased to learn that most participants say they are treated fairly, indicated that they often hear a different story from participants, particularly when the court's individualized responses lead some participants to receive sanctions and other—apparently comparable—participants to receive less severe sanctions, or none at all.

Substance Abuse Treatment Programs

Substance abuse treatment providers across the nation face undeniable challenges. In many communities, the supply of high-quality treatment programs is insufficient to meet the demand for such services, and there are often substantial waiting lists for those services that are available (particularly residential treatment). Treatment agencies working with drug courts face additional challenges, including the need to accommodate larger numbers of referrals, to communicate and coordinate with drug court staff, and to meet courts' reporting requirements.

In light of these many challenges, it is perhaps not surprising that both drug court participants and staff were generally critical of treatment programs.[8] Drug court participants raised a number of issues about treatment providers and the treatment experience, but focused on four principal ones: the overall time in treatment, content of the treatment, scheduling, and compensation.

Many drug court participants felt treatment providers were not forthcoming about how long their treatment would last. They said communication between the treatment facility and court needed improvement, and that the court was led to believe treatment would take several months less than the facility actually planned to retain participants. Participants also disliked assignment to treatment sessions they felt were irrelevant to them. One participant, for example, objected to having to attend a class about heroin use, since he was primarily a marijuana user. He felt that assignment to this class was more about punishment and less about treatment.

Those attending outpatient treatment, many of whom had family, work and school obligations, were critical of the treatment schedules and found it difficult to coordinate the multiple demands on their time. Many drug court participants must pay fees for treatment expenses, and many were generally unenthusiastic about that. Some also felt it gave treatment facilities an incentive to retain them in treatment longer than strictly necessary—"the longer people stay in, the more money the program gets."

Like participants, drug court staff were often critical of treatment programs. Many of the clinical staff noted that, in general, treatment programs have failed to make the adjustments necessary to work effectively with court-mandated populations:

> *The reality is we have this incestuous relationship with the drug treatment community, which gives them permission to be lazy, non-creative, non-welcoming, non-respectful.*

Residential programs, for the most part, are still operating from a model that was based in the 1960s—punitive fear concept—and not much has changed... They're still pretty antiquated in their philosophy when it comes to treating addicts.

Staff also cited a shortage of available treatment services in the community, particularly for special-needs populations such as non-English-speakers and mothers with young children. Staff in all courts spoke at great length about the difficulty of holding treatment providers accountable. Despite being aware of problems with providers, staff felt that their hands are tied due to a lack of alternatives:

We unfortunately have very little discretion about where we send clients because most of the people who go to long-term treatment have to go on Medicaid... we only have one provider ... I have a lot of concerns about what goes on there... it doesn't always coincide with what the drug court would like to do. There's a lot less flexibility there and there's a lot less communication from their staff to the courts.

I say this knowing that our choices are severely limited, but we, to the best of our ability, hold the providers we use accountable to provide at least some level of quality service, and, if they don't, we don't use them anymore, or we sanction the program.

Not all drug court staff expressed concerns about treatment providers that work with the court. One judge, for example, reported there were no significant problems with treatment providers and characterized the court's relationship with local providers as "outstanding."

What works?

Participants were asked what they believe makes drug court programs work. In all focus groups, discussion focused primarily on the hands-on role of the judge and participants' experiences, both positive and negative, in the courtroom. Drug court participants repeatedly noted that they feared sanctions and were nervous when appearing before the judge. At the same time, virtually all also felt that the judge was supportive and helped them stick to the treatment process. One participant noted that he was able to avoid attending treatment while on probation, but he was unable to do so in drug court. Asked to explain, he commented that "regular probation is nothing compared to drug court because you don't go see the judge."

Participants were keenly aware of the leverage the court holds over them and acknowledged that the threat of jail for not completing drug court motivated them to stay in treatment and meet other program requirements. As one participant noted: "You want to use? All right, you can go to jail. You don't want to go to jail? Don't use." They also cited the intensive monitoring and drug testing, which "keeps you on point." This stands in contrast to the typical experience on regular probation that one participant characterized as a "joke" because "they're not testing."

Finally, some spoke about the success of drug court not in terms of specific aspects of the program but rather in terms of the support and motivation it provides individuals who are ready to be free of drugs and alcohol, to make a change in their lives. Drug court "motivates you to do what you need." But participants cautioned that individuals must really want to stay clean: "If you don't want to change, drug court is not for you. The drug court is not the place to just hang around and not go to jail."

The Courtroom Experience

The courtroom experience is critical to the drug court model. In contrast to the traditional courtroom, the drug court courtroom has less adversarial, less formal proceedings, featuring direct interaction between judge and participant. Focus group participants were asked to describe their experience in their courtroom and the impact of those experiences.[9]

Drug court staff hope that praise and criticism from the judge, a figure of authority, will motivate participants to do well. Conversations with participants suggest this is working. Discussion focused principally on the fear of judicial sanctions. Participants reported that they spend time before court preparing for what the judge might say to them. Many get nervous—one said his "stomach [was] in knots" before seeing the judge. Others felt the same way, particularly when they anticipate reprimand or sanction:

> *I used to come to court nervous. I used to smoke a cigarette. It might be my last cigarette.*

> *The hardest part is when you know you are messing up and you have to go see her.*

Over time this nervousness fades, assuming participants are compliant:

> *[The judge is] on you the first, second time there... He gets better though, once he gets to know you, he knows you're coming up clean every time. He gets to be more friend than enemy.*

> *If you know you're clean and you know you're not doing nothing [wrong], you're doing everything that you're supposed to be doing, it's good. I mean, it's not really all that nerve-wracking.*

Although appearing before the judge can be traumatic, participants also expressed satisfaction when they received positive feedback. Praise makes participants "want to think positive." Rewards such as certificates from the judge make participants feel "like [they are] achieving something." Another put it this way: "I like the congratulations. [The judge] always congratulates me and says, 'keep it up, you are doing fantastic.'" Participants in one session noted that the judge "pried" into their lives, but seemed to agree this was part of the judge's job and a sign that he "shows you a real concern" and wants participants to succeed.

The courtroom model also tries to produce an "audience effect"—seeing others receive praise and sanctions from the judge is intended to motivate participants to strive for similar praise and avoid similar reprimand. In all sessions, drug court participants were surprisingly cognizant that an audience effect is intentional and most agreed that seeing others receive sanctions—specifically incarceration—sends a message:

> *[The judge] locked him up for absences... it could happen to me the same way just by doing the same thing he did. That is something we have to understand.*
>
> *I think watching other people go to jail keeps you out... You know these people are not joking.*
>
> *A lot of it kept me sober. Seeing guys go to prison.*
>
> *When you're sitting up there in the courtroom ... you got somebody up there and you see that, the sheriff or the deputy, or whatever, come around... Wow... That could be you.*

Although they had less to say about seeing others do well, participants, when probed on the matter, generally agreed that seeing others rewarded and, especially, attending drug court graduation ceremonies inspired them to do well. Some participants in one court, however, did appear less inspired, with some arguing that rewards (for days clean and sober) were "arbitrary" and not handed out regularly—"too fluctuating."

Suggestions for Improvement

The focus groups also produced a number of thoughtful suggestions from participants and staff about ways to improve their drug court programs. Participants recommended expanding the drug court in different ways—e.g., having more treatment providers work with the court and providing flexible scheduling of classes; enhancing access to education, employment, job training, and other services; and reimbursing for travel so participants can more easily travel between court and treatment and home.

Drug court staff echoed many of these concerns and offered additional suggestions not raised by participants, including the need for more treatment services for women, non-English speakers and the dually diagnosed; more training in addiction issues for judges, attorneys, and other legal staff who work with drug courts (as well as those in other court settings); and more widely available methadone treatment.

Conclusion

Program staff and participants in all three drug courts generally do see eye to eye. Staff were remarkably cognizant about why participants enter drug court, what they like and do not like about it, and what motivates them to remain clean and in the program. The outcome of the research also made clear that these courts, to varying degrees, are willing to take feedback into account when shaping policies and procedures. For example, participants in one focus group told us that the name "drug court" is stigmatizing, branding participants as addicts. After program staff learned what the participants had expressed, the court changed its name to "treatment court." Staff at this court acted on other focus group findings as well. Staff members' knowledge of and concern for the participant perspective likely explains participants' positive impressions of the staff.

CHAPTER THREE

Evaluation of the Staten Island Treatment Court: Implementation and Impacts

KELLY O'KEEFE AND MICHAEL REMPEL

In March 2002, the Staten Island Treatment Court opened to provide an alternative to incarceration for drug-addicted felony offenders.[1] Staten Island is the least populated of the five boroughs of New York City, with a population of just under 450,000. Seventy-eight percent of the population is white, the highest percentage in any of the five boroughs. Also, Staten Island has the lowest poverty rate (10 percent) of the five boroughs. Although part of the city, much of Staten Island is suburban or semi-rural in appearance. This makes the Staten Island Treatment Court a particularly valuable case study, since most of the drug court evaluation literature to date has focused on sites in more densely populated urban areas.

This chapter presents the results of both a process and impact evaluation. The process evaluation focuses primarily on the planning process and the first year and a half of operations (see O'Keefe 2003), although qualitative data was updated in December 2005, spanning a much longer 46-month operational

This research was supported by the Bureau of Justice Assistance, U.S. Department of Justice, as part of an award to the New York State Unified Court System to implement the Staten Island Treatment Court. Opinions and interpretations in this chapter are those of the authors and do not necessarily represents the views of the U.S. Department of Justice or the New York State Unified Court System. The New York State Division of Criminal Justice Services provided criminal history and recidivism data for the evaluation. The authors are solely responsible for the methodology and results obtained with the data.

period. The impact evaluation involves a comparison of recidivism outcomes between participants arrested in the first 40 months of drug court operations (March 2002–June 2005) and an otherwise similar group of defendants arrested in the year before the Staten Island Treatment Court opened (March 2001–February 2002).

This chapter first describes the court's operational model and presents data on participant background characteristics, compliance, intermediate judicial sanctions, and key program outcomes (retention rates and employment or educational outcomes for graduates). We then present the methodology and results for the impact evaluation.

Operational Model

The Staten Island Treatment Court accepts nonviolent, first-time felony drug offenders as well as chronic misdemeanor offenders who are arrested in Staten Island and are addicted to or abusing drugs. It hears cases one day a week and follows a classic drug court model with multiple program phases, intensive case management, frequent appearances before the judge, and sanctions and rewards in response to participant behavior and needs. In addition to the standard drug court graduation requirements of remaining drug-free for a meaningful period of time and completing treatment, participants must make measurable progress toward personal goals such as education or employment. Team members, including the judge, frequently address obstacles impeding personal achievements, and the court requires participants to contemplate personal goals and success in multiple written interviews during their participation. Graduates have the criminal charges against them dismissed, while those who fail are sentenced to a pre-negotiated jail alternative (usually one year).

The Team

The Staten Island Treatment Court team consists of a dedicated judge, project director, senior case manager, senior court clerk, two dedicated assistant district attorneys, two defense attorneys, several dedicated case managers from Treatment Alternatives for Safe Communities (TASC), a nationwide case management agency, and a TASC supervisor. In addition to the treatment court team, there is a steering committee that meets regularly. The steering committee consists of the judge, the D.A.'s chief of the narcotics bureau, the TASC supervisor, the project director, a partner in the law firm that represents treatment court participants, and two staff attorneys from the same firm.

From observation, the treatment court team and steering committee are comprised of remarkably dedicated individuals. They take time out of their schedules to make the court a priority, arranging steering committee meetings either before or after work hours, gathering to review cases weekly over lunch, and fitting in e-mails and conversations throughout the week. The team lacks office space for meetings, and court space is tight. However, those involved in the court maintain good working relationships and a positive attitude toward their mission.

The staff built a sense of teamwork through traveling together, attending trainings, and making difficult decisions regarding eligibility, sanctions/rewards, and logistics. From individual interviews and evaluator observations, it has become clear that team members fundamentally respect one another's experiences, views, and intentions. The group has remained largely intact since its inception and has a relaxed, friendly feel. Members reported that they felt as if they had a voice in meetings and decision making. As one interviewee said, "We sometimes argue or have differences, but in the end, we're all here for the same reason—to help folks stop using drugs."

Eligibility

Defendants are currently considered eligible for the Staten Island Treatment Court if they are 16 years of age or older, either drug-addicted or abusing drugs, and charged with a nonviolent, first-time narcotics felony. Nonviolent misdemeanor offenders with multiple prior misdemeanor convictions are also eligible.

As of December 2005, the treatment court had received a total of 402 referrals. Of these, 179 defendants (45 percent) enrolled as participants. Over the entire 46 months of operations encompassed by this evaluation, the Staten Island Treatment Court has averaged 103 referrals and 47 drug court participants per year. Due to declining arrest volume, these numbers are substantially lower than the court's originally projected rate of intake. The treatment court had planned to screen 400 defendants per year and to enroll 200 new participants per year. But the results are typical of adult drug courts nationwide, which average 40 participants per year (Schafer and Zweig 2004).

Charges

Initially, eligibility was limited to nonviolent, first-time narcotics felony offenders. In March 2004, the treatment court accepted its first nonviolent misdemeanor offender, and subsequently changed its rules to allow other misdemeanor offenders with multiple priors to enroll.

As shown in Table 1, misdemeanors represent 10 percent of all participant charges. Felony drug possession accounts for nearly half of all charges (48 percent) followed by felony drug sales (38 percent). The remaining charges (four percent) were for nonviolent felony level property offenses.

Participant Profile

The profile table (Table 2) details the demographics, socioeconomic status, and drug use/drug treatment history of all enrolled

Table 1. Participant Charges

Participant Charges	Male N	Male %	Female N	Female %	Total N	Total %
Misdemeanor						
Petit larceny	3	6%	4	27%	7	10%
Criminal contempt	1	2%	0	0%	1	1%
Drug possession	6	4%	2	6%	8	4%
Other	1	1%	1	3%	2	1%
Felony						
Drug Sales	53	37%	15	44%	68	38%
Drug Possession	75	52%	11	32%	86	48%
Burglary	2	1%	0	0%	2	1%
Larceny	2	1%	1	3%	3	2%
Robbery	1	1%	0	0%	1	1%
Total	144	100%	34	100%	178	100%

(Missing=2)

participants (as of December 2005). To give context to the profile data, the following discussion makes comparisons to the data reported in the 2003 statewide evaluation of 11 other adult drug courts in the New York state, including the drug courts from all four other boroughs of New York City (Rempel et al. 2003: Chapter 3).

The median age of entry of 22 years at the Staten Island Treatment Court stands out because it is the lowest age when compared to these 11 other drug courts (range = 23–33 years). The participant population in Queens (one of the other New York City programs) is just slightly older with a median age of 23 years.

When examining socioeconomic status, Staten Island Treatment Court participants fare relatively well: 53 percent were engaged in work or school at the time of entry, which compares with a range of 16 percent to 55 percent across the 11 other drug courts examined in the statewide evaluation. And only 11 percent of participants have ever been homeless, a lower percentage than most drug courts both statewide and nationally. However, only 34 percent of the Staten Island Treatment Court participants had a high school diploma/GED at time of entry compared with 45 per-

Table 2. Participant Profile

	Male (N = 128)	Female (N = 25)	Total (N = 153)
Demographics			
Median Age at Entry	22	28	22
Median Age at First Drug Use	15	16	15
Race/Ethnicity			
Caucasian	46%	52%	47%
Black	44%	36%	42%
Hispanic/Latino	9%	8%	9%
Native American	2%	4%	1%
Race/Ethnicity Total	100%	100%	100%
Socio-Economic Status			
Ever Homeless			
Yes	9%	21%	11%
No	91%	79%	89%
High School Degree/GED			
Yes	32%	42%	34%
No	68%	58%	66%
Employed/In School at Entry			
Yes	54%	46%	53%
No	46%	54%	47%
Household at Entry			
Lives Alone	10%	17%	11%
Unmarried partner	9%	4%	8%
Spouse	4%	8%	5%
Children under 18	0%	21%	4%
Parent / Siblings	59%	42%	56%
Other relatives	10%	8%	9%
Foster Care	1%	0%	1%
Friends	3%	0%	2%
Others	4%	0%	3%
Shelter	1%	0%	1%
Drug Use/Treatment History			
Years of Drug Use (Median)	7	10	7
Ever in Treatment	25%	48%	23%
Primary Drug of Choice			
Heroin/Opiates	11%	25%	14%
Cocaine	9%	0%	7%
Crack	6%	25%	9%
Marijuana	65%	43%	61%
Alcohol	4%	4%	4%
PCP	2%	0%	2%
Prescription/Designer	4%	4%	4%

cent in Queens, whose population is generally similar. Approximately 70 percent of treatment court participants live with either immediate family or relatives, indicating some level of social support.

In regards to drug use and drug treatment history, the median length of drug use is seven years. This is slightly lower than the lowest median years of drug use of the 11 drug courts in the statewide evaluation (eight years). On the other hand, the median age of first drug use, 15 years, was well within the range of all 11 other programs (15–17 years). The primary drug of choice is overwhelmingly marijuana (63 percent), and only 23 percent of participants reported any previous treatment prior to drug court entry. The predominant use of marijuana is quite typical of juvenile and young adult drug court populations, but it is unusual for programs that are formally open to adult criminal populations of all ages.

Overall, the results of the participant profile analysis suggest that the treatment court serves a younger, less severely addicted population than most of the state's drug courts and, for that matter, most adult drug courts nationally.

Monitoring Compliance

The Staten Island Treatment Court participation process is divided into three phases. A participant must spend a minimum of four months in each phase in order to move to the next. Incurring sanctions may lengthen the time spent in one phase and/or set the participant back to a previous one. The treatment court team discusses each case individually before allowing it to transition to the next phase.

In the first phase, participants are scheduled to appear before the judge from once a week to once a month (the exact frequency is determined individually for each participant, with the general tendency to gradually reduce the frequency over time). In the second phase, the range is once a month to once every six weeks; and in the third phase the range is once every six weeks to every two months. This frequency is less than for most adult drug courts, which tend to hold judicial status hearings once every month or less throughout participation; however, the less severely addicted and more socioeconomically advantaged character of the Staten Island Treatment Court suggests that fewer status hearings may be as effective (see Marlowe et al. 2004).

The Staten Island Treatment Court states that one of its goals is "to monitor participants' compliance with mandatory periodic drug testing." This goal is achieved through frequent testing at the TASC office and the community-based treatment programs. Initially, participants are drug tested twice a week, once at their treatment program and once at the TASC office. If the participant is noncompliant, testing increases to as many as five times per week. The treatment providers fully cooperate with treatment court requests to increase drug testing. Testing can also decrease in frequency based on compliant behavior.

Of those participants enrolled through December 2005, 73 percent tested positive at least once, including for alcohol use. Most positive tests occurred early in drug court participation—by their 10th drug test, only 11 percent tested positive, and only three percent tested positive for "serious" drugs (cocaine or heroin).

Infractions, Sanctions and Rewards

A formal schedule of sanctions and rewards is clearly spelled out in the Staten Island Treatment Court participant handbook and policy and procedures manual. Each phase has A level, B level and C level infractions, and these infractions have corresponding sanctions that increase in severity with the number of infractions and the phase. Even though the infractions and sanctions policies are clear, the Staten Island Treatment Court team weighs personal and family factors, and previous behavior that may or may not

Table 3. Participant Infractions

	Participants with at least One Infraction
# Participants	**96**
% Participants W/ At Least One Infraction	**53%**
# Infractions	**243**
% Serious Infractions (new arrest & warrants)	**21%**
INFRACTION TYPE	
1. New Arrest	**8%**
2. Warrant	**13%**
Abscond, Voluntary return on warrant (ROW)	2%
Abscond, Involuntary return on warrant (ROW)	4%
Abscond, return unknown	7%
3. Dirty or Substituted Urine	**38%**
4. Program Violation	**38%**
Missed appointment	24%
Rule-breaking	14%
5. Other	**3%**

explain the current infraction, before imposing the indicated sanction.

Table 3 shows that 53 percent of participants committed at least one infraction while enrolled. A serious infraction, defined as a new arrest or warrant, was committed by 21 percent. Table 4 shows that 52 percent of participants received at least one sanction, and 25 percent received at least one jail sanction. The most common types of sanctions were treatment increase (increased case manager contacts or treatment intensity) and jail, each comprising 28 percent of all sanctions imposed. Community service (15 percent of all sanctions) and verbal admonishment (19 percent) were also common sanctions. The court rarely utilized the jury box as a sanction due to space constraints; community providers, case managers, and defense attorneys occupy the jury box during treatment court sessions.

Table 4. Participant Sanctions

	Staten Island
# Participants	180
# Sanctions	222
% W/ At Least One Sanction	52%
% W/ At Least One Jail Sanction	25%
SANCTION TYPE	
1. Verbal Admonishment	19%
2. Essay	3%
3. Jury Box	1%
4. Court Monitoring Upgrade[1]	3%
5. Treatment Increase[2]	28%
6. Community Service	15%
7. Jail	28%
Less than 1 week	27%
7-11 days	10%
More than 11 days	0%
Length unspecified	63%
8. Other	3%

[1] Court monitoring upgrade sanctions include increased court appearances, even daily court reporting.

[2] Treatment increase sanctions include increased contact with case manager, mandatory AA/NA, detox/rehab, increase in frequency of drug tests, increase in modality or treatment level.

Treatment

Staten Island Treatment Court participants are largely placed in outpatient facilities (86 percent). Only 13 percent were placed in long-term residential facilities at the beginning of their treatment; and the remaining one percent were first placed in a 30-day inpatient program and then switched to outpatient. The lack of residential services in Staten Island is a barrier, as participants older than 21 who need such services must be placed outside of the borough. Currently, the court places these participants in upstate New York and other boroughs of New York City. If attending outpatient treatment, participants visit the TASC office once per week to check in and take a drug test.

Community Outreach

The Staten Island Treatment Court has made many efforts to achieve its goal of "outreach continuously to inform the community about Staten Island Treatment Court and seek support for the Staten Island Treatment Court." While still in the planning phase, the court reached out to community providers to update them on the court's work and explain future plans. After the court had been in operation for over a year, the project director engaged in outreach to primary providers to inform them about the court and enlist their support. As a signal of the visibility of the drug court and its accomplishments, the court has received recognition and awards from three local organizations.

Program Outcomes

Graduation Requirements and Outcomes

In order to graduate, participants must complete all requirements of the individual treatment plan, accrue 12 months without sanctions, have made significant and measurable progress toward personal goals such as employment, G.E.D, vocational training or school, and submit a graduation application setting forth accomplishments and goals. The graduation application is completed at the time of an exit interview, conducted by either the senior case manager or the project director. As of December 2005, a total of 73 participants had graduated, 25 had failed, and five had completed their participation with "incomplete" status (resulting from a serious mental or physical illness). Among the graduates, the average time to graduation was 15.6 months.

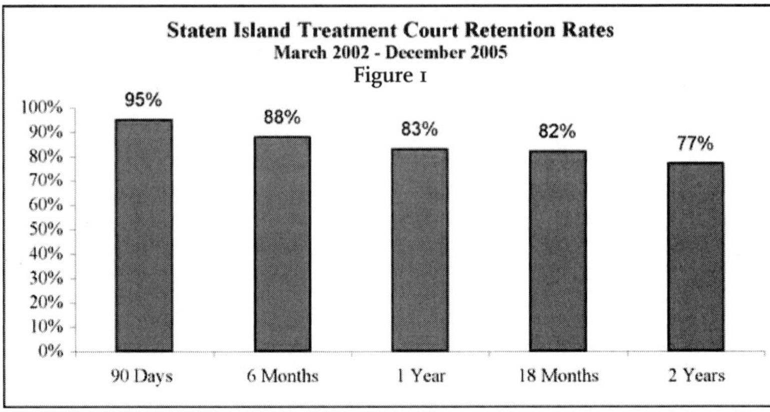

Retention Rates

Retention is a key measure of program success (see Chapter 1). Figure 1 displays retention rates for the court from 90 days through two years after enrollment. The Staten Island Treatment Court maintains high retention rates and suffers very little attrition—from 95 percent retention at 90 days to 77 percent retention at two years post-enrollment. This data shows that the court has exceeded its official planning goal of a 70 percent one-year retention rate. Also, the court's one- and two-year retention rates compare favorably with the drug courts included in the earlier New York state evaluation (Rempel et al. 2003). The 11 adult drug courts examined in that earlier study had one-year retention rates ranging from 47 percent to 82 percent (Staten Island Treatment Court = 83 percent) and two-year retention rates ranging from 32 percent to 78 percent (Staten Island Treatment Court = 77 percent).

The Staten Island Treatment Court set a goal for a 65 percent graduation rate. Based on its two-year retention rate of 77 percent, and the fact that nearly all participants have reached final status as of the two-year mark, it is more than likely that the court is achieving a graduation rate above 70 percent. This exceeds both the Staten Island Treatment Court's own graduation rate objective and average graduation rates for adult drug courts nationwide, which from all available evidence appears to stand at approximately 50 percent.

Other Outcomes for Graduates

Of those graduating, some had achievements in areas outside of substance abuse treatment. A high percentage of graduates already had a GED/high school diploma upon entry into the court (63 percent); and an additional seven participants (10 percent) obtained their GED or high school diploma while in the program. Also, 14 percent of graduates completed a vocational program while in the drug court. As of their graduation date, 69 percent were employed either full-time or part-time, and 36 percent were enrolled in school.

Impact Evaluation

This section examines the impact of the Staten Island Treatment Court on recidivism, case processing efficiency, and sentencing outcomes. The primary research question is whether the treatment court produces a reduction in recidivism as compared with conventional case processing.

Research Design and Methodology

The evaluation involved a comparison of outcomes between Staten Island Treatment Court participants arrested in the first 40 months of drug court operations (March 2002–June 2005) and an otherwise similar group of defendants arrested in the year before the drug court opened (March 2001–February 2002). The participant sample included all 146 participants arrested from March 2002 through June 2005. Recidivism data was obtained after an additional six months, at the end of December 2005, meaning that all participants could be tracked over at least a six-month period. Also, 123 participants could be analyzed over a one-year time frame, and 102 could be analyzed over 18 months.

Diminishing sample sizes made any analysis beyond 18 months unfeasible.

The comparison group was initially defined to maximize its comparability to participants in terms of its current charges and criminal history. Since 86 percent of those in the participant sample were arrested on felony drug charges (the remaining 14 percent were arrested on a wide assortment of other felony and misdemeanor charges), the comparison group was limited to felony drug charges only. Consistent with official treatment court eligibility criteria, defendants were excluded from the comparison group if they had a prior violent felony conviction at any time or a prior nonviolent felony conviction within the preceding 10 years. Also, defendants were excluded if they were arrested on the most serious type of felony drug charge (A1 or A2 felonies, which together comprise less than five percent of all drug felonies in Staten Island). Finally, defendants were excluded if their case did not result in a conviction. This last exclusion was based on the assumption that any defendants with a reasonable probability of having their case dismissed would not, in practice, agree to participate in at least a year of court-mandated treatment. After applying these exclusions to those arrested in Staten Island in the year before the treatment court opened, 223 potential comparison group defendants were identified.

While this initial pool of 223 comparison candidates matched the formal "paper eligibility" criteria of Staten Island Treatment Court participants, this could not by itself guarantee that all of them would truly have entered the drug court if the opportunity existed to do so. Some of these defendants might have been found ineligible for reasons not captured by formal legal criteria (e.g., if not addicted to drugs, or if perceived to be involved in heavy drug trafficking), and others might have refused to participate. Further, it is possible that officially eligible defendants with a certain background (demographics or criminal history) are especially likely or unlikely to end up participating.

Additional statistical methods can be used to determine exactly which types of defendants possess background characteristics most similar to those of real drug court participants and to select a final comparison sample that even more closely matches the participant sample. Propensity score matching techniques are designed to do this. They involve matching each participant to a comparison group candidate whose background characteristics are most comparable. The matching process does not require that each individual characteristic be identical (same age, same race, same prior criminal history, etc.) but that when all background characteristics are considered together, the matched pair shares a similar propensity, or probability, that they would participate in drug court if given the opportunity (see Rubin 1973; and for a detailed discussion of how these techniques may be applied in a drug court evaluation, see Rempel 2006).

For this study, a one-to-one matching method was employed, meaning that each participant was matched to the comparison group candidate with the nearest possible propensity score (most similar set of background characteristics) from among those not previously matched to another participant. By the end of the matching process, 146 Staten Island Treatment Court participants were matched to exactly 146 comparison group defendants.

The data shown in Table 5 demonstrates the dramatic effect of propensity score matching in leading the final samples to be far more comparable than the initial samples. The left-most columns compare the 146 drug court participants to the initial 223 comparison candidates, revealing significant differences in multiple criminal history, charge related, and demographic characteristics. The right-most columns demonstrate the degree to which the final samples became more comparable as a result of the matching process. The final samples were not significantly different on

Table 5. Characteristics of Participant and Comparison Groups Before and After Propensity Score Matching

	Pre-Matching		Final Comparisons		Change in Drug Court/Comparison Sample Differences
	Drug Court	Comparison	Drug Court	Comparison	
Sample Size	(N = 146)	(N = 223)	(N = 146)	(N = 146)	
Criminal History					
Prior Arrests					
Any prior arrest	65%*	75%	65%	59%	-4%
Any prior felony arrest	47%*	58%	47%	52%	-6%
Any prior misdemeanor arrest	57%+	66%	57%	60%	-6%
Any prior drug arrest	55%	61%	55%	56%	-5%
Mean number of prior arrests	3.9	5.1	3.9	4.6	-0.5
Mean number of prior felony arrests	1.5	2.0	1.5	1.9	-0.1
Mean number of prior misdemeanor arrests	2.4	3.1	2.4	2.7	-0.4
Mean number of prior drug arrests	2.0	2.1	2.0	2.0	-0.1
Prior Convictions					
Any prior conviction[1]	48%+	57%	48%	51%	-6%
Any prior felony conviction	2%+	0%	2%+	0%	0%
Any prior misdemeanor conviction	22%*	32%	22%	29%	-3%
Any prior drug conviction	16%	16%	16%	14%	2%
Mean number of prior convictions[1]	2.1	2.7	2.1	2.3	-0.4
Mean number of prior felony convictions	0.0[2]	0.0	0.0[2]	0.0	0.0
Mean number of prior misdemeanor convictions	0.9	1.4	0.9	1.1	-0.3
Mean number of prior drug convictions	0.3	0.3	0.3	0.3	0.0
Current Charges					
Felony drug sales	45%	41%	45%	51%	2%
Felony drug possession	41%**	59%	41%	49%	-10%
Other charges[3]	14%***	0%	14%***	0%	0%
Demographics					
Female sex	17%+	25%	17%	18%	-7%
Mean age	26.2**	28.9	26.2	26.6	-2.3
Race/ethnicity					
Black	43%	43%	43%	44%	1%
White	51%+	42%	51%	51%	-9%
Hispanic / other[4]	6%**	15%	6%	5%	-8%

+ $p < .10$ * $p < .05$ ** $p < .01$ *** $p < .001$ (2-tailed t-test)

[1] Prior criminal history is only considered if there was an arrest at the felony or misdemeanor level. However, felony or misdemeanor arrests that lead to a conviction at the violation level are counted and thus reflected in the totals for any type of conviction.

[2] The actual mean is .0411.

[3] Other charges includes: nine misdemeanor drug possession charges, nine other misdemeanors, and three other felonies.

[4] All defendants in this category are Hispanic, except for two defendants in the drug court sample.

any characteristic (.05 level), except for the probability of having a non-felony drug arrest charge; this one difference is an automatic function of defining the comparison group to exclude such charges.[2]

In the analyses to follow, the participant-comparison match forms the unit of analysis for estimating the drug court's impact. The average difference in outcomes across all matches is used to estimate the overall drug court impact. Whenever a participant is unavailable for a particular analysis—for example, only 102 of the 146 participants in the full sample had accumulated enough time after their initial arrest to analyze over the 18-month tracking period—the comparison defendant with whom that participant was matched is also dropped from the analysis. This maintains similar levels of match comparability across each individual analysis.

Impact on Recidivism

As shown in Figure 2, the Staten Island Treatment Court produced a substantial reduction in recidivism across both the one-year and the 18-month measurement periods ($p < .05$ or better for both comparisons). After one year, 26 percent of drug court participants versus 48 percent of the comparison group were re-arrested; and after 18 months, the difference was 41 percent versus 55 percent. Framed differently, when compared with the initial comparison group level, *the Staten Island Treatment Court produced a 46 percent relative reduction in the re-arrest rate after one year* and a 25 percent reduction after 18 months.

As further shown in Table 6, comparable recidivism reductions were evident when isolating felony, misdemeanor, and drug-related re-arrests. Also, when turning to re-convictions, the magnitude of the recidivism reduction appears to increase. The 18-month re-conviction rate was 23 percent for drug court participants and 41 percent for the comparison group, meaning that the

Figure 2. Impact of the SITC on Recidivism Within One Year and Eighteen Months After the Initial Arrest

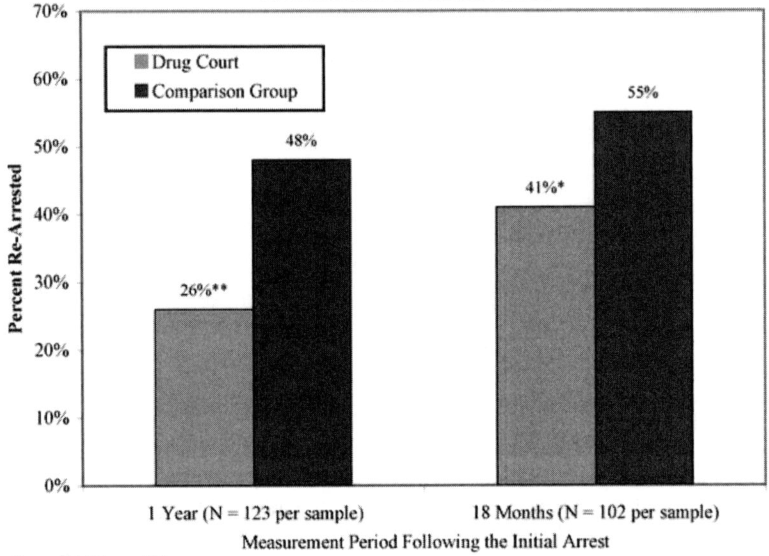

* p < .05 ** p <.001

drug court produced a relative reduction in the re-conviction rate of close to half (44 percent).

When examining the total number of re-arrests and re-convictions, the comparison group had almost twice as many total recidivist events as drug court participants did across most of the outcome measures reported in Table 6. For instance, drug court participants averaged 0.63 re-arrests over the 18-month tracking period, whereas the comparison group averaged almost double at 1.19.

Finally, the drug court appeared to delay the onset of recidivism when examining those with at least one re-arrest within 18 months (this effect was not apparent in the shorter one-year analysis). Of those re-arrested within 18 months, drug court participants averaged 256 crime-free days before their first re-arrest, while the comparison group averaged a significantly lower number, only 164 crime-free days.

Table 6. Impact of the SITC on Recidivism

Recidivism Measure	Drug Court	Comparison Group
Recidivism within One Year of the Initial Arrest	(N = 123)	(N = 123)
Any re-arrest	26%***	48%
Mean number of re-arrests	0.41**	0.87
Any felony re-arrest	17%*	31%
Any misdemeanor re-arrest	14%**	30%
Any drug re-arrest	17%**	34%
Any re-conviction	15%**	29%
Mean number of re-convictions	0.18**	0.44
Of those with at least one re-arrest:	(N = 32)	(N = 59)
Days to first re-arrest	114	136
Recidivism within 18 Months of the Initial Arrest	(N = 102)	(N = 102)
Any re-arrest	41%*	55%
Mean number of re-arrests	0.63**	1.19
Any felony re-arrest	24%*	36%
Any misdemeanor re-arrest	24%*	39%
Any drug re-arrest	25%*	38%
Any re-conviction	23%**	41%
Mean number of re-convictions	0.31	0.63
Of those with at least one re-arrest:	(N = 42)	(N = 56)
Days to first re-arrest	256**	164

+p<.10 *p<.05 **p<.01 ***p<.001 (2-tailed t-test)

Note: An event counts as recidivism if it resulted in a conviction. Technically, the new arrest must have occurred within the given measurement period (e.g., 1, 2 or 3 years), but the conviction may have occurred at a later time. Participant sample sizes vary, because some cases entered drug court too recently to have accumulated sufficient post-arrest time for a three year post-arrest analysis.

Other Predictors of Recidivism

To determine whether other defendant characteristics besides drug court participation status predicted recidivism, a Cox regression analysis was performed. Cox regression assesses both the presence and timing of recidivism (how many crime-free days were there before a re-arrest took place). All 146 defendants from each sample were included in the analysis. None were tracked for longer than 18 months, and for those whose possibility of re-arrest could only be tracked over a lesser period, the Cox procedure takes into account the exact amount of "at risk" time.

The results indicate that significant predictors of recidivism (re-arrest) were as follows (see Table 7):

Table 7. Cox Regression Predicting the Impact of SITC Participation and Other Background Characteristics on Re-Arrest

Maximum Tracking Period	18 Months
Total Sample	292
Drug Court	146
Comparison Group	146
Number of Censored Cases (not re-arrested)	161[1]
	Odds Ratios:
Drug court participant	.691*
Natural logarithm of the total number of prior arrests	1.515***
Arrested on felony sales top charge	1.204
Female sex	.902
Age	.969**
Race/ethnicity[2]	
Black	1.651
White	.896

+p<.10 *p<.05 **p<.01 ***p<.001

[1] All censored casees (not re-arrested) had their number of days set to 547 if they could be tracked for the maximum tracking period of 18 months. If they could not be tracked for that duration, their number of days was set to their number of days "at risk" (i.e., the total number for which they could be tracked).

[2] Race/ethnicity has a third, unlisted "Hispanic" category to which black and white participants are compared.

- *Drug court participation status*: Consistent with the previous results, drug court participation significantly predicted non-recidivism ($p < .05$);
- *Prior criminal history*: The number of prior arrests significantly predicted recidivism ($p < .001$);[3]
- *Age*: Younger age significantly predicted recidivism ($p < .01$).

Impact on Case Processing Efficiency

In addition to the primary goals of reduced recidivism and drug use, the first drug courts established in the early 1990s were also concerned with the goal of increasing case processing efficiency. Improved efficiency actually comprised the primary goal motivating the initial appearance of drug courts, including the Miami Drug Court in 1989 (Cooper 2002). Faced with escalating numbers of drug cases and drug-related incarcerations, court systems throughout the country were under growing pressure to manage their cases more efficiently, reduce case backlog, reduce jail and prison terms for drug offenders, and generate cost savings. Accordingly, research reports on drug courts published through the mid-1990s emphasized the measurement of processing-related objectives (McCoy 2003).

As shown in Table 8, Staten Island Treatment Court participants reached initial disposition after significantly less time than the comparison group. For this analysis, "initial disposition" for drug court participants is defined as the date of the guilty plea that formalized drug court entry; the disposition date for the comparison group is usually the plea date as well, but in some cases can be the date of conviction by trial. Participants averaged 2.1 months to initial disposition, whereas the comparison group averaged twice as long at 4.2 months ($p < .001$).

Of course, from a pure court resources standpoint, the drug court ultimately takes longer to process its cases than conventional prosecution since a "final" drug court disposition is not reached until the date of drug court graduation or failure. Thus as shown in the bottom section of Table 8, drug court participants averaged 16.1 months to graduation or failure, almost four times longer than the comparison group's average time to disposition.

Impact on Sentencing Outcomes

As an alternative-to-incarceration program, most drug courts aspire to reduce the time that defendants spend in jail or prison. Some drug court critics argue that, due to the lengthy jail or prison sentences commonly imposed on drug court failures, drug court participants—when considered all together—face more severe criminal justice sanctions than under conventional prosecution (Nolan 2001). A study of the Baltimore drug court found that while participants spent fewer days in jail than the

Table 8. Impact of the SITC on Case Processing Efficiency

Processing Measure	Drug Court	Comparison Group
Months from Initial Arrest to Initial Disposition[1]		
Average	2.1***	4.2
Median	1.5	2.7
Months from Initial Arrest to Final Disposition[2,3] (defined as graduation or failure date for drug court participants and plea date or other final disposition date for the comparison group)		
Average	16.1	4.2
Median	15.7	2.7

+ p<.10 * p<.05 ** p<.01 *** p<.001 (2-tailed t-test)
Note: Significance tests were not conducted for the median results.

[1] The initial disposition date is defined as the plea date for drug court participants and the plea date or other final disposition date for the comparison group.

[2] The final disposition date is defined as the graduation or failure date for drug court participants and as the final disposition date (identical to above) for the comparison group.

[3] The drug court participant sample for this analysis only includes graduates and failures (N = 98).

comparison group due to their final sentence, they spent substantially more time in jail due to intermediate sanctions for noncompliant behavior; thus when all time was considered, the total number of days spent incarcerated was only slightly lower for drug court participants than for the comparison group (Gottfredson, Najaka, and Kearley 2003). In the statewide evaluation of New York's drug courts, participants in three of the six sites where impact evaluations were conducted averaged significantly fewer days in jail or prison than the comparison group on the initial criminal case; but participants in one drug court spent significantly more time in jail or prison on the initial case; and in the final two sites, there was not a significant difference in either direction (Rempel et al. 2003).

The present analysis began with the 100 drug court participants who had reached a final disposition (graduation or failure) as of the analysis and their 100 matched comparison group defendants. Since six of the 100 comparison defendants and one

Table 9. Impact of the SITC on Sentencing Outcomes[1]

	Graduates	Failures[2]	All Drug Court	Comparison
Available Sample Size	76	26	93	93
Sentence Type				
Incarceration Sentence	0%	96%***	26%	27%
Prison	0%	23%$^{+}$	7%	7%
Straight jail or jail/probation split	0%	73%***	20%	20%
Time served	0%	0%**	0%**	10%
Straight probation	0%	0%***	0%***	15%
Conditional discharge	0%	0%***	0%***	18%
Fine (without any additional sentence)	2%	0%***	1%***	32%
Case dismissed/no sentence imposed	98%	4%[4]	72%***	0%
Sentence Length				
Length of jail/prison sentences[3]				
Average length (across entire sample)	0	208***	58	39
Average length (of those sentenced to jail or prison)	n/a	217	217	159

$^{+}$ p < .10 * p < .05 ** p <.01 *** p < .001 (2-tailed t-test)

Note 1: T-tests were only conducted for the comparisons between: (1) all drug court participants and the comparison group and (2) failures and the comparison group. Graduates always have their case dismissed (with one exception), so statistical tests are unnecessary to demonstrate the clear and distinctive pattern that is applicable to graduates.

Note 2: Percentages do not always add up to 100 percent or to applicable sub-category totals due to rounding.

[1] The total drug court participant sample for this analysis only includes those reaching final dispositional status: graduates (67), failures (21), and incompletes due to mental or physical illness (five).

[2] This category includes both the 21 drug court failures and the five participants with a final status of incomplete due to mental or physical illness.

[3] For prison sentences, time incarcerated is assumed to be the minimum (e.g., one year in a one-to-three year sentence); and for jail sentences, time incarcerated is assumed to be two-thirds of the official sentence, given standard "good time" release policies.

[4] One case that was closed as "incomplete" was convicted, but a sentence was not imposed.

of the drug court participants had missing sentence information, the final samples were then reduced to 93 and 93.

As shown in Table 9 (comparing the two right-most columns), the probability of receiving either a jail or prison sentence is virtually identical for both participants and the comparison group (26 percent and 27 percent). Also, the average time spent serving a jail or prison sentence is less than 60 days for both samples, with small, non-significant differences in the exact numbers.

Although there were not significant differences in incarceration rates when comparing all treatment court participants to the comparison group it turns out that, when isolating drug court failures only, failures were significantly more likely to be sentenced to jail or prison than the comparison group (96 percent versus 27 percent), and averaged significantly more time sentenced to jail or prison (208 versus 39 days). Therefore, there is some legal risk involved in entering the drug court. Graduating means the complete avoidance of a criminal record, since those cases are dismissed, but failing involves a longer average sentence than what would have been imposed had the case been processed using conventional methods. Since the Staten Island Treatment Court has an exceptionally high graduation rate (72 percent of the 100 participants reaching final status as of this analysis), most Staten Island Treatment Court participants receive a clear legal benefit from their enrollment. Also, since the Staten Island Treatment Court produces a significant reduction in recidivism, future incarceration rates can be expected to drop lower eventually for those enrolling in the drug court than for the comparison group. This anticipated future effect is not immediately apparent when examining jail and prison rates only on the initial case that first brought the participants to drug court.

Summary

This process evaluation highlights that the Staten Island Treatment Court team collaborated effectively in implementing a classic adult drug court model, including interagency collaboration, compliance monitoring, judicial sanctions and rewards, and strong legal incentives to succeed—case dismissal for graduates and exact, predetermined jail sentences for those who fail.

The participant profile indicates that the court serves a younger, less addicted population than most of the state's drug courts and, for that matter, than most adult drug courts nationally. To some extent, the court operates as a young adult drug court, with a median age of 22 years, a median duration of drug use of just seven years, and an exceptionally high 63 percent of its participants listing marijuana as their primary drug of choice. Accordingly, the results of this evaluation may pertain to some extent to juvenile as well as adult drug courts.

Of particular note, the court achieved remarkably high program retention rates—from 95 percent retention at 90 days to 77 percent retention at two years post-enrollment. These retention rates compare favorably with the drug courts included in the earlier New York state evaluation and indicate a favorable graduation rate (almost certainly exceeding 70 percent, as compared with a national average of approximately 50 percent).

The impact evaluation demonstrates that the Staten Island Treatment Court produced consistently positive impacts on the probability, prevalence, and timing of both re-arrests and re-convictions. The court produced a 46 percent relative reduction in the re-arrest rate after one year and a 25 percent reduction after 18 months, and reductions of similar magnitude were evident when isolating felony, misdemeanor, and drug-related re-arrests. The treatment court reduced the average number of re-arrests by close to or more than half on all recidivism measures examined; for example, the total number of re-arrests over the 18-month tracking period dropped from 1.19 for the comparison group to 0.63 for drug court participants (a 47 percent relative reduction).

The impact findings are consistent with the broader literature, which shows that most drug courts produce meaningful reductions in recidivism. The high program retention and graduation rates achieved by the treatment court undoubtedly contribute to its positive recidivism impacts—since participants who are retained in treatment for substantial periods are less likely than others to re-offend. For instance, the court's one-year retention rate of 83 percent is higher than any of the 11 New York state drug courts examined in the 2003 statewide evaluation, and the two-year retention rate of 77 percent ranks second. As long as the Staten Island Treatment Court continues to focus on its process, effectively implementing the drug court model and using its collaborative team to address obstacles as they arise, it is reasonable to expect that the program will continue to produce positive outcomes and serve as a model for other drug court programs.

CHAPTER FOUR

Action Research: Using Information to Improve Your Drug Court

MICHAEL REMPEL

Over the past 15 years, drug courts have rapidly joined the mainstream of American jurisprudence. As of this writing, over 1,500 drug courts have opened nationwide, more than triple the number from as little as seven years ago (Office of Justice Programs 2006). Despite the sheer number of drug courts in existence, these projects still face pressure to demonstrate tangible results—more participants enrolled in treatment, less crime and drug use, and cost savings for states and localities. Some jurisdictions have established formal performance indicators, such as annual enrollment figures, numbers of new graduates and failures, and recidivism rates. Elsewhere, drug courts may be held to looser standards, but individual programs may still want some means of monitoring and improving their services. This will almost inevitably mean investing in research. Indeed, research and evaluation have always been among the 10 key drug court components; and funding agencies routinely require an independent evaluation as part of any start-up grant.

Nonetheless, many drug courts find it exceptionally challenging to implement an ongoing program of research. Staff often

A version of this essay was originally published in 2005 by the Center for Court Innovation as a white paper under the same title. Its publication was supported by the Bureau of Justice Assistance, Office of Justice Programs, U.S. Department of Justice. Opinions and interpretations in this chapter are those of the author and do not necessarily represent the official position or policies of the U.S. Department of Justice.

lack both the necessary time and expertise, and even in places where independent evaluations have been performed there is often little thought about creating permanent systems for tracking performance. More often, the evaluator submits a final report without imparting practical data collection or monitoring tools that can be applied in future years. Further, the experience of staff in working with evaluators is sometimes a negative one, producing a sense of relief and finality once the formal evaluation is done. Thus at a roundtable composed of both court administrators and researchers, one administrator compared receiving evaluation results to a "trip to the doctor," lamenting that evaluations rarely provide constructive feedback, but instead focus on "bad news." Others expressed the belief that few evaluations have influenced practice or raised public support; instead, powerful anecdotes or visits by local politicians to graduation ceremonies have been more important (Fox 2004)

While research would seem to have an important role to play in justifying the drug court investment and ensuring continued quality programming at the local level, actual research capacity and interest remains weak in far too many places. How do we change this state of affairs? A first step might be to change the perception that research is only about large-scale independent evaluations. Such evaluations are needed to answer the "bottom line": do drug courts reduce recidivism and drug use, and do they save money over the long haul? But to examine how drug courts work, for whom they work, for how many people they work, and what changes might lead drug courts to work better, we need a different research model, one that gives drug court teams an integral role in defining the questions to be answered. This model is called "action research." It places a premium on using data to inform operations and on creating a sense of vibrant partnership between researchers and administrators.

This chapter will cover:

- What is action research?
- Steps in implementing action research;
- Data collection 101: key categories of data that must be tracked;
- Important drug court performance indicators;
- Participant surveys: easy methods to generate additional feedback; and
- Conclusion: why action research is necessary.

What is Action Research?

Action research is designed to provide immediate and useful feedback about everyday program operations and performance. Action research does not evaluate whether a drug court is working, but how, why, and for whom it is working, and how it can improve. Since drug courts vary in their target populations and operational resources, questions of interest can also vary across different sites. That said, the most common questions include:

Is the drug court meeting its volume projections?

How many defendants are screened, assessed, and enrolled each year? How does this number compare with target objectives? Are certain categories of defendants routinely found ineligible—for instance defendants arrested on certain charges those or with certain demographic characteristics?

What is the profile of drug court participants?

What is the nature of participant background characteristics (e.g., drug use and treatment history, primary drug of choice, demographics, employment status, criminal history, current charges, and mental health status)? Does the actual participant profile mirror the intended target population?

What is the course of treatment and recovery?
How common is relapse? How long does it generally take for participants to become drug-free? Are there key warning signs that a participant is about to fail? What is the average time to graduation?

What are the core outcomes?
How many participants are retained (graduated or still active in the program) one year after enrolling in the drug court? After two years? After three years? What is the graduation rate?

Which participants succeed?
Are certain categories of participants more likely to graduate than others (e.g., based on their drug use, treatment, or criminal histories, demographics, or other characteristics)?

And cutting across all of these questions is:

What are the policy implications?
Are there clear and tangible policy implications that can be drawn from the answers to the above? How can local practice be improved?

Steps in Action Research

There is no easy formula for implementing a program of action research, but a general outline follows. In addition, there is a worksheet at the end of this chapter that is used at trainings to assist drug court teams when they sit down to establish a concrete plan of action.

Identify program goals
Before becoming mired in the details of specific data and findings, it makes sense to step back and examine what the drug

court set out to do in the first place. Why was it established? How did the planners define "success"? Goals define the drug court's general mission. Common goals include: reducing recidivism, rehabilitating addicted offenders, processing cases more efficiently, and making courts more "problem-solving" or "therapeutic" in focus.

Identify program objectives

Objectives are more specific than goals. They define exactly how the goals will be achieved and can be evaluated against quantifiable targets. Objectives are "SMART":

- *Specific:* pertain to a specific task or program;
- *Measurable:* quantifiable—can be tested with numbers;
- *Achievable:* doable within existing resources and constraints;
- *Results-oriented:* focus on short-term activities necessary to achieve longer-term goals; and
- *Time-bound:* include a date by which they should be achieved.

Sample drug court objectives could include: enrolling 100 new participants per year; moving cases from arrest to formal drug court enrollment within one week, moving cases from formal drug court entry to placement in community-based treatment within one additional week, achieving a 60 percent one-year retention rate, achieving a 50 percent graduation rate; or reducing recidivism by 20 percent compared with conventional case processing. It is helpful for objectives to be realistic, so programs avoid setting themselves up for disappointment. For example, based on national findings it is unrealistic to retain 80 percent of a program's participants after one year. More realistic are one-year retention rates ranging from 55 to 70 percent. A later section cites national findings and several other key performance indicators to help drug court staff in determining which objectives may be appropriate for them.

Develop plans to measure the objectives

Once objectives are identified, what information is needed to measure them? Is this information collected in the drug court's own management information system, a system designed for the entire courthouse, or must a new database be created? Can drug court staff collect the required data, or is outside help necessary (e.g., is help needed from courthouse computer staff, or does it make sense to consult with a local researcher to set up a database for future use)? Who is responsible for which data reporting tasks, and when are they due? Should results be updated regularly (e.g., each month, quarter, or year)? In general, if no one is directly responsible, and if deadlines are not set, these tasks will tend to slip through the cracks in the crush of competing demands.

Identify and develop plans to answer other questions of interest

What other information would it be helpful to know about the drug court or its participants that may not have fallen neatly under the above objectives? As examples, do staff suspect that certain categories of participants (e.g., defined by their charges, demographics, drug use, mental health history, or other characteristics) have particular problems or needs? Would staff like information about how long participants take to reach key milestones, such as completing each phase of treatment or graduating? Would staff like to know which sanctions and rewards have been administered, and how often? Having identified the issues of interest, the next steps are once again to identify the required information, where it is housed, who can generate it, and what is the timeline for obtaining results.

Review the findings

One way to pinpoint issues worthy of action research is to ask, "What results, if I had them, might lead to real policy change?" So, once you've produced the findings, the next step is to determine the implications. Findings can be shared through memoranda or simple spreadsheets (e.g., in Excel or QuattroPro). Team meetings can be used to brainstorm implications, propose new initiatives to address problems that become evident in the data, or recommend further action research inquiries to clarify lingering questions. Using a team model to discuss implications is helpful to resolve legitimate differences over what is implied by a finding. Different staff may present alternative ideas—for example, of how to bolster court volume, or alternative explanations for why volume is low. Group discussion might also uncover differing perspectives on such issues as what kinds of supplemental services participants need, or whether graduation requirements should be adjusted if participants are taking too long to complete.

Take action

Where results fall short of objectives or suggest new directions, the next step is to initiate corrective action.

Initiate new inquiries

The final step is to return again to step 3 to initiate new inquiries, test new policies that were implemented, and, in turn, discuss them as above. On some occasions, seeing hard data may even stimulate rethinking goals and objectives (steps 1 and 2) or formulating new ones.

Data Collection 101

Funding agencies often require applicants to specify a "minimum data set." While there are many possibilities, the first step should always be to track the basics: (1) distinguishing drug court participants from those screened but not ultimately participating, (2) clearly tracking each participant's current status in the program (e.g., open, graduated, or failed), and (3) recording key dates of participation.

Distinguishing the participants

At least two well regarded management information systems do not clearly record the most basic fact about a defendant screened at drug court: did the defendant become a formal program participant or not? As a result, participants and other defendants screened but not ultimately enrolled in the drug court may be intermingled in the data, distinguishable only through time-consuming case-by-case inspection. This is a disastrous situation for any analysis. To begin with, the situation leaves the drug court staff unable to reliably answer the first question on the mind of any senior administrator or policymaker: how many people has the program served? Also, since virtually all other important data analyses will tend to focus on only participants, not on ineligible cases, the research capacity of a drug court is irreparably damaged if formal participants cannot be clearly identified. In the statewide system used by New York's adult drug courts, a simple checkbox for when a defendant signs a contract or otherwise becomes a participant—with another box recording the date of this event—is sufficient.

Tracking the current program status of all participants

Once enrolled, participants can graduate, fail due to a new arrest, fail due to repeated noncompliance, voluntarily opt-out, disappear from program contact (and have a warrant issued), leave the program due to medical or mental health reasons, or move and have the case transferred to another jurisdiction; a multitude of different outcomes are possible. While drug court staff may be interested in many of these outcomes, for most research purposes, only five categories matter:

- Open (still active in the program);
- Warranted (absconded/out on a warrant/temporarily disappeared from program contact);
- Graduated (successfully completed all program requirements);
- Failed (dropped out or participation was terminated by the court); and
- Incomplete.

The final "incomplete" category can encompass multiple situations such as having to leave the drug court due to a severe medical or mental health condition or moving to another jurisdiction. But unless the data makes clear who falls into the first four—most importantly, who graduated and who failed—credible reporting will be difficult. For example, drug court retention and graduation rates are key performance measures that cannot be calculated unless nearly all final/case-ending statuses can be clearly grouped under the "graduate" and "failure" categories. It is fine to track more than five categories, but if this is done, it is imperative to make clear how each one maps to the above five; i.e., which are sub-categories of graduation, failure, incomplete, and so forth. Also, keeping the number of participants falling into the "incomplete" category to an absolute minimum is highly desirable.

Recording key dates of participation

Action research often seeks to explore how a drug court changes over time. For example, is the court screening and enrolling more participants this year than last? Have outcomes improved over time? Are participants' drugs of choice changing, perhaps due to changes in the local drug market? By tracking key dates, it is also possible to measure the time between key stages in the drug court participation process (e.g., arrest to intake, intake to formal enrollment, enrollment to placement in a community-based treatment program, and enrollment to graduation or failure). All drug courts should at least record the following:

- Arrest date/probation violation date (i.e., date of the precipitating event);
- Intake date (when the case first reached the drug court for screening and assessment);
- Participation date (when the defendant formally agreed enroll; this can be replaced by the ineligibility date for defendants who are screened but do not ultimately enroll);
- Exit date (date of graduation, failure, or any other final participation status); and
- Warrant dates (dates for all bench warrants and returns on warrant).

The data described above might be termed the absolute minimum data set—the bare essentials for research to proceed. To the extent possible, additional information would be collected as well (e.g., participant demographics and other assessment information, participant attendance at required court appearances, drug test results, sanctions and rewards, and treatment modalities for all community-based program placements).

Key Drug Court Performance Indicators

While drug courts will vary in their specific objectives and action research plans, the following five types of performance indicators are nearly always important: (1) volume, (2) case processing time, (3) retention and graduation rates, (4) time to graduate, and (5) the participant profile.

Volume

The best-run drug court is of little value if few benefit. For this reason, basic volume questions often dominate action research inquiries: is the drug court screening, assessing, and enrolling enough participants? A national survey found that average adult drug court enrollment is a mere 40 new participants annually (Schafer and Zweig 2004). Even allowing that many drug courts are located in small, rural areas, the inescapable reality is that many programs do not reach anywhere near the number of clinically addicted defendants that exist in their jurisdictions. This underscores the need to continually track volume and, as needed, rethink what steps can be taken to serve more cases.

A drug court's volume may be viewed as a simple function of two core factors: the number of referrals—cases referred to the drug court for screening and assessment—and the percentage of referrals that ultimately participate. Either or both factors may contribute to lower-than-expected volume. Referrals may be low because underlying arrest volume may be declining; clerks, judges, or attorneys may be neglecting to refer cases to the drug court when they should; or there may be no formal drug court referral process, leaving referrals to hinge on individual decisions made by specific judges or attorneys. Factors affecting the yield of referrals into full-fledged participants include the reality that a significant percentage of defendants may: have disqualifying medical or mental health issues; refuse to participate; have their eligibility rejected by prosecutors; or be found ineligible for various other legal reasons. The bottom line is that in order to establish what is in fact taking place, it is important to track all referrals, not just participants, and for those who do not ultimately participate, it is important to track the reason for non-participation (e.g., legal ineligibility, not addicted to drugs, severe mental health problems, lack of interest, lack of motivation).

Having pinpointed why volume is low, staff can take corrective action. For instance, if referrals are low, perhaps the situation could be improved by implementing a more formal screening mechanism, whereby cases meeting certain criteria are automatically routed to the drug court before any other case processing activity can proceed. Or perhaps formal eligibility can be widened, as one New York State drug court did by expanding from handling exclusively nonviolent felonies to including certain misdemeanors as well.

On the other hand, if the flow of referrals is acceptable but a large percentage of those referrals ultimately do not participate, the drug court team could explore the possible reasons for this. If the prosecutor is rejecting a large percentage of defendants, the team might meet with the prosecutor in an effort to address any concerns the prosecutor may express. If a large percentage of defendants are refusing to participate, the team might meet with the defense bar to discuss which requirements are leading the program to be perceived as undesirable. For example, action research led one New York State drug court to shorten the jail sentences imposed on its drug court failures; this action was taken in response to evidence of a high defendant refusal rate coupled with evidence that the jail alternatives for failing drug court involved significantly more jail time than the typical sentences imposed on defendants who opted not to enroll. Shortening the jail alternative thus made this program more appealing to defendants, and the yield went up accordingly.

Initial case processing time

Research shows that immediacy—engaging participants as soon as possible after the precipitating arrest (or probation violation)—is critical to drug court success. For instance, across five New York State drug courts, participants who avoided disappearing from program contact and having a warrant issued within the first 30 days after entry were far more likely to graduate than those warranting within that initial 30-day period (Rempel et al. 2003). In interpreting this finding, researchers concluded that early warranting reflects both the quality of participant compliance (noncompliant participants are more likely to warrant) and the drug court's speed of early case processing (participants able to begin treatment right away due to rapid case processing are much less likely than others to warrant). This means that it is partly within the drug court's own control to initiate policies that can minimize early warranting. For example, in one New York State drug court, evidence that initial treatment placement delays had increased the program failure rate led to the establishment of daily "pre-placement groups" run by case managers at the courthouse, designed to keep participants more engaged while waiting for their first community-based placement.

Retention and graduation rates

Retention is a key measure of success. Research finds that higher retention rates not only indicate success in treatment but also predict future success in the form of lower post-treatment drug use and criminal re-offending.

How is a one-year retention rate calculated? First, it is necessary to consider only participants who entered the program at least one year prior to the analysis. Of those who have been enrolled for at least a year, it is then necessary to obtain their program status as of their one-year anniversary date. Having done this, the retention rate simply adds the percentages of participants that are still open as of the one-year mark or that have graduated by that point; those on warrant or who have failed by the one-year mark are, conversely, considered to be not retained. If there is a final category of participants whose status is "incomplete" for reasons such as having to leave the program due to illness, or transfer to another jurisdiction, they are similarly grouped in the not retained category. Even if all of the required data is unavailable, it is still possible to construct a reasonable estimate. For example, if available data does not isolate when participants are on warrant status, one could count everyone as retained except those reaching a final status of failure as of the one-year mark. This method is not ideal because it may overestimate the retention rate but is preferable to no calculation at all.

Two- and three-year retention rates are calculated in an equivalent fashion; for example, the two-year retention rate considers only participants who have been enrolled for at least two years and determines their retention status as of their two-year anniversary date. Importantly, since most participants have reached their final graduation or failure status by the three-year mark, it is generally legitimate to report the three-year retention rate as the drug court's graduation rate. As the preceding explanations of how to construct a retention rate hopefully clarifies, careful tracking of key dates—date participation began, date of program graduation or failure, and dates of all warrants and returns on warrants—is essential.

For a one-year retention rate, the national drug court average has been estimated at 60 percent (see Belenko). In a recent New York State study, eight of 11 drug courts exceeded 60 percent, and the median retention rate (the one achieved by the middle or sixth best drug court of the 11) was 66 percent (Rempel et al 2003). In general, any drug court with a one-year retention rate of higher than 60 percent is likely to be performing effectively, while any falling below 50 percent is likely to benefit from initiating a reflection process on how to improve.

Drug courts falling in between these markers (e.g., 50 to 60 percent) may also want to reflect on possible program refinements. A critical caveat, however, is that some drug courts have lower retention rates than others because they work with more difficult-to-change populations (e.g., higher addiction severity, longer history of criminality, deeper level of involvement with deviant peers). Therefore, it is incorrect to compare the retention rates of several drug courts and automatically assume that the one with the lowest rate is having the least impact on its participants relative to conventional case processing. For example, a 50 percent one-year retention-rate with a population that is highly addicted, possesses a low socioeconomic status, and has a lengthy prior criminal record very likely signifies a significant positive impact relative to the status quo. The point is not to use retention rates to pass final judgment on a program but as a tip for whether further thought and investigation of existing policies may be worthwhile.

Time to graduation

Average time to graduation is an important performance measure. Drug courts typically establish minimum participation requirements (e.g., one year clean and sober); but in fact, graduates often take much longer to complete the program due to interim relapses and setbacks. Without looking squarely at the numbers, it is difficult to know exactly how much time and commitment the drug court truly requires of its participants. For example, if a drug court's minimum time to graduation is one year, but successful graduates in fact average two years before completing, perhaps the court's requirements are too onerous to be finished in the originally anticipated amount of time. If the drug court retention rate also turns out to be low, that might indicate that downgrading the graduation requirements could actually produce better outcomes. John Roman, one of the nation's foremost drug court researchers, has cautioned that overloading graduation requirements may be detrimental to drug court efficacy (Roman 2005). As a benchmark against which individual drug courts can compare their own results, both a study of 11 New York State drug courts and a national survey across all 50 states found that, on average, graduates spend 15 months in the program (Rempel et al. 2003; Schafer and Zweig 2004).

Participant profile

One of the easiest and most rewarding types of action research inquiries involves generating a profile of the demographic, drug use, criminal history, and other background characteristics of participants. While such a profile is not truly a "performance indicator" *per se*—one would not judge the performance of a drug court based upon enrolling participants in certain demographic categories—a profile still has a large number of practical uses. First, it yields an overall social portrait of the actual participants coming through the program. This can help staff to understand the nature and severity of the problems participants face (with substance abuse, mental health, housing, or employment issues) and how their drug court's profile compares with others. If two drug courts in the same region discover that their participants have similar needs, they might initiate further discussions. For example, an interim evaluation of a new drug court in one borough of New York City showed that its participants had an extremely distinctive profile (a largely young and marijuana-addicted clientele) that was similar to the profile of a drug court in a nearby borough; this led staff from the newer drug court to seek information from the one that had a demonstrated record of success serving a comparable population.

Second, a profile indicates to what extent a drug court's anticipated target population matches the real one. For example, if the target population is predominantly black or Hispanic, but the drug court ends up mainly enrolling non-Hispanic Caucasians, that information could lead the drug court to explore why such a disparity arose and possibly to initiate outreach to the defense bar or others in a position to bring a wider pool of arrestees into the program. Or if a jurisdiction established a drug court to address a perceived crack epidemic, but most participants are addicted to marijuana, that might trigger a reexamination of drug-use problems in the community or a reexamination of why those addicted to crack are not making it to the drug court (e.g., perhaps because they tend to be arrested on ineligible charges or to have ineligible criminal histories).

Third, a profile can suggest a need for supplemental services. For example, if more participants than anticipated speak Spanish, that might suggest a need to establish more linkages with treatment programs serving a Spanish-speaking population (or a need for more Spanish-speaking programs in the community). If a large percentage of participants are unemployed and have a poor work history, staff might consider seeking funds to establish on-site vocational or employment services, or for establishing more links with community-based treatment programs that offer such services. If many participants suffer from co-occurring mental health disorders, the drug court could seek to add programming for the dually diagnosed. Often, drug court staff will understand the special needs of their participants from everyday experience, but objective data can still be used to verify these experiential impressions as well as to justify funding requests for concrete supplemental services.

Other Questions

While the aforementioned performance indicators are likely to prove important to a large number of drug courts, action research is not only about tracking standard indicators but also about brainstorming to identify new questions with real policy ramifications at the local level. The specific questions to be addressed should flow from the interests and concerns of the team, but in general, some of the most valuable types of inquiries that have yet to be illustrated concern the treatment and recovery process.

Sample questions can include:

- How common are relapses and other types of noncompliance during drug court participation?
- How frequently are participants sanctioned, and which sanctions are most often imposed?
- How long does it take to reach key milestones (e.g., 90 days clean, promotion to Phase Two, promotion to Phase Three)?
- Are certain categories of participants, defined by their demographic, criminal history, substance abuse history, or other characteristics, more likely than others to require residential as opposed to outpatient treatment?
- What are critical warning signs of failure? And
- How far into the drug court participation process does drug court failure tend to occur (near the outset or at important later stages)?

The Use of Surveys

Action research need not only involve the analysis of "hard" data. Drug court staff can also gain valuable information through the use of simple survey instruments designed to elicit participant feedback and recommendations. One easy suggestion is to build into graduation activities an opportunity for all participants to fill out a survey with questions designed to probe how they perceived various aspects of their drug court experience: the quality and accuracy of the information they received about the drug court program before agreeing to participate, the role of their attorney and of the prosecutor; the experience of appearing regularly before the judge, receiving positive rewards, receiving sanctions, speaking with their case manager; and attending treatment at a community-based program. If possible, it would be ideal to make such surveys available to participants who fail the drug court as well to elicit their views concerning why they did *not* succeed and what improvements might have helped them.

Besides a "catch-all" exit survey, drug courts can also implement special topics surveys whenever specific concerns arise. A few common examples would be:

> *Treatment program feedback* If staff would like more information about the participant experience at their treatment programs, and what if any unmet service needs still exist (e.g., in employment, education, counseling, health care, or other areas), they could design a special survey for this purpose. Such a survey might ask participants to rate various aspects of their treatment program (on a 1–5 scale) and might add a series of open-ended questions to probe in greater detail what is most and least helpful about treatment.

> *Consequences of graduation and failure* If staff is unsure whether participants understand what the legal effects of graduating and failing will be (e.g., how much jail would result), they could design a brief survey to check whether participants in fact have accurate knowledge, who conveyed that knowledge, how often participants were reminded, and how concerned they were to obtain the legal

benefits of graduating and to avoid the legal consequences of failing.

Civil legal needs If staff believes many participants have additional legal needs due to simultaneously occurring family or other civil cases, and that these other issues might pose a barrier or source of stress that could interfere with recovery, a survey could be implemented on the prevalence of various civil legal needs.

Case manager survey Besides the participants themselves, case managers or probation officers working for the drug court can be a valuable resource, particularly when it comes to questions concerning the quality and availability of local treatment programs, both in general and for special needs populations (e.g., participants with co-occurring disorders, Spanish-speaking participants, women with children); drug court teams might consider designing a survey for their own staff to obtain feedback in a more systematic way than through informal conversations.

If drug court teams are having difficulties wording the questions or figuring out what information to obtain with a closed-ended format (e.g., with yes/no or 1-5 scaled options) and what information to obtain with more probing, open-ended questions, it may take only a short consultation with a local academic to improve the quality of an instrument.

When implementing surveys, it is important to bear in mind that the results are likely to be of greater value, and the process to be better at protecting the rights of the respondents, if they can be submitted anonymously, without names and without drug court staff having the ability to view the surveys exactly when they are dropped off.

CONCLUSION

Having become empowered to ask real questions about drug court data and performance, drug court practitioners themselves can become action researchers, using data to monitor performance and solve practical problems. While certain inquiries may require at least a rudimentary knowledge of research methods, much can be done without specialized expertise simply by tabulating aggregate numbers from official court records or information systems.

Action research may well play a critical role in the future of drug courts. Innovations often lose some of their potency after they are institutionalized and run by new staff who may not be as familiar with the founding ideas and practices. However, simple performance monitoring protocols can help to ensure that program volume remains high and performance is maintained at original levels. Further inquiries can contribute to challenging old routines and initiating new innovations in program areas that were perhaps taken for granted in the past. In this way, the drug court intervention can continue to flourish.

APPENDIX: ACTION RESEARCH WORKSHEET

1. What are the major goals of your drug court? (Goals identify the overall mission and purpose of the program, not specific methods or numeric targets.)

2. What are the major objectives of your drug court? (Objectives explain how the goals will be achieved. They are specific, realistic, and lend themselves to quantitative performance measures.) For each objective, try to develop quantifiable targets.

3. Were you able to develop realistic quantifiable targets for each objective? If not, what information do you need to develop these targets? How do you propose to obtain it?

4. Develop an action research plan: What data or results do you need to see if you are meeting each of your objectives? How can you obtain that data? Can your staff do it, or do you need outside help (e.g., courthouse clerical staff, administrative staff able to obtain aggregate data from a drug court management information system, or others)? What should be the deadline for reporting the results? Should results be updated regularly (e.g., each month, quarter, or year)?

5. What is missing? What other information would it be interesting or helpful for you to know about your program and its participants that may not have fallen clearly under the above objectives? Develop a plan for obtaining and reporting that information.

6. Can practice change? Think about your research plans. Brainstorm examples of drug court practices or policies that you might rethink depending on what results you obtain. Who else would need to be at the table in discussing possible policy changes?

Domestic Violence Courts

Some observers have questioned whether domestic violence courts are truly a "problem-solving" model. On first consideration, the connection is unmistakable. Like addiction, mental illness, juvenile delinquency, and other problems addressed by problem-solving courts, domestic violence is a dire social malady—hence a clear candidate for a focused court response. Just as drug courts began as a specialized docket designed to handle a massive influx of drug cases, domestic violence courts began in part as an efficient response to a massive influx of domestic violence cases throughout the 1980s and 1990s. Growing domestic violence caseloads originated with the efforts of the feminist and victim's movements to put violence against women on the national agenda and encourage all criminal justice agencies (police, prosecutors, probation, and the courts, working in tandem with community-based agencies) to develop a more coordinated response.

Despite the unmistakable parallels to other problem-solving courts in terms of history and approach (specially trained judge, specialized docket, dedicated court team, outreach to community partners, etc.), domestic violence courts are also unique. For instance, unlike drug and mental health courts, many domestic violence court proponents do not subscribe to the view that the offender's behavior stems from underlying problems that treatment or services can remedy. Indeed, victim safety and offender accountability are usually prioritized over and above offender rehabilitation. In fact, domestic violence courts are the only problem-solving justice experiment considered in this volume where the needs of victims are paramount.

As a movement, domestic violence courts are also distinguished by decentralization and local adaptation. Unlike drug courts, with their well established goals and nationally disseminated key components, domestic violence courts do not subscribe to nearly as unified a model. Domestic violence courts lack a national professional association or information clearinghouse to facilitate information sharing and dissemination of best practices. It is not even known for certain how many such courts exist nationwide, although most believe that they number somewhere in the hundreds.

In short, domestic violence courts pose a profound array of both conceptual and empirical questions, many of which are taken up in the chapters that follow.

In Chapter Five, Chandra Gavin and Nora K. Puffett present a comparative study of the goals, policies, practices, and stakeholder perspectives in New York City's five misdemeanor domestic violence courts. By accumulating the distinct perspectives of each core stakeholder—judge, prosecutor, defense attorney, victim advocate, and court staff—this chapter reveals the essential programmatic elements of domestic violence courts, and seeks to stimulate further reflection on the advantages, challenges, and fault lines surrounding the nation's domestic violence court experiments.

In Chapter Six, Melissa Labriola, Michael Rempel, and Robert C. Davis report the results of a randomized trial testing the effectiveness of one of the principal elements adopted by many domestic violence courts nationwide—court mandates to batterer programs. (This chapter reproduces the executive summary of a more in-depth report.) Some see batterer programs strictly as a tool of accountability and monitoring, designed to provide a mandatory sanction that the offender must complete, while others hope that batterer programs can achieve more, reducing re-abuse and making victims safer. The study's results call into serious question this second, more ambitious, perspective.

In Chapter Seven, Amanda B. Cissner examines a novel adaptation of the domestic violence court model to younger offenders, ages 16 to 19. Evidence indicates a high rate of intimate partner violence among victims from their late teens to early twenties. This chapter introduces the problem of teen dating violence and provides a comprehensive process evaluation of an experimental pilot, the Brooklyn Youthful Offender Domestic Violence Court. The evaluation is careful to highlight lessons learned that may be broadly applicable, beyond Brooklyn, to other jurisdictions interested in replication.

CHAPTER FIVE

Specialized Domestic Violence Courts in New York City: A Comparative Study

CHANDRA GAVIN AND NORA K. PUFFETT

In the decade since the passage of the Violence Against Women Act in 1994, jurisdictions across the country have sought to redefine their response to domestic violence. The act led local legislatures to institute new measures such as pro-arrest policies, and provided substantial funding for specialized prosecution and police units. In many states, district attorneys were encouraged to pursue cases even without victim cooperation—cases they might previously have declined—through the practice of "evidence-based" prosecution that relies on physical evidence and 911 tapes, rather than complainant testimony.

A heightened public awareness of domestic violence coupled with these new arrest and prosecution policies led to an overwhelming influx of domestic violence cases into the courts. The complexity of these cases in turn led to the development of specialized domestic violence court dockets. The judges and staff assigned to these new domestic violence courts received expert training in domestic violence issues and gain the benefit of experience through their specialization in domestic violence cases.

This chapter is based on a research report published in 2005 by the Center for Court Innovation as "Criminal Domestic Violence Case Processing: A Case Study of the Five Boroughs of New York City." Its publication was supported by the Office on Violence Against Women, U.S. Department of Justice. Opinions and interpretations in this chapter are those of the authors, or, where attributed, of those interviewed as part of the research, and do not necessarily represent the official position or policies of the U.S. Department of Justice.

While domestic violence courts began to emerge only in the mid-1990s, by 2000 one survey identified 160 courts nationwide that had at least some type of "specialized process" for handling domestic violence cases (Keilitz 2000). Today, while precise figures are unavailable, domestic violence courts undoubtedly number in the many hundreds. Most handle adult criminal cases, although recent models have been designed to handle juvenile cases, civil restraining orders, or custody and visitation cases where there are underlying allegations of domestic violence. In addition, an "integrated" model, recently piloted in New York, Florida, and several other jurisdictions, involves a single multi-jurisdictional judge handling all of a family's overlapping criminal, family, and matrimonial cases involving domestic violence.

The rapid rise of domestic violence courts is perhaps nowhere more apparent than in New York State, the home of 63 such courts as of 2006. The first of these courts, which opened in Brooklyn in 1996, was also the first in the country to specialize in felony-level domestic violence cases (see Newmark, Rempel, Diffily, and Kane 2001; and Wolf, Aldrich, and Moore 2004). The court implemented many of the core principles and features that have come to embody domestic violence courts nationally: a single presiding judge, a dedicated prosecution team, victim advocates to provide support and resources to complainants, and a resource coordinator to monitor defendant compliance with orders of protection and mandates to batterer programs. The court was also envisioned as one component of a larger coordinated community response to domestic violence. The judge and court staff met regularly with prosecutors, defense attorneys, probation, victim advocates, batterer program providers, and others to coordinate policies across institutions.

The favorable response to the court was such that it was soon expanded to a second dedicated felony court in Brooklyn, and plans were made to adapt the model for misdemeanor cases as well. The state's first misdemeanor domestic violence court opened in the Bronx in 1998, with other misdemeanor courts shortly following in the other four boroughs, as well as outside of the New York City metropolitan area.

In New York State, domestic violence courts were only the latest development in a larger movement toward problem-solving courts and alternative sentencing (see Berman and Feinblatt 2001; Casey and Rottman 2003). However, domestic violence courts differ substantially from other problem-solving initiatives such as specialized drug courts, mental health courts, and community courts. For one, the nature of domestic violence makes it unique among criminal behaviors, and accordingly difficult to prosecute. The complainants are often the only witnesses to crimes that have left no physical evidence. Yet the complainants—whether due to fear for their safety, concern for their children, pressure from the defendant, or a genuine disinclination to press charges—often decline to cooperate, thereby severely limiting the prosecution. In these cases, the prosecutor must decide whether to dismiss the case, try it on the strength of what little material evidence there may be, or subpoena the complainant as a hostile witness.

In addition, unlike other problem-solving initiatives, many domestic violence courts do not seek to rehabilitate the offender. The primary goals of New York State domestic violence courts are victim safety and offender accountability—not offender reform (Mazur and Aldrich 2003). The complainant is a central concern of the prosecution and the court, and interventions such as batterer programs are often used more for monitoring and punitive purposes than for rehabilitation. Yet this creates ambivalence about the goals of the court among some stakeholders, who ask, "Isn't rehabilitation of the defendant the best guarantor of victim safety?" Logically it might seem so (and complainants often suggest an interest in rehabilitation), yet the existing literature casts doubt over the effectiveness of rehabilitative programs (see Chapter 6; Feder and Wilson 2005).

Study Methods and Purpose

The current study sought to document existing domestic violence court policies and practices, to understand their underlying rationale, and to elicit stakeholder perspectives regarding the strengths and weaknesses of domestic violence courts. The five misdemeanor domestic violence courts of New York City served as case studies.

The analysis relied upon courtroom observations and individual interviews conducted by one of the authors in the spring and summer of 2002. Interviews were conducted with the primary stakeholders in the misdemeanor domestic violence courts of all five boroughs: the Bronx, Brooklyn, Manhattan, Queens, and Staten Island. Only one person declined to be interviewed. Interview subjects included judges and court staff—clerks, resource coordinators, defendant monitors—permanently assigned to the domestic violence court parts, as well as assistant district attorneys, defense attorneys, and victim advocates. Additionally, quantitative data on borough demographics and domestic violence case outcomes were collected from the United States Census and the New York State Office of Court Administration.

Overview of the Domestic Violence Court Model

Domestic violence courts are generally understood to include a fixed, trained judge and prosecutor, and permanently assigned, trained court staff to assist in case coordination and transmittal of information among parties, attorneys, the judge, and community and law enforcement agencies. Advocacy and services for complainants are provided by the prosecutor, the court, or community agencies; lethality assessments and safety planning are perceived as essential (Keilitz 2000). Close judicial oversight of defendant behavior is maintained through frequent court appearances and regular information exchange with probation, programs, police, and others (Healey, Smith, and O'Sullivan 1998; Mazur and Aldrich 2003; Sack 2002; Steketee, Levey, and Keilitz 2000). Defendants are frequently mandated to batterer programs and sometimes to other types of programs, such as substance abuse treatment, mental health, or parenting classes. However, the courts do not necessarily view program mandates as treatment; they may instead use them as a monitoring tool, with program attendance comprising a regular responsibility that the defendants must perform while under court oversight. Many domestic violence courts employ additional staff, with titles such as resource coordinator, defendant monitor, or case manager, to link defendants with programs and monitor their compliance. The courts may operate full time, or may function more as dedicated calendars heard at a fixed time on a regular schedule, usually once a week or month. By definition, such courts hear all domestic violence cases in a jurisdiction, with screening mechanisms established by the prosecutor or court clerks to identify eligible cases (Mazur and Aldrich 2003; Sack 2002; Weber 2000).

All of the practices discussed above are time- and labor-intensive. Accordingly, domestic violence courts often demand additional resources. Judges, attorneys, and staff must receive continuous training; close monitoring requires additional and more frequent court appearances, and outreach by court staff to advocates, programs, and others for information; and maintenance of system-wide consistency necessitates regular meetings of all stakeholders. Given these demands, one might reasonably ask to what extent the benefits of domestic violence courts outweigh their costs. Advocates, defense attorneys, judges, and other stakeholders have expressed a number of additional concerns about domestic violence courts: that they will divert offenders from prosecution to treatment, that they may jeopardize judicial neutrality, and that they will have unintended consequences for complainants, such as increasing the number of complainants prosecuted for failure to protect their children from violence (Keilitz 2000). More optimistically, these stakeholders generally hope that domestic violence courts will result in greater consistency in prosecutors' and judges' treatment of cases, more advocacy and relief to complainants, and increased offender compliance with court orders (Keilitz 2000).

Research on Domestic Violence Courts

There have been few rigorous evaluations of domestic violence courts, but much of what research does exist has been encouraging. Much more than conventional courts, domestic violence courts link complainants to advocacy and services (Harrell, Schaffer, DeStefano, and Castro 2006; Henning and Klesges 1999; Newmark, Rempel, Diffily, and Kane 2001) and are perceived by complainants to do a good job of case handling, to produce fair outcomes, and to be generally more satisfactory than conventional courts (Eckberg and Podkopacz 2002; Gover, MacDonald, and Alpert 2003; Hotaling and Buzawa 2003). Interestingly, while complainants appear to be satisfied overall, the research literature suggests that satisfaction hinges not only on the outcome of the case, but on a broad range of factors, including complainants' perception of having been treated fairly, their personal motivation to end the relationship, and even the criminal history of the offender (Henning and Kesges 1999; Hotaling and Buzawa 2003). This implies that the court experience itself is only a small percentage of the complainant's total experience with the case.

Concerning the idea of a "domestic violence court," complainants reported overwhelming support for the idea in principle, with almost three-quarters of respondents in one study saying that they believed such a court would benefit them, and that knowing of the existence of such a court would increase their chances of reporting future violence (Smith 2001). Yet, it is important to note that even as complainants have in theory and practice approved of the domestic violence court as an improvement over standard case processing, at least one study found that 40 percent of complainants still found the court experience "embarrassing" and said they would not return to court if they experienced another incident of domestic violence (Hotaling and Buzawa 2003).

Regarding the impact on defendant outcomes, the introduction of a domestic violence court has been found to result in significant reductions in case dismissal rates (Davis, Smith, and Rabbitt 2001; Harrell et al. 2006; Henning and Klesges 1999, Newmark et al. 2001), to increase attempts to prosecute domestic violence cases, to increase the percentage of defendants mandated to batterer programs, and to increase the frequency and regularity of judicial monitoring (Harrell et al. 2006; Newmark et al. 2001), as well as to increase the incidence of jail sentences (Ursel and Brickey 1996).

The impact on recidivism, however, remains ambiguous. One study found no effect on misdemeanor offender re-arrest rates (Henning and Klesges 1999); another found no reductions in re-arrests among felony offenders, but suggested that this might have been partially attributable to the court's increased knowledge of defendant behavior, which made it more likely that they would learn of re-offending (Newmark et al. 2001). Three other studies (one of a program targeted to substance-abusing domestic violence offenders) found small to significant reductions in re-arrest rates among misdemeanor offenders (Goldkamp, Weiland, Collins, and White 1996; Gover et al. 2003; San Diego Superior Court 2000). Finally, a 2006 study found a significant reduction in the re-arrest rate over a one-year post-disposition period, but linked this finding to increased probation revocation rates for technical violations—leading more defendants to be re-incarcerated—rather than to a decreased probability of re-arrest among those "at risk" in the community (Harrell, Schafer, DeStefano, and Castro 2006).

Synthesis and Comparison of Findings

This section compares the policies of the five misdemeanor domestic violence courts in New York City. In a more extensive report stemming from this same study, the policies of each court are detailed in separate chapters (Gavin and Puffett 2005).

Demographic Context

Table 1 describes the makeup of each borough's population, and their relative wealth, as of 2000 (U.S. Census Bureau 2000). The gaps between the boroughs are evident, with the Bronx at one extreme and Manhattan at the other. Overall, the populations of Queens, Manhattan, and Staten Island are significantly more prosperous than Brooklyn and the Bronx. Incomes and poverty rates further confirm these differences; in Brooklyn and the Bronx over one-quarter of residents live below the poverty line, while poverty rates are much lower in Manhattan, Queens, and Staten Island.

Case Volume and Sentencing Patterns

Table 2 compares the 2002 domestic violence caseloads of each borough, including case dispositions and sentences. It is interesting to note that differences in arraignment and disposition volume do not strictly correspond to population size. For instance, Queens, with a population nearly the size of Brooklyn's, has substantially fewer arraignments and dispositions. This is probably due to its more restricted definition of domestic violence, leading

Table 1. Borough Demographics

	Bronx	Brooklyn	Manhattan	Queens	Staten Island
Total population	1,332,650	2,465,326	1,537,195	2,229,379	443,728
Race					
Caucasian	32%	43%	57%	47%	78%
African-American	38%	38%	18%	21%	10%
Native American	1%	0	1%	1%	0
Asian/Pacific Islander	3%	8%	19%	19%	6%
Other	26%	11%	12%	12%	6%
Ethnicity					
Hispanic/Latino	51%	21%	28%	27%	12%
High school diploma	62%	69%	79%	74%	83%
B.A. degree or higher	15%	22%	49%	24%	23%
Per capita income	$13,959	$16,775	$42,922	$19,222	$23,905
Percent of population living below the poverty line	31%	25%	20%	15%	10%

Source: U.S. Census.

some cases to be classified as "domestic violence" in Brooklyn, but not Queens (see further discussion below).

Most district attorneys' domestic violence bureaus strive for low dismissal rates. Bronx stakeholders, however, were careful to point out that while their dismissal rate appears relatively high (44 percent), they have a very low rate of adjournments in contemplation of dismissal (ACDs), nearly all of which are eventually closed as dismissals either six or 12 months after the disposition. Brooklyn prosecutors, who have the highest rates of both straight dismissals (51 percent) and of ACDs (30 percent) emphasized that their commitment to pursuing every possible case took precedence over dismissal concerns. Since Brooklyn pursues cases that would have been declined for prosecution in other boroughs, this inflates its dismissal rate; but Brooklyn prosecutors believed that initiating prosecution provides complainants with opportunities and services that advance their safety, even if their cases do not result in a conviction.

Table 2. Domestic Violence Case Volume and Sentencing, 2002

	Bronx	Brooklyn	Manhattan	Queens	Staten Island
Arraignments	5,491	6,976	4,063	4,676	960
Disposed at arraignment	2%	2%	1%	3%	5%
Dispositions	6,467	9,157	4,627	5,248	1,031
Pleas	48.90%	17.60%	33.50%	55.50%	35.30%
Convicted	0.40%	0.30%	0.70%	0.50%	0
Acquitted	0.50%	0.10%	0.60%	0.30%	0.30%
ACD	2.70%	30.00%	13.30%	21.80%	23.10%
Dismissed	44.40%	51.00%	47.80%	19.60%	39.80%
Other	3.00%	0.10%	4.10%	2.40%	1.60%
Sentences	3,477	1,675	1,722	3,133	373
Community Service	0.60%	5.10%	9.70%	0.70%	0.80%
Fine	0.60%	1.10%	2.70%	0.60%	6.70%
Imprisonment	38.90%	35.30%	35.20%	21.20%	30.00%
Probation	4.70%	7.30%	5.60%	3.10%	3.80%
Conditional Discharge	55.50%	50.90%	46.50%	74.10%	58.20%
Other	0.10%	0.20%	0.10%	0.20%	0.50%

Source: Office of the Administrative Judge of the New York City Criminal Court

Domestic Violence Court Policies

While court size and resources vary among the boroughs, all of the courts share similar structural and operational elements. As shown in Table 3, features on which there is the most variation include funding and staffing, and charges and pleas accepted.

Staffing and Resources

All of the stakeholders agreed that the biggest challenge for domestic violence courts is the lack of resources. All courts labor under substantial caseloads. In courts without a resource coordinator, an additional burden is placed on the court clerks, prosecutor, or judge to select, screen, and communicate with potential programs.

Three of the five boroughs (the Bronx, Brooklyn, and Queens) have resource coordinators, but only two (the Bronx and Queens) have the added staff resource of defendant monitors, who can assess and link defendants to programs and then obtain compliance reports in time for regularly scheduled judicial status hearings. And only the Bronx has a project director with the time to

Table 3. Domestic Violence Court Features

	Bronx	Brooklyn	Manhattan	Queens	Staten Island
Year opened	1997	1999	1999	1997	1997
Additional funding	STOP grant from VAWO	None	None	2 grants, one from DA, one from Safe Horizon[1]	None
Dedicated court parts	3: All-purpose, trial, compliance	3: All-purpose (2), compliance	1: All-purpose & compliance	2: All-purpose & trial, compliance	1: All-purpose & compliance
Project director?	Yes	No	No	No	No
Resource coordinator?	Yes	Yes (as of 2003)	No	Yes	No
Defendant monitor?	Yes	No	No	Yes	No
Cases with felony charges heard?	No	No	No	Yes, through felony waiver plea	No
Conditional pleas taken?	No	Yes	No	Yes	No
Defendants mandated to programs?	Yes	Yes	Sometimes, at victim's request	Yes	Yes
Separate compliance part	Yes	Yes	No	Yes	No
Victim advocacy provider(s)	DA, Safe Horizon[1]	DA, Safe Horizon[1]	DA	Safe Horizon[1]	Safe Horizon[1]

Note: This chart is valid as of 2004.

[1] Safe Horizon is a local victim assistance agency serving all five boroughs of New York City.

manage the court's other specialized staff, while developing and implementing new policies and services. The greater resources of Queens and the Bronx are further complemented by grant funding obtained by partner organizations: in both boroughs, Safe Horizon is funded to provide enhanced victim advocacy, and in Queens the District Attorney's Office has funding to provide additional services at intake.

Charges

All of the courts except Queens accept only misdemeanor and violation charges. (Brooklyn and the Bronx have separate Felony Domestic Violence Courts; felony domestic violence cases in

Manhattan and Staten Island are prosecuted on general dockets.) Queens, by contrast, processes both felony and misdemeanor cases in the misdemeanor domestic violence court, keeping the felony cases through indictment or felony waiver plea. Queens stakeholders argue that this creates a consistent judicial response to domestic violence at all levels of the criminal justice system, as well as a pool of assistant district attorneys with multiple levels of experience. (Since this study was completed, a restructuring of the criminal courts in the Bronx led that borough also to handle both felony and misdemeanor cases in the same court.)

Conditional Pleas

Plea bargaining occurs in all boroughs, but only in Brooklyn and Queens does the court routinely accept what are known as "conditional pleas." These require that the defendant plead guilty to both an A-level misdemeanor charge and a violation; the former is dropped if the defendant successfully completes a program mandate. If the defendant fails to comply, the judge imposes the maximum sentence (one year on the A misdemeanor). This practice gives the court substantial added leverage to coerce defendants to comply with program mandates. Conditional pleas are most commonly used in Queens; it is unclear why they are only infrequently used in Brooklyn and not at all in the other boroughs. Stakeholders in the other boroughs did not identify the use of conditional pleas as a practice that they wished to introduce, nor as one to which there had been opposition or objections.

Programs and Compliance

All of the courts mandate defendants to a range of program types, but rely most heavily on batterer programs. The most often used program is Safe Horizon's Domestic Violence Accountability Program, which follows an accountability model that stresses

Table 4. Prosecutorial Policies

	Bronx	Brooklyn	Manhattan	Queens	Staten Island
Definition of domestic violence: Persons who: · are related by blood; · have children in common; or · are, or have been, married, living together, or involved in an intimate relationship.	Yes	No Persons who are intimate partners (inc. same-sex couples and couples not living together).	Yes	No Persons who have children in common, or are or have been married or living together.	Yes
Dedicated DV Bureau?	Yes	Yes	No	Yes	Yes
Dedicated DV staff	17 ADAs	14 ADAs	1 supervisor	9 ADAs	3 ADAs
Involved in post-sentence compliance monitoring?	No	No	No	Yes	No

defendant attendance and compliance with program rules, coupled with transparent and reliable procedures for reporting any noncompliance to the court. However, until 2005 Brooklyn mandated a higher percentage of its defendants to a shorter program with a more therapeutic orientation, Interborough Developmental and Consultation Center. Not surprisingly, the two courts that have long had resource coordinators and defendant monitors, Queens and the Bronx, draw on the greatest number of programs, demonstrating the value of additional staff in exploring and maintaining relationships with community resources.

All of the courts conduct compliance monitoring through regular post-sentence court appearances, but they vary in their approach. In Manhattan and Staten Island, compliance is conducted by the presiding judge in the single court part dedicated to domestic violence. In the Bronx and Brooklyn, however, a separate compliance part presided over by a judicial hearing officer (usually a retired judge) is dedicated to compliance monitoring. Queens has a dedicated compliance part and judicial hearing officer as well, but the sentencing judge may decide in select cases to monitor compliance herself. While there may be advantages to consolidating all compliance cases on a single calendar, there are also disadvantages to having that calendar heard by someone other than the sentencing judge. In particular, judicial hearing officers are unable to impose legal sanctions, and so must refer noncompliant defendants back to the sentencing judge, a sometimes lengthy process that would seem to undermine the ideal of swift and certain consequences for noncompliance. A study of such judicial monitoring in the Bronx found that it did not deter re-offending (see Chapter 6).

Orders of Protection

The courts are extremely consistent in their policies and practices regarding orders of protection; all routinely issue full orders in all cases, granting very few limited orders, and then often only at or after sentencing.

Victim Services

Most of the courts refer complainants to victim advocates from Safe Horizon, although Manhattan routinely uses victim advocates in the District Attorney's Office. The Brooklyn District Attorney's Office employs social workers to work with high-risk complainants at intake. The Queens District Attorney's Office has additional intake victim advocacy provided by Safe Horizon. All courts appear to successfully link complainants to victim advocates, regardless of their agency affiliation. Among the district attorneys' offices that maintain victim advocates, only Manhattan does not extend services to complainants who choose not to prosecute, referring them to Safe Horizon instead.

Prosecutorial Policies

Some of the primary differences between domestic violence courts result from the policies and practices of the district attorneys. Each borough has a unique approach to prosecuting domestic violence cases (see Table 4).

Definition of Domestic Violence

The New York City Police Department defines domestic violence as any violence occurring either within a family or between intimate partners, regardless of the duration of the relationship. The district attorneys' domestic violence bureaus, however, are not bound by these definitions, and may impose stricter criteria. Judges, also, may decline to hear a case that they do not feel falls under their jurisdiction. However, most counties respect the police definition. As a result, most courts are hearing cases involving not only intimate partners—married, dating, and former couples—but also cases involving relatives, primarily siblings or parents and their older children.

The Queens Domestic Violence Bureau is unique in its adherence to a narrow definition of domestic violence, which results in the Queens Domestic Violence Court seeing proportionally fewer cases than the other counties. The Queens Bureau's definition of domestic violence is limited to couples, regardless of gender, who are legally married or who have been legally married, who are living together or who have lived together, or who have children in common. This definition excludes all non-intimate partner violence. This definition also excludes intimate partner violence among dating couples who have never lived together. While Brooklyn also excludes non-intimate partner violence cases, Brooklyn does not exclude intimate partner cases where the partners have never lived together. There are advantages and disadvantages to these restrictions. Issues such as child and elder abuse are distinct from domestic violence, and ideally should be addressed by experts in those areas; but in a less than ideal world, judges' training in domestic violence might provide them with more insight into these issues than is enjoyed by judges with no extra training. As one judge said in reference to a case in which an adolescent boy was accused of abusing his parent: "I know he's not strictly domestic violence, but another [court] part is not going to have the understanding that I do, or the resources."

Intake Process

Most counties make first contact with the complainant over the phone, and may draft the accusatory instrument without meeting with the complainant in person. In Staten Island, the police review their reports with assistant district attorneys in the complaint room; an assistant district attorney from the Sex Crimes/Special Victims Bureau usually contacts the complainant within a few days. In Brooklyn and Manhattan, the police transmit their reports to the district attorneys' offices' general intake units, which conduct preliminary telephone interviews and draft the accusatory instrument. General intake then forwards all information to the domestic violence bureau. In Manhattan, the only borough which does not have a specialized domestic violence bureau, the assistant conducting the general intake is assigned the case and may draft the accusatory instrument without speaking to the complainant. Finally, in the Bronx and Queens, an assistant district attorney from the domestic violence bureau always interviews the complainant in person before drafting the accusatory instrument. Those domestic violence bureaus that have placed an emphasis on connecting with the complainant as early as possible assert that this practice helps to ensure the complainant's safety and cooperation: complainant safety, because the domestic violence bureau is able to provide resources ranging from information on the case to relocation assistance; and complainant cooperation, because it allows the domestic violence bureau to forge a relationship with the complainant close to the point of crisis, when trust and cooperation may be more easily established.

Decision to Prosecute

The cooperation of the complainant is usually the critical factor in deciding whether there is sufficient evidence to prosecute the case. By New York State law, if prosecution is based on the police report rather than complainant report, the complainant must corroborate the report within five days if the defendant is incarcerated, or 90 days if the defendant is released. At that time, the prosecution must either produce the corroborating statement or declare its readiness to continue with an evidence-based prosecution, without the assistance of the complainant. The frequency with which district attorneys pursue the latter course varies. The Bronx is the only borough to explicitly require victims to sign a complaint before the district attorney will proceed with prosecution. On the other end of the spectrum, the Brooklyn District Attorney's Office attempts to pursue all cases under the theory that the prosecution period may be an important one for promoting the safety of complainants and linking them to services—even if most of the criminal cases are eventually dismissed (Peterson 2002).

Vertical Prosecution

Once the process begins, most boroughs attempt to practice some degree of vertical prosecution—assigning a single prosecutor to follow the case from beginning to end—but only Queens and Manhattan strictly implement the practice. In Queens, an assistant district attorney conducts an interview with the complainant at the time of the incident, and then appears at arraignment and all court dates. The same is true in Manhattan, with the exception of arraignment, where the assistant district attorney assigned to arraignments for the day will take the case. In the Bronx, Brooklyn, and Staten Island, the case goes through general intake, after which the Domestic Violence Bureau Chief assigns it to an assistant district attorney. This attorney will not appear at arraignment, and may not necessarily appear at subsequent court dates; instead, one or several assistant district attorneys are assigned to the courtroom for the day, representing all cases on the calendar. However, these bureaus will attempt to have the assigned prosecutor appear in court if the appearance is expected to be particularly complex or significant. Court observations indicated that it was not unusual for the judge to request the presence of the assigned assistant district attorney. While it is possible that the handling of the case by different assistants has no effect on processing, court observations indicate that assistant district attorneys who stand up on cases not their own often lack even basic information, leading to delays.

Compliance Involvement

All five boroughs will have their assistant district attorneys return to court if they become aware of a violation of an order of protection, an act of violence, or a new arrest. However, most domestic violence bureaus do not remain involved in the case after sentencing, and are therefore unlikely to know if any infractions have occurred. The exception is the Queens Bureau, which continues to meet with the complainant and monitor the defendant, receiving monthly updates about the defendant's conduct directly from the mandated program. This means that the assistant district attorney is able to alert the complainant if the defendant has not been compliant and might pose a danger. It also makes Queens assistant district attorneys more likely to be aware of any violations of the order of protection.

Stakeholder Perceptions

Stakeholder interviews addressed several broad topics on the levels of both theory and practice. In particular, stakeholders were asked to explain their perceptions of the domestic violence court's purpose, to consider its strengths and weaknesses, and to discuss the use and impact of program mandates for defendants and victim services for victims. Most believed strongly that domestic violence courts provide tangible benefits in the areas of victim safety and defendant accountability. Others cited practical benefits resulting from the structure of the courts. The most significant benefit cited by stakeholders was the enhanced training of staff and stakeholders, and the experience that comes from handling the same types of cases every day. Most stakeholders reported that domestic violence court judges and staff are attuned to the complexities of domestic violence cases, and know what issues to expect and how to respond. Many felt that this level of expertise enhanced the consistency of the court's response, a development perceived to benefit not only victims and the community but also attorneys, who reported that they could more accurately predict the behavior of the judge in a specialized part. This consistency enables defense attorneys to better advise their clients, thus benefiting defendants as well.

While there was a great deal of agreement about the benefits, there were also differences in emphasis. Stakeholders also raised a number of concerns in the course of their responses. The following sections detail the findings.

Goals and Objectives

The official goals of all five domestic violence courts under investigation are to promote defendant accountability and victim safety. However, particular actors may be overwhelmingly concerned with only one of the primary goals (e.g., victim safety), or with goals of their own (e.g., speedy case processing or defendant rehabilitation). Perceptions of goals were generally consistent within each role. Differences emerged more often between roles than boroughs.

Each of the judges and judicial hearing officers had slightly different perceptions. Goals articulated by judges and judicial hearing officers included: uphold the law, protect the complainant, punish the defendant, and rehabilitate the defendant. As the last two items from this list illustrate, the articulated goals sometimes seemed to be at odds.

Prosecutors were concerned with prosecuting the defendant to the fullest extent of the law, and with finding the best and safest outcome for the complainant. Some offices balanced these two objectives, while others assigned primacy to one or the other, or seemed to believe that the first guaranteed the second. Some prosecutors felt that their goals were sometimes at odds with those of other stakeholders. One assistant district attorney stressed that processing cases quickly, while relevant, was not the primary concern of the office, because a quick disposition might not be in the best interest of the complainant, or might not result in the most appropriate sentence.

The defense attorneys were unanimous in adhering to a narrower focus on the "fairest" court outcome for the defendant. While they disagreed on whether "fairest" was always a dismissal, or whether some cases merit a conviction and sentence, they consistently perceived adjudication in the domestic violence court to be prejudicial (an objection that will be examined more closely below).

In general, victim advocates were not as invested in the court process as other stakeholders. Their primary concern was the safety of the complainant, which, in their minds, takes precedence over the court case.

Interestingly, none of the stakeholders interviewed mentioned a reduction in re-offending as an explicit goal or benefit of the court; when asked, none had any substantive information on re-offending rates in their court, and few were confident about the court's impact on re-offending. One prosecutor suggested that the court may produce a reduction in re-offending over time, but for now, many stakeholders agreed with one who observed that "I've been seeing a lot of defendants over and over again."

Defendant Accountability

Most stakeholders felt that the domestic violence court model increases defendant accountability. However, while nearly everyone felt that the court possesses the appropriate mechanisms to respond to noncompliance, the judges consistently expressed doubts regarding the accuracy and timeliness of the information they receive regarding infractions and new arrests; and other stakeholders shared this concern. Stakeholders agreed that the court is most likely to be aware of, and is best able to respond to, noncompliance at a mandated program (e.g., not attending the program, or exhibiting disruptive behavior). However, many defendants are attending a program for half or less of the duration of their conditional discharge, and some receive no program mandate at all. Concerns pertaining to resources and information sharing (see below) further undermined the perception that the court promoted accountability.

Batterer Programs and Other Program Mandates

Most jurisdictions have formed relationships with batterer programs, in part to obtain more information about their philosophies, policies, and practices. However, almost all stakeholders expressed uncertainty regarding the value of the programs, and said they would welcome research on their effectiveness.[1] In particular, some judges and prosecutors were concerned about mandating an intervention that has not been proven effective. Victim advocates were concerned that these programs have no effect, or even a negative effect, on victim safety. (Echoing some of these concerns, the research literature generally casts doubt on the potential for batterer programs to change offender behavior; for example, see Davis, Taylor, and Maxwell 2000; Dunford 2000;

Feder and Dugan 2002; Feder and Wilson 2005; and Labriola et al. 2005).

Almost all stakeholders mentioned that there are very few high-quality batterer programs available, and very few that accept female batterers. In addition, many stakeholders commented on the need for a greater diversity of program models. Counties with sufficient resources have made an effort to provide culturall competent batterer programs for members of different ethnic communities. Unfortunately, not all counties have access to these types of programs, or the staffing resources to evaluate their appropriateness.

Many domestic violence courts also mandate other types of programs, primarily substance abuse treatment, as part of the conditional discharge. Some stakeholders felt that this was inappropriate; in the words of one judge, "This is the domestic violence part. While substance abuse may have been a contributing factor, it did not cause domestic violence, and not sentencing the defendant to a batterer program sends the wrong message." Other stakeholders cited the cost of drug and alcohol programs as prohibitive. Defense attorneys also felt that the potentially fluid nature of the drug treatment mandate was unfair to their clients (that is, if there is no completion date for drug treatment established at the time of the mandate, the defendant does not know how long he will have to remain in treatment).

In contrast, stakeholders who supported the use of different types of programs argued that the court should offer the most appropriate solution for each family. Some felt that it would be difficult for defendants to benefit from the batterer program without first becoming sober. Explained one defense attorney, "The philosophy of the office is that in cases where the defendant has substance abuse or alcohol abuse issues, these issues should be dealt with either prior to entering the batterer intervention program, or concurrently with the batterer intervention program."

Since very few facilities offer a concurrent batterer program/substance abuse treatment curriculum, and since defense attorneys are likely to resist a mandate involving two programs as excessively onerous, the result is that defendants are often mandated to substance abuse treatment only.

Additional arguments for the use of substance abuse treatment mandates were that many batterer programs will not admit addicts, and that some defendants have strictly alcohol- or drug-related issues and would not benefit from the batterer program at all. Finally, a small group felt that it is better to send defendants to a program type that, unlike batterer programs, has at least been proven effective.

Victim Safety

There was pronounced disagreement among stakeholders regarding the ability of the court to promote victim safety. Judges felt very positive about the court's ability to secure victim safety. However, two judges said that they do not have adequate information about victim outcomes to evaluate whether or not the court is actually accomplishing this goal.

Concerns about victim safety extended to the courthouse itself. Although courtroom safety was a concern for most stakeholders, some felt that the courts did not translate these concerns into safe practices. Indeed, courtroom observations revealed that defendants and complainants often wait in close proximity to one another. Although Safe Horizon provides safe waiting spaces in all courthouses, many complainants do not take advantage of them, whether because they do not know about them, do not feel they need them, or have other concerns (most commonly, that they will miss their court appearance—waiting on another floor requires the complainant to coordinate communication between victim advocates and the assistant district attorney, which may be difficult).

More than one stakeholder recommended periodic sweeps of the courtroom and waiting areas to identify complainants who may require information or services. However, there is disagreement about who should be doing this, and how often. In one borough, one stakeholder complained that it was not being done, while on the same day another reported that periodic sweeps of the courtroom were a regular practice. One stakeholder regretted that courtroom outreach by advocates is "not as structured as it should be."

One stakeholder criticized the common prosecutorial policy of requiring the complainant to attend all pre-disposition court appearances, and announcing the complainants' names in the courtroom, feeling that it made complainants vulnerable to their abusers. Prosecutors' reasons for doing this include allowing the complainant to settle any disagreements about order of protection preferences, and giving the assistant district attorney and complainant the opportunity to meet in person. However, one district attorney's office eliminated this policy and now sees complainants prior to the defendant's court date whenever possible.

The complainants who attend court and do not take advantage of the safe waiting areas expose themselves to the defendant and defense attorney. Stakeholder testimony and court observations indicate that defense attorneys frequently initiate contact with complainants; defendants and their family members and friends may also subtly (and not so subtly) harass them. Complainants may be unaware that they can notify court officers or the assistant district attorney about this harassment.

Resource Constraints

Most stakeholders agreed that domestic violence court volume is overwhelming, especially given the complex nature of the cases they are hearing. Besides the sheer number of domestic violence cases, most stakeholders agreed that the prosecution of such cases requires more work than other types of cases for several reasons. First, domestic violence cases require more nuanced decisions and more interaction with the other parties than is customary in standard court parts. In addition, evidence-based prosecution is more time-consuming than prosecution based on complainant testimony, and requires judges and attorneys to be intimately familiar with the rules of admissible evidence. Some stakeholders also observed that the specialized part seems to prolong the life of the case and the number of appearances—according to one stakeholder, where equivalent non-domestic violence cases would be dismissed at arraignment or at first appearance, domestic violence cases are often dismissed three months later, after a minimum of three court appearances. (District attorneys, however, generally justify these practices in the belief that the intervention of the court, even when it does not result in conviction, enhances the safety of the complainant through monitoring of the offender, and the threat of a harsher penalty if the defendant is re-arrested and returned to court.) In addition, the frequency with which program mandates are included as an element of conditional discharge and probation sentences requires stakeholders to be familiar with community programs. Finally, a recurring theme among stakeholders pertained to resource constraints in later stages of the case, when attempting to monitor offenders after sentencing. Those courts with enhanced staff positions (project director, resource coordinator, and defendant monitor) cited these as a significant contribution to their success, while those courts without additional staff perceived the lack as a significant obstacle. In some of the courts without additional staff, judges have taken on some of the work that a resource coordinator or project director would normally do, such as training court staff in domestic violence issues and searching for appropriate programs.

While there was universal acknowledgement of problems posed by high case volume and limited resources, there was no consensus among stakeholders regarding possible solutions. Some stakeholders believed that the courts should narrow their definition of domestic violence, usually recommending the elimination of cases that do not involve intimate partners (as is practiced already in Queens and Brooklyn). Some—mostly defense attorneys—go even farther, arguing that some intimate partner cases should not be heard in the domestic violence court if they do not qualify as "textbook" domestic violence. And many stakeholders outside of the well-staffed courts in the Bronx and Queens were interested in adding staff resources (project director, resource coordinator, and/or defendant monitors).

Flow of Information

Some stakeholders emphasized that additional staff resources are particularly helpful in facilitating the sharing of information, if only because there is a staff position (e.g., resource coordinator) that is explicitly responsible for such coordination. A few stakeholders noted that information-sharing about general policy questions is also facilitated by holding semi-regular "partners meetings" attended by judges, court staff, attorneys, victim advocates, and service providers from the community. At these meetings the focus is not on individual cases but on larger issues, such as sentencing trends and program availability, that affect domestic violence courts.

Stakeholders disagreed about the adequacy of the information available to them. Judges, in particular, were not sure that they were receiving all of the information they desired about defendant conduct, compliance with orders of protection, and new arrests. This was true even in counties with defendant monitors and other resources to expand contact with the complainant. Judges were also not confident that they were reliably receiving information from either Safe Horizon victim advocates or the prosecution. Finally, in the three counties where the district attorney's office and Safe Horizon both provide victim advocacy, stakeholders reported occasional problems with the overlap of services. However, most stakeholders were confident that the two agencies communicate well enough that the complainants receive access to services without redundancy.

Complainant and Defendant Understanding of the Process

Stakeholders identified established mechanisms for explaining the court process, requirements, and potential consequences to the complainant and the defendant. In theory, the court process is first explained to the complainant by the assistant district attorney, and then again by a victim advocate. In addition, many judges make a point of informing the complainant to stay away from the defendant when explaining an order of protection, even though the order does not formally enjoin the complainant. Nonetheless, stakeholders agree that the parties are often confused and uninformed. Those who work in direct service confirm that the parties are often oblivious to the ramifications of courtroom proceedings. Stakeholders reported that complainants were most likely to misunderstand the significance of signing the corroborating statement, or the implications of an order of protection. They also observed that complainants rarely understood that the case would not necessarily be dropped just because they declined to cooperate.

As for defendants, stakeholders reported that they often do not realize that the order of protection supersedes the complainant's stated wishes. In addition, stakeholders reported that defendants often misunderstand instructions to attend a program or to appear for the next court date, although those instructions are usually explained first by the judge and then again by the defense attorney. In courts with enhanced staffing resources, the defendant also receives these instructions from the defendant monitor, and possibly the resource coordinator. In spite of this, defendants often appear at programs or court on the wrong day, or not at all. Some attend no program, others the wrong program. One defense attorney attributed this to "wishful thinking," noting, "They block out all of the bad stuff, how bad this is. I'm more concerned about their cases than they are."

Evidence-Based Prosecution

Some stakeholders cited the no-drop policies of many district attorneys as potentially harmful to complainants. Critics, mostly defense attorneys and victim advocates, argued that removing complainants' ability to make free choices could undermine their sense of agency, while instilling in them distrust for the criminal justice system. Some victim advocates further stated that the complainant is in the best position to know whether or not it is safe to pursue the criminal case. One prosecutor pointed out that complainants in misdemeanor cases rarely want to go forward with cases, and that this phenomenon is not unique to domestic violence courts: "If we only prosecuted cases where people wanted to testify, we wouldn't prosecute anything at all."

Subgroups

All stakeholders agreed that the courts could improve their response to parties who do not fit the standard model of abuser and victim. Some stakeholders mentioned the lack of batterer programs for female batterers, both homosexual and heterosexual. Several stakeholders expressed concern about the lack of victim advocacy services for male complainants, both heterosexual and homosexual. (Most stakeholders were satisfied with the victim service advocacy for homosexual women.) A few stakeholders also mentioned the lack of support for heterosexual women who are single or working.

Assistant District Attorneys

Many stakeholders cited the inexperience of assistant district attorneys as a concern. Stakeholders reported that junior assistant district attorneys tend to work more slowly, and are often unwilling to make difficult decisions without consulting a supervisor, leading to unnecessary adjournments and additional court appearances. Everyone interviewed qualified these criticisms with the acknowledgment that prosecutors labor under large and difficult caseloads, made more difficult when the complainant is uncooperative. Whatever the reason, the frequency with which assistant district attorneys appear in court without having spoken to the complainant was a source of particular frustration for judges. Another common concern was that some assistant district attorney practices, such as requiring complainants to appear in court on the same day as the defendants, may put the complainant at risk. A similar, more widespread complaint involved conferencing with clients in hallways and other public locations. Many stakeholders attributed this to excessive caseloads, which may prevent the assistant district attorney from contacting the complainant prior to the court date, and to the lack of available space for meeting with clients in the courthouses.

The Defense Bar

The role of the defense bar was a subject of extensive discussion in many interviews. These discussions generally divided into two areas: problems with the defense bar as expressed by other stakeholders and problems of the defense bar with the domestic violence court model.

None of the other stakeholders believed that the defense bar was fully supportive of the domestic violence court model. Many felt that defense attorneys were exclusively interested in reducing clients' charges and sanctions, consistent with their traditional role. The defense bar's lack of enthusiasm about the domestic violence court may stem in part from the lack of any defense attorneys who specialize in domestic violence practice. No defense attorneys reported handling these cases differently: "We don't believe there's a unique specialty to trying a D.V. case," explained one. In most counties, the domestic violence court has a dedicated judge, clerk, and prosecutor. In no borough, however, are there defense attorneys permanently assigned to the domestic violence court. This means that often the judge, prosecutor, and court staff are ready to hear a case but must wait for the defense attorney to appear. Although several stakeholders expressed irritation with the delays—"Everyone sits around and waits for defense counsel"—none were able to offer a solution other than dedicating specific defense attorneys to the part, which did not appeal to the attorneys themselves: "It's not necessary, and even if it was, I couldn't get anybody to do it, to hear these cases all day, every day."

Another concern was the belief of many stakeholders that defense agencies are not providing appropriate services to their clients. One stakeholder asked, "If they have social workers, why aren't they using them?" Defense attorneys indicated that they make extensive use of their in-house social workers to provide resources and referrals to clients. However, they admit that they may intentionally conceal these efforts from the court. One reason is that the service referrals sometimes run counter to the goals of the domestic violence court model. For instance, the defense counsel might refer a defendant to an organization that does couples counseling because "a lot of times if you can get the two of them into counseling together, the complainant will not follow through with the prosecution." Also, defense counsel may by habit simply be reluctant to share any information with the prosecution and the court if not required by law to do so.

For their part, besides responding to practical criticisms of their participation, some defense representatives sought to challenge the philosophy at the foundation of the domestic violence court model. The criticism voiced most strongly concerned the model's perceived abrogation of the defendant's legal and constitutional rights. According to one defense attorney, "My client is guilty the minute he walks in the door. I have no problem with the process post conviction, but the 'batterers court'—you haven't proven that he's a batterer yet." The defense bar often expressed that the presumption of guilt is made evident at arrest, and continues throughout the court proceedings. Indications of this attitude include the orders of protection issued at arraignment and the tendency to refer to complainants as victims, as well as the focus on the complainant throughout the process. Some defense attorneys believed that this concern for the safety of the complainant, while admirable in an individual, is not appropriate in the legal system, which is supposed to presume defendants to be innocent. The perception of some defense attorneys is that domestic violence courts are designed to save the few complainants who are in imminent physical danger, at the expense of many defendants who are wrongly accused. Of note, many of the defense attorneys interviewed did not object to the special handling of domestic violence cases post conviction, only before. The few who did object to post-conviction programs did so based on their uncertainty about the cost and efficacy of batterer programs, not based on general philosophical objections.

Most defense attorneys further opined that judges' perceptions are biased. One prosecutor acknowledged this possibility as well: "If I were the defense lawyer, that [judge's attitude toward domestic violence] would be my concern." In jurisdictions where the domestic violence court judge also presides over bench trials, some defense attorneys believed that it is even more difficult for their clients to receive fair treatment: "The defendant's only remedy is to plead not guilty, upon which the D.A. reduces the charges to the B[-level misdemeanor] and waives jury trial, resulting in the bench trial in front of the same judge." Some of these defense attorneys report that it is rare to win a bench trial; others find the bench trial process fair. Most defense attorneys believed that the judge's behavior is the result of the publicity that domestic violence cases receive when they go wrong. Others attributed it to the judge's perception of the defendant's innocence or guilt and belief about what message a lenient sentence would send to the defendant: "Judge is thinking... D.A. may not have proved it beyond the shadow of the doubt, but I think he's guilty; if I release him, that gives him *carte blanche* to go home and beat the crap out of her."

Summing up much of the defense argument, all of the attorneys interviewed believed that the courts are essentially "victims' courts." Most other stakeholders did not share this perception, however, arguing that domestic violence courts still operate within a criminal justice system that protects the rights of the accused. One assistant district attorney argued that it was actually a defendants' court because the judge interacts with the defendant and not the complainant, and because there is no penalty to the defendant or the defense bar for not being ready. The prosecutor, on the other hand, is legally required to meet certain time constraints: "The defendant can show up late, the bench warrant is vacated, and the case is adjourned." This stakeholder reported that, while judges are able to penalize the defense counsel for a failure to be ready, most of them are not willing to do so (an assertion supported by court observations).

The issues raised by the defense bar are likely to persist as domestic violence courts continue to expand to new jurisdictions. Although some members of the defense bar were completely hostile to domestic violence courts, others expressed interest in becoming more involved, for instance, in the post-conviction monitoring phase. The interviews yielded a sense that there is a potential for collaboration that has not been fully realized.

Conclusion

Specialized domestic violence courts are now established in all five boroughs of New York City—and their number is rapidly growing across the country. Yet domestic violence courts seem to have been slower to coalesce as a national movement driven by common goals, priorities, and practices, especially compared with other problem-solving court models. The forces influencing their creation are clear: with the volume of criminal domestic violence cases ballooning in the 1980s and 1990s, many court systems created specialized calendars, enabling the judges and staff assigned to them to gain needed expertise. The coincident rise of other specialized courts (drug, mental health, and community courts) offered further impetus for the specialized handling of domestic violence cases. Yet, unlike drug courts, for example, domestic violence courts lack a national informational clearinghouse, training institute, or professional association to coordinate and inform national practice.

In this context, the present study sought to clarify and compare the prosecution and case processing methods of five New York City domestic violence courts, to establish the rationales of various players in creating court policies and practices, and to identify any weaknesses or conflicts within the domestic violence court model as it stands today. Of note, this study found considerable consistency in court operations across the boroughs, and slightly less in prosecutorial practices. It also revealed frustration over a perceived dearth of information about domestic violence courts' impacts on victim safety, defendant rights, and long-term outcomes. A few particular challenges echoed frequently in stakeholder interviews:

Resources All New York City domestic violence courts struggle with exceptionally high case volume coupled with a shortage of resources. Since domestic violence cases require frequent court appearances and some means of obtaining accurate information concerning compliance with program mandates, the need for case management and administrative staff is acute. Some judges reported that they were routinely unable to get through the calendar by the end of the business day. In a related vein, much was made of the overwhelming caseload faced by assistant district attorneys, and of the negative impact this caseload has on case progression. Indeed, research has found that the size of prosecutors' caseloads strongly predicts dismissal rates and sentence severity; the more cases prosecutors have, the less effectively they are able to pursue them (Belknap, Graham, Hartman, Lippen, Allen, and Sutherland 2000).

Flow of Information Most of the courts could increase and improve communication among stakeholders. In almost all of the five courts under investigation, the stakeholders interviewed appeared to be unfamiliar with the policies and practices of many of their partner agencies, and this uncertainty sometimes extended to their understanding of their respective roles.

Function of Program Mandates All five courts officially privilege the goals of victim safety and defendant accountability, yet this left some stakeholders in a state of ambivalence over the role of program mandates. Some seemed to believe, at least implicitly, that program mandates are for changing behavior but then were uncertain about whether batterer programs, the most common program types, do in fact achieve this goal. Some suggested that domestic violence courts should consider using/mandating other program types, substance abuse treatment especially, while others believed that substance abuse treatment was inappropriate, given the focus of the court on domestic violence and not addiction.

Role of the Defense Bar The defense bar has not always been well integrated into the domestic violence court team, a fact reflected in some of the fundamental criticisms leveled by and about the defense bar.

Challenges notwithstanding, most stakeholders spoke positively about the general role of domestic violence courts in the justice system. Many perceived that the courts had substantively improved victim safety as well as defendant accountability. Stakeholders praised the increased training and information available to judges, court staff, and partners, added resources that enable them to handle cases more consistently and to monitor offender behavior more closely.

Despite many cross-borough differences in specific policies, the broad outlines of a generally accepted domestic violence court model could be detected—in, for instance, the consistent focus on policies designed to promote victim advocacy, orders of protection, and post-conviction judicial monitoring of defendant compliance. As a coherent model continues to coalesce, future research evaluating the impacts of different policies and practices will enable stakeholders to make more informed assessments of the criminal justice system's emerging response to domestic violence.

CHAPTER SIX

Testing the Effectiveness of Batterer Programs and Judicial Monitoring: Results from a Randomized Trial in the Bronx

MELISSA LABRIOLA, MICHAEL REMPEL, AND ROBERT C. DAVIS

Over the past two decades, the criminal justice system has reshaped its response to the crime of domestic violence in an effort to protect victims and hold offenders more accountable. In particular, a growing number of courts have come to rely on batterer programs as their mandate of choice, especially when the legal issues in a case preclude the imposition of jail. To date, only four previous randomized trials have evaluated the effects of batterer programs (Dunford 2000; Feder and Dugan 2002; Palmer, Brown, and Barerra 1992; and Davis, Taylor, and Maxwell 2000). Even fewer studies have considered the effects of judicial monitoring, although many courts are now devoting substantial resources to monitoring, both pre- and post-conviction. Some believe that monitoring can deter recidivism by sending a message that the court is closely watching over the offender and will

This chapter was originally the executive summary of a research report published in November 2005 by the Center for Court Innovation under the title, "Testing the Effectiveness of Batterer Programs and Judicial Monitoring: Results from a Randomized Trial at the Bronx Misdemeanor Domestic Violence Court." Its publication was supported by the National Institute of Justice, U.S. Department of Justice. Official criminal history and recidivism records were provided by the New York State Division of Criminal Justice Services. The methodology and any opinions or interpretations in this chapter are those of the authors and do not necessarily represent the official position or policies of the U.S. Department of Justice or the New York State Division of Criminal Justice Services.

discover and sanction any noncompliance, but this belief has not been rigorously examined.

Accordingly, this study seeks to provide a more definitive test of the effectiveness of batterer programs and varying intensities of judicial monitoring in a single randomized trial. The research was carefully designed to ensure that the effects of batterer programs and judicial monitoring could be distinguished, so that the impact of one practice would not be mistakenly attributed to the other (see Labriola, Rempel, and Davis 2005 for the complete research report).

Research Design

The study was implemented at the Bronx Misdemeanor Domestic Violence Court, with enrollment running from July 23, 2002, through February 27, 2004. All eligible offenders were arraigned on a domestic violence misdemeanor, convicted of a violation, and sentenced to a conditional discharge with a one-year protection order in favor of the victim. This was the most common legal status when completion of a batterer program was also a condition of the sentence. The study proceeded in two parts, the primary randomized trial and a quasi-experimental design.

Design for the Randomized Trial

The trial involved a two-by-two factorial design (see next page), in which offenders were randomly assigned to one of four conditions: (1) batterer program plus monthly judicial monitoring, (2) batterer program plus "graduated" monitoring (less frequent court appearances in response to compliance and more frequent appearances in response to noncompliance), (3) monthly monitoring only, and (4) graduated monitoring only. Since all four conditions involved monitoring, the design isolated whether a batterer program requirement (for groups one and two) produces

	Batterer Program	No Batterer Program
Monthly Monitoring	N = 102	N = 109
Graduated Monitoring	N = 100	N = 109

any additional protective value in the form of lower recidivism rates. Further, the trial examined whether the specific approach to monitoring makes a difference: is it more effective to require domestic violence offenders to return to court as a matter of routine each and every month, or to offer incentives by adjusting the required frequency of court appearances as a direct response to past compliance? By using random assignment methods, considered the "gold standard" in social science research, findings can be deemed valid with a high level of certainty. A total of 420 offenders were randomly assigned in this fashion.

Other key components pertaining to the implementation of the trial were as follows:

Sampling frame To be eligible for random assignment, both the prosecution and defense had to be prepared to accept a conditional discharge sentence with a batterer program. The sentencing judges could exclude eligible offenders at their discretion, but used this option in only 14 percent of all eligible cases. Subsequent analysis detected few significant differences (in only two out of 67 baseline comparisons) between the characteristics of offenders in the randomized trial and those excluded by the judges.

Batterer program curricula The offenders assigned to a batterer program attended one of two 26-week programs, with classes meeting weekly for 75 minutes. Both programs are typical of batterer programs run for groups of men nationwide. They seek to educate participants about the roots of battering in societal norms that support male abuse of women and, through a combination of instruction and discussion, encourage participants to take responsibility for their anger, actions, and reactions. One of the programs also includes a substantial cognitive-behavioral module that focuses on identifying early warning signs of abusive behavior and developing skills for managing responses in appropriate ways.

Duration and content of judicial monitoring For those assigned to a batterer program, the monitoring period runs through program completion, which averages seven months (allowing for three unexcused absences). For those not assigned to a program, monitoring was similarly set at seven months. The offenders appear in a specialized compliance part before a judicial hearing officer (a retired judge), who possesses information about batterer program attendance (if applicable), re-arrests citywide, violations of any orders of protection, and any victim reports of re-abuse conveyed to a victim advocate.

Implementation of graduated monitoring Offenders on the graduated schedule were required to report to court less frequently when in compliance (e.g., four, 10, 18, and 26 weeks after sentencing) and more frequently when out of compliance (two and four weeks later), but we found that only the former of these rules was consistently implemented.

Research interviews with victims One year after sentencing, attempts were made to contact the victim in the case, and 106 interviews were completed. Although the contact rate was only 25 percent, there were no significant differences in the characteristics of cases for which the victims were and were not interviewed.

Design for the Quasi-Experimental Comparison

Since all four experimental conditions included judicial monitoring, the randomized trial could not test whether judicial monitoring produces any additional protective value in comparison with the complete absence of monitoring. However, in the second part of the study, offenders in the randomized trial were compared with another pool of offenders convicted of the same offenses during the same period of time but who, as a result of normal sentencing deliberations, were sentenced to a conditional discharge involving neither a batterer program nor monitoring. This served to add a true "nothing" condition to the study, albeit without the methodological benefits of random assignment.

To minimize the risk of bias, we implemented a propensity score matching technique designed to ensure the comparability of the two samples. This technique served to limit the final "no-monitoring" sample only to those offenders whose background characteristics (e.g., demographics, criminal history, current charges, and relationship to victim) closely matched those of the offenders in the randomized trial. After completing the matching process, 387 offenders from the initial trial were matched to 219 offenders in the no-monitoring group. (Thirty-three of the initial 420 offenders in the randomized trial had to be removed due to missing data on key characteristics required for matching; also, the 219 offenders in the final control sample represented the best matches from a much larger initial pool of 599.) A comparison of the two final samples showed not a single significant difference in their baseline characteristics, suggesting a high degree of internal study validity.

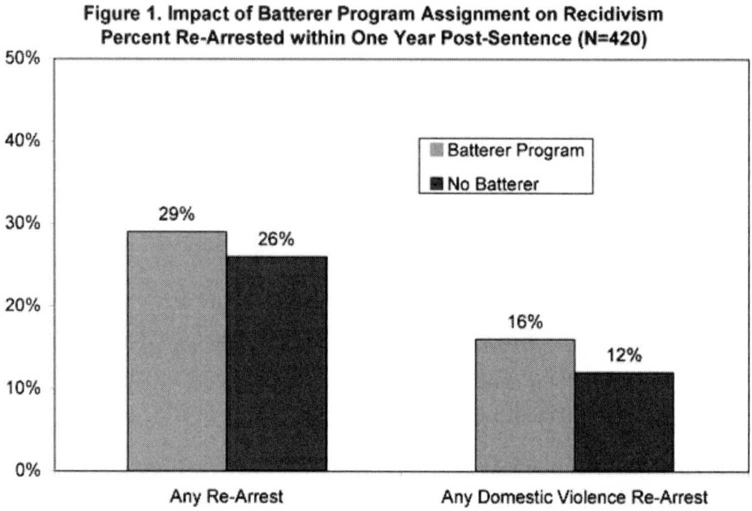

Results

The offenders were tracked for one year after sentencing. Most were also tracked over a longer 18-month period, a shorter "in program" period (when the offenders were actively monitored), and a one-year "post-program" period (after monitoring had ended). However, we did not detect any notable differences based on the time frames examined, and, for that reason, the results reported below are all for the one-year post-sentence period.

Official Re-Arrest Records

Impact of batterer programs on re-arrest

Batterer programs did not produce a reduction in re-arrests (Figure 1). There were no significant differences between those assigned and not assigned to a batterer program in the probability of re-arrest for either any offense (29 percent and 26 percent) or for domestic violence (16 percent and 12 percent).

Figure 2. Impact of Judicial Monitoring Schedule on Recidivism: Percent Re-Arrested within One Year Post-Sentence (N=420)

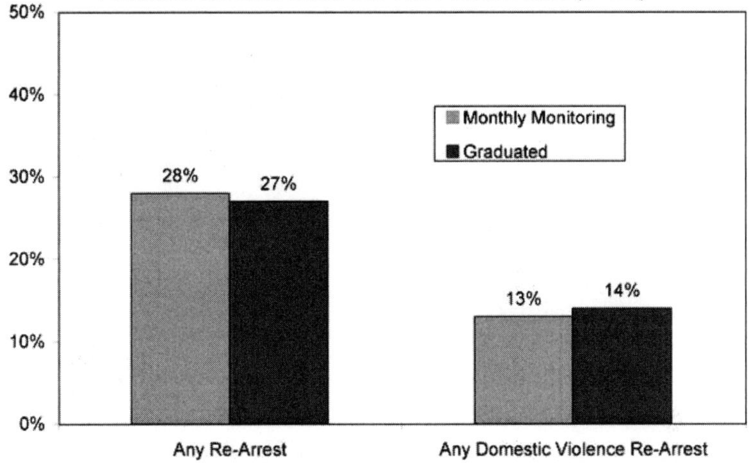

Impact of judicial monitoring schedule on re-arrest

Neither form of monitoring proved more effective than the other (Figure 2). There were no significant differences between those assigned to monthly and graduated monitoring in the probability of re-arrest for any offense (28 percent and 27 percent) or for domestic violence (13 percent and 14 percent).

Impact of judicial monitoring on re-arrest (compared with the complete absence of monitoring, based on the quasi-experimental design)

Judicial monitoring did not produce a reduction in re-arrests (Figure 3). There were no significant differences between those in the randomized trial, all of whom were monitored, and those in the no-monitoring sample in the probability of re-arrest for any offense (27 percent and 24 percent) or for domestic violence (13 percent and 14 percent). Judicial monitoring appeared to produce a modest reduction in the total number of domestic violence re-arrests ($p < .10$), but this was the only outcome measure whose impact began to approach statistical significance.

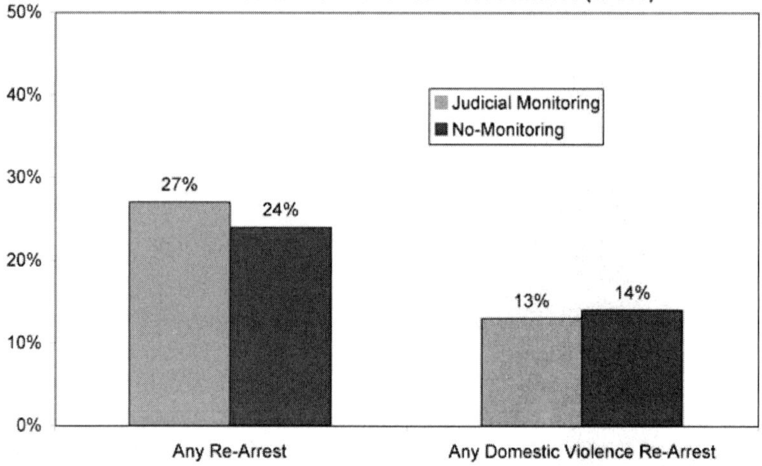

Figure 3. Impact of Judicial Monitoring on Recidivism: Percent Re-Arrested within One Year Post-Sentence (N=606)

Survival analysis

None of the interventions under examination outperformed any other in delaying the onset of recidivism; there were no significant differences in the average number of crime-free days prior to first re-arrest. For all samples, of those re-arrested over the one year tracking period, approximately two-thirds were re-arrested within the first six months after initial sentencing.

Predictors of recidivism

The strongest predictors of future recidivism were prior criminal history, younger age, lack of a "stake-in-conformity" (e.g., stemming from employment or living with the intimate partner), and more serious current arrest charges. However, taken together, these measures more strongly predicted re-arrest for any offense than for domestic violence in particular; hence domestic violence offending appears to involve dynamics that are less easily captured by standard social background variables.

Victim Reports

Prevalence of victim reports of re-abuse

Forty-six percent of the women interviewed reported experiencing at least one incident of re-abuse in the year after sentencing: 15 percent reported physical abuse, 18 percent reported threats, and 44 percent reported other forms of abuse (harassing phone calls, confrontation, denial of access to money, isolation from friends, stalking, threats of suicide, or threats of harm to children or other people they know).

Impact of random assignment conditions on victim reports of re-abuse

Whether the cases were assigned to a batterer program or not, or to monthly or graduated monitoring, these measures had no significant effects on victim reports of re-abuse (either in general or concerning each specific form of re-abuse: physical, threats, or other).

Impact of batterer programs on victim satisfaction with the sentence in the case

Victims whose cases were assigned to a batterer program were more satisfied with the sentence in the case (77 percent) than victims whose cases were not assigned to a program (52 percent). The type of judicial monitoring schedule had no impact on victim satisfaction.

Conclusion

The preponderance of evidence now accumulated in the field calls into question the effectiveness of batterer programs based on the most prevalent national models. Indeed, the main findings from our randomized trial are consistent with other recent trials, of which none found that mandating offenders to a batterer program produced lower rates of re-abuse. We did find a beneficial impact of a batterer program mandate on victim satisfaction with the sentence in the case; however, in the absence of a reduction in re-abuse, this finding is difficult to interpret. It may only indicate that victims whose partners are mandated to a program are imbued with optimism that is in the end unjustified; alternatively, it is equally plausible that the victims recognize that the batterer program does not make them safer but want the offenders held more accountable by having to attend it as an added sentencing requirement. Indeed, nearly half (49 percent) of the victims who were dissatisfied with the sentence expressed that they held this view because the sentence was not severe enough.

Contrary to our expectations, we did not find that judicial monitoring leads to lower re-arrest rates, nor did we find that the specific monitoring schedule (monthly or graduated) affects the recidivism outcomes. Our findings are qualified, however, by the nature of judicial monitoring at our site in the Bronx. The feedback conveyed by the judicial hearing officer during monitoring appearances was generally brief, matter-of-fact, and often couched in legal terminology that some offenders may not have understood. While there was some use of positive incentives with offenders on the graduated schedule, noncompliance did not consistently and immediately trigger sanctions—jail or other—designed to enforce the court's conditions and deter future noncompliance.

This study's findings therefore call into question the efficacy of the simple surveillance of domestic violence offenders through ongoing court check-ins, but we did not test the effects of a truly robust form of judicial supervision. Also, whereas our batterer program results affirm those obtained by other experiments, the previous literature is more limited with respect to monitoring. Hence we believe there is a need for replication of our monitoring results, preferably involving a test of a more rigorous judicial supervision regimen in which information is more clearly conveyed to the offenders about their responsibilities, and compliance is enforced through the consistent implementation of sanctions and incentives.

In light of our findings, courts may now wish to consider new experimentation with judicial monitoring (e.g., involving more rigorous applications of positive and negative incentives to foster compliance), changes in program mandates (e.g., involving mandates other than standard batterer programs with an educational or cognitive-behavioral emphasis), a greater emphasis on accountability rather than rehabilitation when batterer programs are used (e.g., consistently imposing consequences in response to noncompliance), and a re-focus on victim services (e.g., involving efforts to develop new resources and methods to assist victims and spread community awareness about the harms of domestic violence). Regrettably, our study suggests that some of the most prevalent court responses to domestic violence crime may be ineffective, but perhaps these findings can liberate the justice system to innovate in as-yet unexplored ways and promote a new period of reflection and experimentation.

CHAPTER SEVEN

Confronting Teen Dating Violence: An Evaluation of the Brooklyn Youthful Offender Domestic Violence Court

AMANDA B. CISSNER

Despite growing awareness of the issue of domestic violence, teenage dating violence has only recently emerged as a focus of domestic violence programming and research. According to the U.S. Department of Justice, women ages 16 to 24 are the most vulnerable demographic to non-fatal intimate partner violence (Rennison 2001). In New York City, the domestic violence hotline receives an average of 375 calls a month from teenagers seeking help with an abusive relationship. Ten percent of domestic violence victims treated at New York City hospitals are under the age of 20 (Commission to Combat Family Violence 1999). These numbers indicate that teen dating violence is a serious problem.

In response, the New York State Unified Court System in collaboration with the Center for Court Innovation launched the Brooklyn Youthful Offender Domestic Violence Court in December 2003. The Brooklyn Youthful Offender Domestic Violence Court builds on the model of adult domestic violence courts (see Chapter 5) but with an eye to the special needs of adolescent offenders and victims. A single judge presides, sitting for

This chapter is adapted from a research report published in 2005 by the Center for Court Innovation under the title, "Process Evaluation of the Brooklyn Youthful Offender Domestic Violence Court." The research for this article was supported by the Bureau of Justice Assistance, Office of Justice Programs of the U.S. Department of Justice. Any opinions are those of the author or, where attributed, the stakeholders and research participants. They do not necessarily represent the official position or policies of the U.S. Department of Justice.

regular court appearances as well as continued compliance monitoring. The hope is that by handling all misdemeanor teen dating violence cases, the judge gains a specialized understanding and sensitivity and is able to promote a more consistent court response. Both the judge and potential back-up judges receive specialized training on the unique needs and challenges of adolescent victims and perpetrators of relationship violence.

In addition to the single judge, the Youthful Offender Domestic Violence Court features a dedicated prosecutor, a victim advocate (working through the District Attorney's Office), and a resource coordinator. The resource coordinator prepares case information for the judge, facilitates contact between service providers and the court to ensure swift and accurate reporting, and helps in the identification of eligible cases. Beyond specialized staffing, the court relies on a free 12-week batterer program designed for teen perpetrators (STEPS to End Family Violence, hereafter STEPS), continued court monitoring, specialized staff training, and the involvement of community partners. Through a collaboration of service providers, prosecutors, the local defense bar, and court personnel, the court aims to create a multi-level response to teen dating violence.

This chapter presents a process evaluation of the first 15 months of the Youthful Offender Domestic Violence Court, from December 2003 to March 2005. After outlining the state of the current literature and the evaluation methodology, the chapter provides a chronological account of the court: planning, implementation, operations (eligibility, screening, court procedures, volume and characteristics, victim services), the courtroom experience, and offender outcomes. Major findings and lessons learned are included throughout.

The State of the Literature

The prevalence of teen dating violence is difficult to determine. A

2001 study by Silverman and colleagues found that one in five female high school students reported being physically or sexually abused by a dating partner (Silverman, Raj, Mucci, and Hathaway 2001). A poll conducted by Kaiser Permanente found that 40 percent of girls between the ages of 14 and 17 reported knowing someone their age who had been hit by a boyfriend (Kaiser Permanente 1995). O'Keefe and Treister (1998) found an even higher incidence of dating aggression among teens: 45 percent of high school girls and 43 percent of high school boys reported experiencing some physical aggression in a dating relationship.

However, Molidor and Tolman (1998) warn against reading such findings to indicate gender parity in dating violence. Adolescent girls in their study reported that in 70 percent of violent incidents, it was the male who initiated the violence. Additionally, female and male responses to violence were dissimilar: female adolescents most frequently reported fear, followed by emotional hurt, while male adolescents most commonly reported amusement or anger. In a later study, Molidor and colleagues found that adolescent males were also less likely to be injured through intimate partner violence than were adolescent females (Molidor, Tolman, and Kober 2000). Similarly, O'Keefe (1997) concluded that teenage females are more likely than males to use violence as self-defense. The City of New York (1998) estimated that nearly 80 percent of girls who are physically abused in their intimate relationship continue to date their abuser.

Several studies have found indications that abuse in the home may predict future teen dating violence (e.g., Roscoe and Callahan 1985; Wolfe, Scott, Wekerle, and Pittman 2001). However, a longitudinal study by McClosky and Lichter (2003) did not find a significant relationship between exposure to domestic violence during childhood and later dating violence.

Despite the risk of intimate partner violence for adolescents, there are few programs designed for either youthful victims or perpetrators. Even fewer evaluations are available to determine the effectiveness of teen-specific programs. Of seven evaluations included in a review of the literature by Hickman, Jaycox, and Aronoff (2004), all but one were school-based prevention programs targeting the general student population. The results of these evaluations are mixed, but generally indicate that programming can have some impact on knowledge about dating violence. Likewise, an independent evaluation of the Mentors in Violence Prevention program found that it resulted in significant attitude changes among both male and female high school student participants (Northeastern University's Center for the Study of Sport in Society 2001). However, it is difficult to draw conclusions about changes in attitudes and behaviors or the longevity of any potential impacts. The single community-based program included in Hickman and colleagues' review targeted teens at risk of dating violence, rather than teens generally, and was found to be effective in reducing dating violence (Wolfe et al. 2001). However, Hickman et al. warn that caution should be exercised in generalizing the findings of all program evaluations to date, as methodological problems are common across studies (Hickman et al. 2004). None of the programs evaluated in the Hickman review utilized the justice system in combination with community partners to target the issue of teen dating violence.

Sagatun-Edwards and colleagues (2003) provide a rare examination of such a collaboration in their evaluation of the Santa Clara County Juvenile Domestic and Family Violence Court. This specialized court targets youthful perpetrators of both dating violence and family violence through the Family Court system. Similar to the Brooklyn Youthful Offender Domestic Violence Court, the Santa Clara court hopes to promote victim safety and offender accountability. In addition, the court aims to reduce future violence through developmentally appropriate programming. The evaluation reveals that those juveniles seen in the specialized court were more likely to be mandated to a batterer program, were more likely to successfully complete this program, were subject to more monitoring, were more likely to receive a no-contact protective order, and were more likely to abide by orders of protection than the comparison group (offenders with similar domestic or family violence charges during the two years preceding the opening of the specialized court). The court was not found to be as successful, however, when it came to affecting future offending. Juveniles who completed the batterer program were less likely to violate their probation or have a new offense up to two years after program completion than the comparison group. But when all program participants (graduates and failures) were compared to the control group, providing for a more methodologically appropriate comparison, those offenders seen in the specialized court part were significantly more likely to have a new adult domestic violence-related arrest (Sagatun-Edwards, Hyman, LaFontaine, and Nelson-Serrano 2003).

Research Methodology

All analyses included in this chapter are based on stakeholder interviews, structured courtroom observations, operations meetings observations, quantitative database analysis, redacted STEPS intake interviews, interviews with defendants in the STEPS program, and a stakeholder communication survey.

Stakeholder interviews were conducted with representatives from both the Brooklyn District Attorney's Office and the defense bar, as well as with the two judges presiding over the Brooklyn Youthful Offender Domestic Violence Court in its first year, the court's resource coordinator, the victim advocate, the chief clerk of Brooklyn Criminal Court, a representative from STEPS, a STEPS facilitator, and the Brooklyn Youthful Offender Domestic

Violence Court coordinator from the Center for Court Innovation.[1] In addition, 15 key stakeholders completed communication surveys reporting the frequency of their interactions with other stakeholders as well as rating the overall quantity and quality of communication between stakeholders.

The researcher conducted a total of 25 days of structured courtroom observation over one year. Also, databases were maintained by the program staff, tracking program and compliance data, victim participation, and background information on both parties. For the evaluation, this data was supplemented with criminal history and court appearance data.[2] Finally, interviews were conducted with 13 defendants, all of whom were enrolled in the STEPS batterer program.[3]

Implementation

Planning and Operations Team

The collaborative nature of this project is reflected in the number and diversity of justice system and community stakeholders involved in the planning and continued operations of the Youthful Offender Domestic Violence Court. In December 2002, one year prior to opening, the Center for Court Innovation convened a group of stakeholders to initiate the planning process. Included in this planning group were several representatives from the Brooklyn Criminal Court, the Domestic Violence Bureau of the Brooklyn District Attorney's Office (which oversees the prosecution of all domestic violence cases), and victim services agencies. Also participating was the domestic violence coordinator from the New York City Criminal Court Administrative Judge's Office, who works to help plan and implement domestic violence projects in New York City. When a victim advocate for teenagers and a dedicated STEPS facilitator were hired during the court planning process, these parties began to participate in operations decisions as well. Although representatives from the two principal public defender agencies in Brooklyn were invited to participate in court planning, miscommunication between planners and defense representatives led the defense bar to feel excluded from the early planning process. Due to this miscommunication, the defense bar was not part of initial court planning.

In order to examine the communication patterns among stakeholders, all key players were asked to complete a communication survey when the court had been operating for about six months. When asked to rate both the frequency and quality of communications between stakeholders, 93 percent of respondents reported being satisfied or very satisfied with both. However, during interviews, several stakeholders voiced concern over what they perceived as the defense bar's lack of engagement and the failure to integrate the defense into the operations team.

After struggling for several months to find ways to bring the defense bar to the table, the judge and project coordinator decided that reaching out to defense agencies and providing them with a chance to have their concerns heard might help allay some of their fears. Therefore, in late 2004 and early 2005 the judge and coordinator gave a presentation at both the Legal Aid Society and Brooklyn Defender Services, providing background information and answering questions. In this way, the judge and project coordinator were able to ameliorate some of the defense bar's earlier resistance to the project.

Key Findings

Stakeholder Communication The vast majority of stakeholders reported satisfaction with both the quantity and quality of communications among key players.

Stakeholder Outreach Communications problems with the defense bar led to unnecessary friction during the court's early operations and necessitated labor-intensive peace-making. Such discord may be minimized by including all the necessary players early on.

Program Goals

When asked about the underlying goals of the court, stakeholders had somewhat disparate impressions. In particular, there seemed to be some uncertainty about whether the court is designed to produce behavioral change. While some stakeholders identified reducing teen dating violence and recidivism as being among the goals of the court, others maintained that such ambitious aspirations were likely beyond the scope of the program.

According to the project coordinator, confusion over the goals of the specialized court may stem from the fact that goals were not clearly laid out to stakeholders or discussed among them during the planning process. Additionally, as a demonstration project, the Brooklyn Youthful Offender Domestic Violence Court is among the first projects of its kind. Although establishing and sharing a clear set of goals during the planning process may have reduced later confusion, the very nature of a demonstration project involves learning by trial and error. Therefore, it is reasonable to expect that the project goals may change in response to unforeseen circumstances arising during operations. For future projects of its kind, an open, continuous discussion of key project goals and objectives may be what is needed.

Other than the issue of defendant behavioral change, stakeholders reported widely similar perceptions of program goals. Several saw the court as "a place that is finally [taking teen dating violence] seriously." Additionally, multiple stakeholders mentioned the goals of defendant accountability and monitoring; services targeted at the often difficult to reach population of teenage victims, ideally resulting in increased victim safety; and programming specially developed for teen batterers.

Key Finding

Establishing Goals Establishing or at least discussing clear goals early in the planning process and making these goals known to all key players might minimize later confusion. An operations manual might be useful for codifying goals for stakeholders and others interested in future replication of the model.

Eligibility and Intake

All misdemeanor cases in Brooklyn involving intimate partner violence in which the defendant is between 16 and 19 years of age are eligible for the specialized court. Additionally, English-speaking male defendants without severe addiction or mental health issues are considered STEPS program-eligible. The D.A.'s office may have additional stipulations for offering STEPS as part of a plea bargain, such as a limited criminal history, no open felony cases, cooperation of the complaining witness, and current charge severity.

In practice, there was initially some confusion regarding eligibility requirements. In particular, the eligibility criteria for the Youthful Offender Domestic Violence Court were sometimes confused with the more restricted criteria for the STEPS batterer program; because non-English speakers and female defendants are not eligible to enter the 12-week STEPS program, their cases were not always adjourned to the specialized court. Similarly, non-intimate partner cases with defendants in the target age group were frequently incorrectly adjourned to the court. Several memos outlining eligibility criteria were sent to stakeholders and clerks, which somewhat helped to alleviate this problem.

There has also been continued confusion about who is responsible for flagging eligible cases so that they may be properly adjourned to the Youthful Offender Domestic Violence

Court. Particularly in a large urban court with numerous special programs such as Brooklyn Criminal Court, getting all players to remember the requirements for specialized parts is taxing, as noted by one stakeholder:

> *There are a million memos about which cases go where—there's a lot of screening to be done and, in arraignments, they're not sitting down to carefully assess each case. I think that it would also help if the clerks were trained to flag these cases, but again, the clerks are already flagging for so many things, [I] don't know that they're going to flag for one more thing. The more eyes looking out for it, the better chance it will end up in the right place.*

The result is a system where arraignment judges who know about the Youthful Offender Domestic Violence Court adjourn eligible cases to the specialized court part and the clerks flag some cases, leaving the resource coordinator working in conjunction with the D.A.'s office to locate additional eligible cases and get them properly adjourned. Several attempts to replace this inefficient system with a more streamlined, clerk-initiated system of screening were made with varied success. Yet, some eligible cases continue to be adjourned to the wrong part and must be brought over to the court by the resource coordinator.

Key Findings

Eligibility During the initial operations period, there was continued confusion over eligibility criteria. Repeatedly defining the criteria for all stakeholders helped to reduce confusion somewhat.

Screening Cases Identifying and flagging eligible cases continued to be a problematic issue well into the court's operations. Working to train clerks, arraignment judges, and other key players proved insufficient to catch all cases. This problem may be particularly relevant for other high-volume urban courts where clerks already flag for a number of specialized parts (e.g., drug courts, mental health courts, and/or adult domestic violence courts).

Defendant Characteristics

During the first 15 months of Brooklyn Youthful Offender Domestic Violence Court operations, 279 defendants with 360 separate cases were found eligible and adjourned to the court. Table 1 describes the background characteristics of these defendants. Despite their young age, less than half reported being enrolled in school. Eighty-four percent had completed no more than eleventh grade. However, many defendants hope for higher educational attainment—of those who have not graduated high school, were not currently in school, and did not already have a general equivalency diploma (GED), 80 percent reported wanting to get their GED. Less than a third of defendants reported some amount of drug use and only slightly over a third reported alcohol use. Marijuana was the only drug defendants reported using. None of these defendants were excluded from STEPS based on their drug or alcohol use. Nearly half of defendants have a child in common with the complaining witness. Anecdotally, defendants in the Youthful Offender Domestic Violence Court experience a relatively high level of violence in their daily lives; within the first 15 months of operations, one defendant was shot and killed in an unrelated incident, one defendant was charged with an attempted homicide that left the victim paralyzed, and another defendant was stabbed multiple times.

Key Finding

Additional Service Needs The Youthful Offender Domestic Violence Court defendant population was not likely to be in school. Defendants were likely to have children in common with the complaining witness. In addition, defendants' lives reflected a high level of general violence. The court might address these issues by providing additional voluntary service referrals.

Victim Services

Victims of domestic violence are notoriously difficult to engage due to a variety of issues including reluctance to prosecute, mistrust of the criminal justice system, economic dependency, fear, children in common with the abuser, and a desire to remain in a relationship with the abuser. Teen victims pose an even greater challenge, as teens are frequently wary of authority figures. Despite these obstacles, a critical component of the Youthful Offender Domestic Violence Court is victim outreach, through which adolescent victims of relationship violence are offered information, safety planning, and support. The victim advocate is responsible for reaching out to all teen complainants, linking them to counseling, safety planning, and access to other services. In addition, the advocate is available to discuss and explain the victim's participation in the criminal justice process and to provide information about the status of the case.

By explaining the court process and the various orders of protection available to victims, the victim advocate hopes to make the experience more comprehensible and less overwhelming for victims and to overcome victims' reluctance to prosecute cases. Additionally, the advocate explains the STEPS program to complaining witnesses, being careful to remind them that no program is a cure-all for violence. The advocate continues to check in regularly with victims throughout the course of each case.

Table 1. YODVC Volume 12/2003-3/2005

Total Cases Heard in YODVC	360
Total Defendants Seen in YODVC	279
Average Number of Cases per Defendant	1.3
Descriptive Statistics	
Average Defendant Age	18.3
Male Defendant	88%
Defendant and Complaining Witness have a Child in Common[1]	48%
Defendant has Non-Sealed Prior Arrests[2]	34%
Average Number of Prior Arrests[2,3]	1.8
% of Defendants Currently in School[4,5]	46%
Median Highest Grade Completed[5]	11
Completed 8th Grade or Below[5]	2%
Completed 9th Grade[5]	16%
Completed 10th Grade[5]	25%
Completed 11th Grade[5]	44%
Completed 12th Grade[5]	14%
% of Defendants with a GED[4]	6%
Of those w/ No GED, % Wanting a GED[4]	80%
% of Defendants Reporting Drug Use[4]	26%
% Reporting Daily Drug Use[4,6]	33%
% Reporting Weekly Drug Use[4,6]	40%
% Reporting Rare Drug Use[4,6]	27%
% of Defendants Reporting Alcohol Use[4]	34%
% Reporting Weekly Alcohol Use[4,6]	20%
% Reporting Monthly Alcohol Use[4,6]	50%
% Reporting Rare Alcohol Use[4]	25%
Top Charge[7]	
Assault	68%
Criminal Contempt	17%
Menacing	10%
Harassment	5%
Criminal Mischief	3%
Weapons	2%
Other	6%
Mean Days from Arrest to YODVC Entry[2]	36.0
Mean Days from Arraignment to YODVC Entry[2]	33.5

[1] Or the CW is pregnant.

[2] Includes data for only the 264 cases that are not dismissed and sealed.

[3] Of defendants with any unsealed priors.

[4] Data from 65 STEPS screening interviews conducted between 4/15/2004 and 3/31/2005.

[5] Includes high school, trade school, and GED classes.

[6] Of those reporting any use.

[7] Top charge on any case. Because many defendants have multiple cases, percentages are out of the total 360 cases seen in the YODVC, rather than the 279 defendants seen in the part.

The victim advocate's outreach has resulted in many complaining witnesses signing corroborative affidavits, strengthening the district attorney's case against defendants and increasing the chances that defendants will be offered (and will accept) the STEPS program. As illustrated in Table 2, 39 percent of all complaining witnesses with cases in the Youthful Offender Domestic Violence Court signed a corroborative affidavit. If the victim advocate was able to successfully establish contact with the complaining witness even once, this percentage jumped to 68 percent. This finding underlines the importance of successfully establishing contact with victims of domestic violence. When comparing defendants offered STEPS to those not offered the program, cases in which a corroborative affidavit was signed were significantly more likely to be offered STEPS (60 percent versus 25 percent, $p<.001$).

In her interview, the victim advocate stressed the importance of measuring success not solely with signed corroborative affidavits. For some victims, signing an affidavit may result in the deportation or incarceration of someone with whom they have children and from whom they need continued support. Regardless of whether victims are interested in signing an affidavit or in having their partner attend the STEPS program, the victim advocate listens to their service needs and connects them with service providers:

> *College tends to be a thing that comes up with a lot of them. A lot of them do have children, so a lot of them dropped out of high school or didn't finish high school, didn't go to college, so that's a big thing.*

> *[Sometimes they are living] with the defendant, sometimes they're living by themselves, sometimes they're living with their families, but it's just more that he knows where they live.*

Although there is no data available to document the additional services provided by the victim advocate, she reports that educational and housing concerns top the list of issues victims want to discuss.

Key Finding

> *Victim Outreach* Complaining witnesses the victim advocate was able to contact at least once were much more likely to sign corroborative affidavits than those witnesses never successfully contacted. This finding suggests a link between effectiveness of victim services and case prosecution.

Participation in the STEPS Batterer Program

During the planning process, it was expected that most eligible defendants would be mandated to participate in the STEPS batterer program as a pretrial release condition (i.e., prior to a conviction). However, the defense bar was unhappy with this arrangement and the judge wanted to avoid setting a hard-and-fast policy, leaving himself free to make decisions on a case-by-case basis.

After operations began in December 2003, it became apparent that the reluctance of several stakeholders to implement a pre-plea mandate necessitated a new system. The flexibility of the stakeholders enabled the planning team to develop a post-plea system, whereby STEPS is offered as a part of plea bargain to defendants with appropriate criminal charges and histories.

In the final policy arrangement, defendants who accept a plea bargain including STEPS are mandated by the court to complete the program and face criminal justice consequences if they do not complete. As indicated in Table 3, 38 percent of all Youthful Offender Domestic Violence Court defendants were offered

Table 2. Complaining Witness Cooperation

Total Cases Heard in YODVC	360	
Total Defendants Seen in YODVC	279	
Corroborative Affidavits		
Complaining Witnesses tracked by VA[1]	191	68% [2]
Total % C/Ws Signing Corroborative Affidavits	108	39% [2]
Of C/Ws Successfully Contacted by VA, % Signing Corroborative Affidavits	107	68%
% of C/Ws Never Successfully Contacted	121	43% [2]
C/W Reported a History of Abuse[3]	110	85%

[1] Not all complaining witnesses for all YODVC cases are tracked by the victim advocate. The victim advocate does not have access to those cases in which there is a cross-complaint or cases that are not in the DA's Domestic Violence Bureau, for instance.
[2] Percent based on total number of *all* defendants (i.e., N=279).
[3] With the defendant or others. Percent is out of the 130 C/Ws contacted by the VA who answered this question.

STEPS and 65 percent of these defendants entered the program. Table 3 further indicates that of those defendants who had entered STEPS as of the March cut-off date for this report, and whose cases are closed, 62 percent successfully completed. It would generally be unsurprising to find teenage abusers less likely to complete their program mandate than older defendants, as younger age is generally correlated with program failure. Indeed, the 62 percent completion rate is slightly lower than the completion rate of 70 percent found for adult defendants mandated to one of two batterer programs in the Brooklyn Criminal Court (Cissner and Puffett 2006).

During defendant interviews, respondents were asked whether they felt that the decision to enter STEPS was their choice to make. When making the decision between jail and the program, many defendants felt they would get more out of STEPS than they would from jail:

> *I thought that if I went to the program, that would help me... better than me being in jail... That really wouldn't help me with the problem that I had at the time. Jail, that's just another way to make people be down, not teaching them anything. But the program has taught me a lot since I've been there... Every week*

Table 3. STEPS Entry and Completion

Total Cases Heard in YODVC	360	
Total Defendants Seen in YODVC	279	
Defendants Offered STEPS	105	38%
Took STEPS [1]	68	65%
Open Case	11	17%
Successfully Completed	34	52%
Failed	21	32%
Successful Completion Rate [2]	62%	
Defendant was Given Two Chances to Complete STEPS [3]	25	45%

[1] Of defendants offered STEPS.
[2] (Successfully Completed Cases)/(Successfully Completed Cases + Failed Cases)
[3] Of those who have completed (or failed) STEPS.

> *when I go to the program, it's like, I'd rather be in the program, going there every week, than to be locked up every week and not being outside, for me doing something that I know I shouldn't do.*

However, two defendants reported that the decision between jail and a program wasn't much of a real choice:

> *I mean, yeah, you've got a choice—you either go to STEPS for 12 weeks or go to jail for 15 days. [Laughs.]... [The program is] a lot of people who were like, 'I'm not going to jail, I'm going to do the program.'*

> *I had no choice. I was going to get 15 days [jail]... With the 15 days, I would have lost my job.*

Key Findings

Program Completion Consistent with planners' expectations, 62 percent of defendants in STEPS successfully completed the program. This outcome is slightly lower than studies of adult domestic violence offenders in Brooklyn, though successful program completion is routinely associated with older age.

Table 4. The Courtroom Experience

Days of Court Observations	25
Cases Observed	355
Length of Appearance	
Mean, 1st call (minutes)	3.6
Mean, 2nd call (minutes)[1]	4.5
Mean, total time before judge (minutes)	4.1
Judicial Interaction	
Judge Spoke Directly to Defendant	44%
Judge Gave Positive Feedback	37%
Judge Gave Negative Feedback/Lecture	19%
Judge Gave General Instructions/Facts of Case	44%
Defendant present at 1st call	82%
Defendant present at 2nd call	75%
Bench Warrant Ordered	10%
Bench Warrant Vacated	26%
Returned On a Warrant	1%
Defendant Is in Custody	7%
Defense Attorney[2]	
Legal Aid Society	62%
18B	13%
Brooklyn Defender Services	11%
Retained	2%
Other/missing	5%
Average minutes spent on non-YODVC cases[3]	18.2

[1] Of the 68 cases that were second called.
[2] Attorney information taken from CRIMS. Percentages are out of total number of YODVC defendants whose cases have not been dismissed and sealed.
[3] Based on 11 court observations.

Program Entry Defendants largely reported that they felt their STEPS participation was their own decision.

The Courtroom Experience

The Youthful Offender Domestic Violence Court is in session Thursday afternoons. Table 4 presents some basic information about the structure of 355 court appearances that were observed while conducting the evaluation. This table reveals that the majority of defendants were available in court the first time their case was called, although nearly one-fifth missed first call. However, a bench warrant was ordered by the judge in only 10 percent of cases, reflecting the observation in court that missing defendants often have their cases second-called with no warrant ordered, providing them with a second opportunity to arrive. Defendants spent an average of just over four total minutes in front of the judge. During that time, the judge spoke directly to 44 percent of the defendants rather than communicating to defendants through their attorneys, with positive feedback for 37 percent and negative feedback for 19 percent.

Judicial Interaction

In her usual interaction with defendants, the judge utilizes positive reinforcement to encourage continued compliance and negative reinforcement in response to noncompliance. Positive feedback may involve encouraging statements such as "keep up the good work," wishing defendants good luck in completing STEPS, and praising defendants who complete their program obligations. The judge frequently told compliant defendants that not only should they be learning from the program, but that other STEPS participants would learn from their positive example and active participation in STEPS classes. Defendants frequently noted the judge's praise during interviews, citing the praise as added motivation:

> *"It makes me feel good. Makes me feel happy. Makes me feel like I accomplished something. Like I'm really starting to learn... Making me feel... wiser."*

Defendants saw the connection between their compliance and the judge's positive feedback:

"When I used to go to court, I was going to court nervous, because I didn't know what they judge was going to do to me. Now I can say I'm going to court with confidence like the judge is going to give me a nice compliment this time because I was never late, I was always early, always on time, I have yet to miss a day."

Several defendants saw the judge's praise as an indication that she wants them to succeed:

"[The judge] gave me more feedback... 'How you doing?', 'I...hope you finish this program, you're almost done.'... Because she wants to see me do good, you know, get out of here."

However, a few defendants were less impressed by the judge's praise. One defendant saw the judge's consistency as impersonal:

The judge says positive things, but it's just the same speech for everyone... it's just the speech that she gives to everybody... I sit in court for almost three hours, everybody's just doing the same thing as me, just coming up for a checkout. You know what I mean—it's just the speech.

The flip side of judicial praise is the negative feedback defendants receive when they are noncompliant. Frequently, this came as a warning to defendants that the jail alternative would be imposed if they continued to be noncompliant. Several defendants mentioned negative feedback and the threat of jail time from the judge as a motivating factor that helped them get in line with the court's expectations.

[The judge] told me... 'One more time, if you miss even one time, if you even come late once, I'm giving you the maximum time—15 days in jail.' So that's when I really took [the program] serious.

Her comments was, most of the time, they was bad. So it was like, I took them bad comments and then alright, I said to myself, that comments is not getting you nowhere but a longer stay in the program and jail time. So it was like, to get all of it over with, just go to the program, be on time, don't miss no days, and... just sit back and learn, participate. And so far that's what I've been doing... Right now, I can't wait 'til I go to court... I know she's gonna have something good to say to me, about me.

Not only does the negative feedback from the judge impact those at whom it is directed, but defendants sitting in court also hear the judge's responses to others' noncompliance. When asked about seeing others get lectured or remanded, most defendants felt that those not living up to the program requirements got what they deserved:

Yeah, that [defendant] got remanded 'cause he kept sleeping. He'll have a lot of time to sleep [in jail]... Everybody's accountable for their own actions, that's the first thing you learn when you come to this class—accountable for your own actions. You fall asleep, you've got to know to expect it.

It's... [their] fault. It's up to them... this ain't nothing. I mean, it's 12 weeks. You can do this, get it out of the way. Go ahead with your life. You the one choose to mess it up. She gave it to you—you get a second chance. If you mess up for the second chance, you should go to jail. Cause it ain't nothing. Not like you have to stay for years... you're just waiting for twelve weeks.

Defendants reported being motivated by seeing others receive positive feedback from the judge:

I was slipping up. So every time I went into court, [the judge] was saying bad stuff about me, but [I saw] the judge give people compliments in court, so I figure like, if I can do this, she'll give me compliments when I go to court. Some people go in, 'Oh, you're doing good, I see you have such and such weeks. Good job.' And then that's it. When I go up there, I [am] standing in front of her for maybe like 15, 20 minutes [because I am non-compliant]. When the next person goes up, they won't even be standing there a minute because of the compliments that they [are] doing good.

Likewise, seeing others complete the program served as a motivation for this defendant:

When I first came, like three people completed... They completed it, they was finished already. So when I seen them completing it, I looked and I realized, ... if they can do it, why can't I do it? I know I can do it.

Infractions, Sanctions, and Incentives

During the early stages of the Youthful Offender Domestic Violence Court, there was much discussion of what to do with defendants who failed to attend STEPS. The STEPS policy allows each defendant to miss one class without negative repercussions. Absences are excused in the case of hospitalization or a death in the family with proper documentation. Additional unexcused absences result in a discharge from STEPS. However, deciding on a court policy to address additional absences took some time. Initially, the court was frequently inconsistent in upholding the absence policy. Defendants missing more than their one allotted absence were typically allowed to re-enter the program, but some defendants were allowed to pick up where they left off while others had to start over. That is, if two defendants had both attended eight of 12 classes and then missed two classes, one defendant might be readmitted to STEPS and ordered to complete his four remaining classes, while the other defendant might be readmitted to STEPS and ordered to complete an entire 12 classes, as though he had never attended STEPS before.

In interviews, several defendants noted the inconsistent absence policy. At least one defendant noted the down side of such a policy, holding that he had little motivation to go to STEPS, knowing he could always be readmitted:

> *If you was late and you had a legit excuse for it... [you'd get] another chance... That's what kept me in the program for so long... being given chances... [The policy] didn't work because I felt like, it's okay to slip up.*

After the court had been operational for several months, the team agreed on a more consistent policy. Defendants are allowed the single unexcused absence. Any additional absence without documentation indicating a true emergency results in the defendant being discharged from STEPS. Defendants discharged for the first time are given another chance to complete the program. However, when defendants return to the program for a second time, not only are they required to complete any classes remaining in the 12 weeks, they also have to attend an additional three weeks, resulting in 15 total weeks in the program. It is the judge's policy to be very clear about what will happen if defendants who are starting the program for a second time miss another class.

The judge instructs defendants that while she believes that everyone deserves a second chance, she does not believe in third chances. This warning has become a standard explanation given to defendants readmitted to the program. As indicated in Table 3 above, nearly half of those who completed STEPS were given two chances to do so. Of those given a second chance, 45 percent went on to successfully complete the program, while 55 percent ultimately failed.

In addition to the new absence and re-admittance policy, the judge began to set strict jail alternatives for all defendants entering the program. When they accept the prosecutor's offer of STEPS, defendants are told exactly how much jail time they can expect if they do not successfully complete. For most defendants, this jail alternative is 15 days, although it may be higher for defendants facing more serious criminal charges. Defendants noted the change in policy. Although defendants found the new policy strict, they reported feeling that it is fair:

> *A lot of people haven't done what they have to do, but [the judge] gives them a second chance. [The judge] wants us to succeed.*

About six months into court operations, the judge began to use case calendaring as a tangible incentive for those doing well in STEPS. Particularly as the court calendar became increasingly heavy, defendants could spend a good deal of time waiting for their case to be called. As an added incentive for those in compliance, the judge and the resource coordinator worked to call compliant defendants early in the afternoon, so they could have their cases heard and leave. Occasionally, if a defendant is not in court when the case is called, this method is not possible, but compliant cases tend to be called early. One exception is that the judge also wants STEPS participants sitting in court to see what happens to non-compliant cases. Therefore, defendants who are being remanded also tend to be called fairly early.

All defendants make a final court appearance after completing the STEPS program. The judge's final feedback has changed over the course of the court's operations. Initially, the judge praised completing defendants on their hard work and wished them good luck. Based on feedback from the victim advocate, who worried that complaining witnesses observing this praise might feel that such a positive reaction made light of the defendant's violence, the judge altered her completion speech. Now, in addition to commending defendants for their commitment to finishing, the judge reminds defendants that violence is never acceptable and that violence against an intimate partner is particularly intolerable. In addition, the judge instructs defendants that should they ever appear in her court again, the repercussions of repeated violence will be more severe.

Key Findings

Judicial Interaction Program participants reported that both personal interactions with the judge and a set jail alternative motivated them to complete the STEPS program. Additionally, seeing others receive praise from the judge made an impression on many defendants.

Court Policy Inconsistent readmit policies for non-compliant defendants led to confusion among stakeholders and program participants. Although new policies were stricter, defendants reported appreciating the consistency offered by the more structured policy.

Procedural Justice

When asked if they felt that they were treated fairly in the Youthful Offender Domestic Violence Court, defendants responded largely in the affirmative:

> *"I think it's fair. The only way I wouldn't think it was fair is if the judge give somebody else two more chances. Like if she didn't terminate them... That's the only thing that would be unfair to me."*

The majority of defendants not only reported that they felt that they were treated fairly in court, but that the judge treated them with respect. In large part, this sense of respect seemed to stem from the personal interactions between the judge and defendants:

> *[The judge is] actually looking at me and talking to me... [I felt] well respected. Because he's actually talking to me and not the attorney coming back to me while they are just talking right in front of me.*

> *[The judge] talks to us, she tells me, she talk to me over and over and tell me, she tell me the consequences. It's like she don't really want me ... to mess up. Know what I mean? She want me to do this and get it over with.*

Key Finding

Defendants generally felt that they were treated fairly and with respect in the Youthful Offender Domestic Violence Court. Seemingly, regular judicial interaction and judicial consistency contributed to defendants' overall sense of justice.

Outcomes

Table 5 presents the criminal justice outcomes for Youthful Offender Domestic Violence Court defendants. Because many

Table 5. YODVC Outcomes

Total Cases Heard in YODVC	360	
Total Defendants Seen in YODVC	279	
Final Disposition		
ACD on Any Case [1]	42%	
Plead Guilty on Any Case	28%	
Charges Plead To [2]		
Harassment	58%	
Criminal Contempt	10%	
Disorderly Conduct	8%	
Attempted Assault	7%	
Menacing	6%	
Criminal Mischief	5%	
Petit Larceny	2%	
Drug Charge	2%	
Attempted Criminal Contempt	1%	
Charge Level Plead To [2]		
E Felony	1%	
A Misdemeanor	23%	
B Misdemeanor	9%	
Violation	66%	
Conditional Discharge on Any Case	19%	
Jail on Any Case	11%	
Community Service on Any Case	4%	
Another Program on Any Case	4%	
Violation of Conditional Discharge on Any Case	3%	
Probation on Any Case	1%	
Time Served on Any Case	1%	
Split Sentence on Any Case [3]	1%	
Average Days in Jail [4]	96	
Median Days in Jail [4]	30	
Cases Dismissed and Sealed	96	27%
Reason for Dismissal		
30/30 [5]	54%	
ACD [1]	31%	
Mutual Dismissal [6]	7%	
DA/Weak Case	5%	
Defendant Found Incompetent to Stand Trial	1%	
Other	4%	
Defendants Adjourned or Dismissed [7]	66%	

[1] Of the 116 defendants who received an ACD, only 28 had had their case dismissed by the time of the analysis. The number under Reason for Dismissal: ACD reflects only the 28 whose cases had been dismissed.

[2] Totals are out of the 86 pleas entered. Although 77 defendants entered guilty pleas, several defendants plead to multiple charges.

defendants have more than one case in the court, final dispositions represent the percentage of defendants who had a given disposition on any case. While 66 percent of defendants still had a case either dismissed or adjourned in contemplation of dismissal, 28 percent pled guilty to a charge on at least one case. The charges to which defendants pled are also indicated in Table 5. Thirty-two percent of defendants who pled to a charge pled to a misdemeanor.

Table 5 further indicates that 27 percent of Youthful Offender Domestic Violence Court cases were dismissed and sealed. While more than half of these cases were dismissed because the D.A.'s office was unable to gather sufficient evidence to prosecute the case within the 90 days required by law (this usually indicates that there is insufficient evidence for prosecution), a sizeable number were adjourned in contemplation of dismissal. Because defendants who successfully complete STEPS are frequently given an adjournment in contemplation of dismissal, this level is reflective of the numerous defendants who have entered the STEPS program. In fact, defendants in STEPS are significantly more likely to have received an adjournment in contemplation of dismissal than those not in STEPS ($p<.01$) and are more likely to have received a conditional discharge as well ($p<.001$, with the condition that defendants attend STEPS). In fact, these differences reflect that, rather than "getting off with nothing," a large percentage of defendants receiving adjournments in contemplation of dismissal and conditional discharges are entering the STEPS program.

Conclusion

Awareness of the issue of teenage dating violence is growing. As an effort to target both teenage perpetrators and teenage victims, the Brooklyn Youthful Offender Domestic Violence Court expands on the pre-existing model of adult domestic violence courts by utilizing specialized services developed with a teen population in mind. This model is among the first of its kind and relies on targeted outreach to the difficult-to-engage population of teenage victims as well as developmentally appropriate batterer programming.

This process evaluation of the first 15 months of court operations reveals some key findings of interest for jurisdictions interested in drawing on the model implemented in Brooklyn:

- *The Brooklyn Youthful Offender Domestic Violence Court provided specialized attention to the issue of teen dating violence.* Every aspect of the specialized court was developed with a teen population in mind. Having a specialized court shows offenders and victims that these cases are taken seriously. Additionally, developmentally appropriate programming and services work to engage the teen population.

- *Collaboration was key to the success of the Brooklyn Youthful Offender Domestic Violence Court.* The Youthful Offender Domestic Violence Court team worked together to provide a coordinated response to teen dating violence. Stakeholder flexibility was crucial in overcoming many of the challenges faced during the planning and early implementation of the project. In the one instance where a collaborative approach was not fully implemented—early exclusion of the defense bar—this proved to be an important barrier to implementation, overcome through subsequent outreach.

- *Unanticipated complications arose related to eligibility, case screening, and other policies.* The logistics of identifying and flagging eligible cases, mandating defendants to the STEPS program, adjourning cases, scheduling trials, implementing program attendance policies, and even delivering the judge's graduation speech had to be developed over time. While the planning team anticipated many of these issues before the court was operational, it was impossible to plan for every contingency. Again, the collaboration among stakeholders proved essential in addressing complications as they arose. While other jurisdictions may want to consider a policy manual, such formalization should not prevent altering policies to address new or unanticipated circumstances.

- *A permanently assigned judge with a strong, consistent, and fair judicial style motivated defendants to comply with court orders.* Defendants reported that both positive and negative judicial feedback encouraged them to comply with program mandates. In addition, defendants reported that the judge's consistency across cases increased their sense of procedural justice. This model of judicial interaction varies greatly from business as usual in the adult domestic violence court in Brooklyn, where compliance cases are heard by a judicial hearing officer rather than by the sentencing judge and where sanctions and/or judicial lectures do not directly follow infractions and are likely not given in front of an audience.

- *A set of clear goals and objectives was not agreed upon or explicitly discussed early in the planning process.* Without a clear set of goals, measuring the success of a project is a difficult task. Other jurisdictions may want to consider formalizing goals and objectives in a program manual or having sessions devoted to reaching consensus about their project's "definition of success."

- *Establishing contact with teenage victims was difficult, as anticipated.* However, once this contact was established, the victim advocate was able to link many victims with services and to increase victim cooperation in court proceedings. Other jurisdictions may want to investigate additional methods for gaining accurate victim contact information as well as ways to maximize victim advocacy.

- *Both teenage victims and perpetrators faced a number of unforeseen service needs.* The population seen in the Brooklyn Youthful Offender Domestic Violence Court was less likely to be in school, more likely to have children, and more likely to have additional housing and employment needs than anticipated. Again, stakeholder flexibility allowed some of these additional needs to be met. Other jurisdictions may want to examine opportunities for collaboration with additional service providers.

While this research offers an analysis of the planning and operations of Brooklyn's experimental model, additional questions remain. First, the replicability of the model in other jurisdictions has yet to be determined. Moreover, enough time must pass to determine the ultimate impacts of the Brooklyn Youthful Offender Domestic Violence Court relative to standard practices in Brooklyn. Future research should consider the model's effects on defendant case outcomes and re-arrest rates while continuing to explore its ability to serve the unique needs of teenage victims.

Community Courts

Whereas drug and domestic violence courts both specialize in a type of problem, community courts are defined instead by geography. Most commonly, they address the pressing issues of a specific neighborhood within a large city. There are now 30 community courts nationwide and a growing number opening in other parts of the world.

The community court mission has important implications distinguishing it from the other models under consideration in this volume. First, community outreach is an indispensable element. (Many believe that all problem-solving models should engage the community, but only with community courts is it an imperative following directly from its core mission.) Court planners, judges, and attorneys are expected to venture out into the community, conduct needs assessments, discern citizen priorities, and establish mechanisms for ongoing community collaboration. This represents a radical departure from the traditional role of the court but is consistent with recent trends in criminal justice policy, such as community policing and community prosecution.

Second, since each community court is designed to target the particular needs of its community, these innovations can vary enormously from site to site. In practice, most community courts process low-level misdemeanor criminal cases, but not all do, and some are multi-jurisdictional. For instance, the Red Hook Community Justice Center in Brooklyn, New York, has a single judge who presides over an adult criminal court, a housing court, and a family court hearing juvenile delinquency cases.

Like other rehabilitation-oriented problem-solving models (drug and mental health courts especially), community courts seek to treat their litigants fairly, to provide an individualized form of justice, and to link litigants with services designed to improve their life situation. On the other hand, the community, not the individual litigant, is the model's ultimate target. This leads many community courts, in practice, to make extensive use of community service mandates that are designed to restore the community but focus less on the individual litigant's needs. Also, when litigants are linked with services, the frequent use of short mandates (often as little as one to three days) makes the achievement of real rehabilitative outcomes, including reductions in recidivism, far more difficult to achieve than in drug or mental health courts, with their longer and more intensive mandates.

Although the current research literature is by no means extensive, a small number of comprehensive evaluations of community courts have been completed, providing a wealth of information about how community courts work, their impacts, and whether they save money for courts and communities. In Chapter Eight, Dana Kralstein synthesizes findings from seven such evaluations spanning four community court sites. Among other results, this meta-analysis highlights reductions in local crime, improvements in case processing, and improved confidence in justice.

In Chapter Nine, M. Somjen Frazer reports the results of a study examining how defendants processed at the Red Hook Community Justice Center perceive their court experience compared to similar defendants processed at a centralized, "downtown" court. Based on structured defendant interviews, the study includes separate measures of how defendants perceived the judge, prosecutor, defense attorney, and court officers; and measures of overall fairness and several underlying dimensions (communication, interpersonal treatment, and helpfulness). The study comprises a first-ever empirical test of how community courts are perceived by defendants. The study suggests that the community court succeeded in improving perceptions of fairness among defendants—an important finding given other studies that document that defendants are more likely to comply with court orders when they perceive their treatment as fair.

In Chapter 10, the focus turns from the perceptions of individual defendants to the larger role of community courts within the neighborhoods they serve. Kelli D. Moore reports the results of a citizen survey implemented in Red Hook, Brooklyn, and several surrounding communities. The results—which include improved attitudes toward criminal justice agencies and reduced levels of fear—serve as a community needs assessment, informing programming at the Red Hook Community Justice Center. Also, since the survey was implemented after the court opened, it illuminates the court's impact on community conditions and public perceptions of the criminal justice system.

CHAPTER EIGHT

Community Court Research: A Literature Review

DANA KRALSTEIN

Nationally, there are 30 community courts in the United States. The first one opened in Midtown Manhattan in 1993. Focusing on quality-of-life offenses such as drug possession, shoplifting, vandalism, illegal vending, and drug possession, the Midtown Community Court combines punishment and help by sentencing low-level offenders to perform visible community restitution and receive on-site social services, including drug treatment, individual counseling, and job training. The community courts that followed seek to achieve many goals, such as increased engagement between citizens and the courts, improved perceptions of neighborhood safety, reduced crime, and a greater level of accountability among low-level, "quality-of-life" offenders.

No consensus has emerged regarding how to best measure the goals of these programs, primarily due to the large variety of models adopted by different courts. To date, there are notable evaluations focusing on four community courts—the Midtown Community Court in Manhattan; Red Hook Community Justice Center in Brooklyn, New York; Hennepin County Community Court in Minneapolis, Minnesota; and Hartford Community Court in Connecticut. This paper summarizes the basic findings from these evaluations.

While sharing similar goals overall, the four community courts studied have a variety of differences, both in the types of

---

A version of this chapter originally appeared as a white paper with the same title published in 2005 by the Center for Court Innovation.

court cases they hear and in their programmatic emphasis. It comes as little surprise that a variety of methodologies have been used for evaluation. The most common is some form of community survey (e.g, phone interviews, door-to-door surveys, focus groups) designed to measure community perceptions of community court success. This was the primary method of two Red Hook studies (Moore 2004; Frazer 2005). In addition, the studies of Hennepin (Weidner and Davis 2000; Eckberg 2001), Midtown (Sviridoff, Rottman, Ostrum, and Curtis, 2000; Sviridoff, Rottman, and Weidner, 2002), and Hartford (The Justice Education Center 2002) included offender interviews or focus groups and utilized stakeholder interviews to gather the perceptions and opinions of court staff and treatment providers. The two Hennepin studies and both Midtown studies also gathered administrative/court data to do larger-scale quantitative analyses. As a result, Midtown and Hennepin, unlike Hartford, have been a subject of both process and outcome evaluations. The 2000 Hennepin and 2002 Midtown studies included cost-benefit analyses as well.

What follows is a review of what the literature tells us with regard to community court success in meeting its primary goals—holding offenders to a greater level of accountability for quality-of-life crimes, increasing communication between the community and the criminal justice system, improving community perceptions of safety, increasing case processing efficiency, and reducing certain types of crimes in certain neighborhoods.

Holding Offenders Accountable

One of the original goals of the Midtown Community Court was to reduce the number of "walks" given for quality-of-life crimes—sentences such as "time served" or a conditional discharge with no conditions. Midtown achieved this goal for all of the most common charges handled by the court—between one percent and 12 percent of Midtown offenders were given a "walk" for the top four charges compared to 23 percent to 55 percent of offenders whose cases were heard at Manhattan's centralized criminal court. Instead, offenders sentenced at the Midtown Community Court were at least twice as likely to receive a community or social service sentence as opposed to offenders sentenced in downtown Manhattan.

In addition to changing sentencing practice, the Midtown Court also sought to improve compliance with community-based sanctions. Researchers found that the Midtown Court's community service compliance rate was 75 percent—compared with about 50 percent in the centralized courthouse downtown—the highest compliance rate in all of New York City.

Finally, the 2000 community survey in Hennepin reported that community members thought the most important feature of the community court was that compliance with community service sentences was closely monitored by the court (3.73 on a scale of 1.0 to 4.0).

Community Perceptions

Many community members in Midtown and Hennepin reported that they were willing to reallocate their tax dollars, or even pay more in taxes, to support a community court. In Midtown, 64 percent of respondents were willing to pay some amount of additional taxes to support a court with features like the Midtown Community Court. Of those willing to pay more in taxes, 52 percent were willing to pay up to $100 extra per year.

In the 2000 Hennepin study, 66 percent of community residents who were surveyed were willing to reallocate their taxes, and 64 percent were willing to pay more in taxes to support a community court. Of those willing to pay more in taxes, 73 percent were willing to pay up to $25 more annually in taxes. Significantly, those residents who had heard of the community court or who owned their residence were most likely to be willing to contribute to the court.

A 2005 study of Red Hook, Brooklyn, reported that 78 percent of respondents had a positive feeling about having a community-based court in their neighborhood. A similar community survey conducted in Hennepin in 2001 found that almost two thirds of respondents (66 percent) thought that the county was not harsh enough with criminals.

Processing Efficiency

The Midtown study documents speedier case processing in the community court, as does the 2000 Hennepin study. In the first three years the Midtown Court was open, the average arrest-to-arraignment time was 18.9 hours compared with 29.2 hours at the downtown Manhattan court. The Hennepin Court also achieved quicker case processing, even though more appearances were required before disposition. The average number of days from court filing to disposition was 78.9 for the Hennepin community court defendants, compared to 80 and 124 for the two comparison groups used in that study. However, from arraignment to disposition, the community court needed 6.4 appearances compared to only 3.2 and 4.2 for the comparison defendants. The authors of the Hennepin study observe that the increased number of appearances in the community court are, in large part, due to the increased number of compliance monitoring appearances needed to hold offenders accountable.

Reduced Crime

The Midtown study is the only one to tackle the impact on crime in the community, documenting encouraging results: prostitution arrests were down 56 percent and illegal vending arrests were down 24 percent following the opening of the community court. Data from ethnographic observations and individual interviews confirmed this drop in criminal activity. However, drop in crime cannot be linked exclusively to the Midtown Court. The researchers considered likely a "displacement effect" whereby the drop in such crimes in the Midtown area coincided with increased violations in other areas that were subject to less enforcement efforts.

Cost-Benefit Analysis

The 2000 Hennepin study includes a comprehensive cost-benefit analysis. Overall, the community court was found to be more expensive than regular case processing, costing an additional net $704.52 per case, but the authors noted that there are many additional benefits that cannot be quantified in monetary value to offset the costs. The only benefit that was included is the value of community service performed by defendants. Other benefits included the improved quality of life in the neighborhood and the improved quality and efficiency of decision making due to increased information sharing.

The Midtown study includes a cost-benefit analysis as well, but that analysis is, by the authors' own admission, limited due to an inability to quantify fully all benefits and costs. What the Midtown study did find are significant monetary benefits to the court system—including approximately $100,000 in reduced costs due to decreased pre-arraignment detention, $500,000 in reduced costs due to reduced use of jail, $570,000 in future reduced costs due to reduced prostitution arrests, and $150,000 in benefits derived from the community service of defendants—for a total of approximately $1.3 million annually.

Offender Perceptions

The Hartford study included interviews with offenders to document their perceptions of their experience. Overall, offenders thought the community court was a good idea (96 percent), that their sentence was fair (73 percent), that the community court was helping Hartford neighborhoods (83 percent), and that all people were treated fairly at the community court (61 percent). Similarly, the Red Hook community survey (Moore 2004) found that the majority (56 percent) of those who had had a case at the Justice Center reported a positive experience. The Hartford offenders also thought that the prosecutor was fair (76 percent) and an overwhelming majority (91 percent) thought that they were treated with respect by the judge. As is typical in Connecticut for misdemeanor cases, most defendants had no legal representation (79 percent). Many thought they needed a lawyer (84 percent).

The Midtown study included interviews with female prostitutes who had been arrested and brought to the Midtown Community Court. These women had both positive and negative comments about the Court. On the positive side, they commented that, compared to the traditional downtown court, the community court processed their cases quicker, the holding cells were cleaner, the food was better, and the staff more sympathetic. On the other hand, the women complained that the alternative sentences at Midtown made it more difficult for them to "work"; furthermore, many women mentioned that they would continue to engage in prostitution, but would move out of the Midtown catchment area. (In response, the Midtown Court made several efforts to combat the potential displacement effect. Most notably, the Court now handles all prostitution arrests in Manhattan.)

Both Hennepin studies included offender interviews or focus groups. The 2000 study included a handful of semi-structured interviews with defendants who had been sentenced to community-based services. These four defendants felt that the community court gave them the opportunity and the help they needed to break out of the cycle of criminal justice involvement.

Finally, the next chapter of this volume reports the results of a study of defendant perceptions at the Red Hook Community Justice Center; this is the first study to compare defendant perceptions of a community court to a conventional court, lending added methodological vigor. The results are encouraging, demonstrating high levels of perceived fairness among defendants processed at Red Hook.

Stakeholder Perceptions

The 2000 Hennepin study included focus groups and interviews with stakeholders of the community court, including staff and treatment providers. The treatment providers in particular were pleased with the court's linking of offenders to services, holding them accountable, and locating key service providers in the same building.

In Hartford, staff felt that reacting strongly to quality-of-life crimes prevents future offenses because offenders know these actions are going to be taken seriously. Similar to Hennepin, Hartford staff liked the balance between punishment and help and thought accountability was important. Overall, Hartford staff thought that the community court provides an "opportunity for a second chance" with "a client-centered" social service delivery system. The Hartford study also included interviews with staff that documented the implementation challenges and barriers in opening an innovative program within the criminal justice system.

Conclusion

As the community court model spreads across the country, it is important for the evaluation literature to catch up. There are several methodologies highlighted here, but, to date, no one single study has covered all aspects of evaluation—process evaluation, outcome evaluation, community impact survey, offender perceptions, and cost-benefit analysis. Future analysis should seek to give a more comprehensive picture of these complex projects and initiate further attempts to compare community court outcomes with those achieved by conventional courts.

CHAPTER NINE

Defendant Perceptions of Fairness at the Red Hook Community Justice Center

M. SOMJEN FRAZER

Public confidence in the criminal justice system is remarkably low when compared with other institutions. Scholars attribute this to a variety of factors, some of which are largely out of the control of the system itself. These include rising public expectations, declining trust in government in general, the discrediting of criminal justice expertise and professionalism, and inaccurate information about the workings of the criminal justice system (Garland 2001; Hough and Park 2002; Sherman 2001).

How can public confidence be improved? One approach is to ensure that criminal defendants feel that they are treated fairly. If those most affected by the workings of the criminal justice system come out believing that the system treated them fairly, that may help to convey a broader public message that the system can be counted upon to administer justice. Citizens generally hold favorable views toward institutions that are perceived as unbiased, while holding negative views of institutions that are believed to be partisan or discriminatory (Tyler 1990). Not only can a focus on fairness improve public confidence, but research has shown that, as confidence in the criminal justice system grows law-abiding behavior increases (e.g., Thibault and Walker 1975; Tyler 1990, 1997; Tyler and Huo 2002). This means that a

This study was supported by a grant from the Bureau of Justice Assistance of the U.S. Department of Justice. Any opinions or interpretations expressed in this publication are those of the author and do not necessarily reflect the views of the Department of Justice.

fair process has the potential to create both generalized benefits via improved public confidence and specific benefits through the improved compliance of the particular defendants who experience the process.

Accordingly, this study examines defendant perceptions of fairness in two types of criminal courts: a traditional "downtown" court located in a large urban metropolis, and an experimental "community court" located in a smaller and geographically distinctive urban neighborhood. The study considers overall perceptions of the court process as well as perceptions linked to each of several key criminal justice system representatives, including the judge, prosecutor, defense attorney, and court officers. The study also considers several distinct but interrelated concepts that may predict perceptions of fairness: communication (clearly explaining the court process to defendants and giving them an opportunity to be heard), respectful and fair treatment in the courtroom, and helpfulness (responding to the defendant's individual needs).

The study's major findings include:

- *The community court was considered to be more fair than the traditional court.* In addition to offering a wider range of non-incarcerative sentences (including social and community services), community courts such as the Red Hook Community Justice Center offer a more transparent and collaborative atmosphere for defendants. The services, transparency, and collaboration characteristic of the community court model heighten defendant perceptions of fairness.

- *Defendant responses to the traditional criminal court were also relatively positive.* Although defendant responses to Red Hook were generally more positive than they were to the traditional court, at least 70 percent of defendants were satisfied with nearly all of the court actors and court processes in both courts.

- *Defendant perception of the judge was the most important predictor of overall perceptions of the court's fairness.* Defendants who perceived that the judge treated them with respect, helpfulness, and objectivity were more likely to say their experience was fair overall. This effect was stronger at the Red Hook Community Justice Center, presumably because the judge plays a more crucial role in the community court model, offering support and praise to successful defendants, sanctions for those who are noncompliant, and services and referrals for all defendants. Although the treatment of defendants by other court actors, including the defense attorney, prosecutor, and court officers, was also important, perceptions of the judge were overwhelmingly more important to determining perceptions of overall fairness.

- *The quality of communication that defendants experienced in the courtroom had a significant effect on their overall perceptions of the court's fairness.* Clear communication was slightly more important to defendants' overall perceptions of fairness than respectful and helpful treatment from court staff, although these were also important elements. This suggests that efforts to improve communication and enable defendants to express their own perspectives can create more positive perceptions.

- *Defendant perceptions of fairness varied less across survey respondents in Red Hook than in the traditional court, and demographic backgrounds mattered less in Red Hook in deter-*

> *mining these perceptions.* Defendants at Red Hook were not only more generally satisfied than those at the traditional court, but there was less variation by race and socioeconomic status. Also, having had a case dismissed did not significantly affect Red Hook defendants' perceptions.

The rationale for implementing the study in two sites was to test the potential of the community court model to improve upon existing defendant perceptions. Community courts are explicitly interested in improving public confidence in the criminal justice system (Berman and Feinblatt 2005). They seek to accomplish this by responding to community concerns while simultaneously addressing the service and treatment needs of individual defendants (Berman and Feinblatt 2005; Casey and Rottman 2003; Kralstein 2005). Community courts include a far greater range of dispositional and sentencing options than are commonly available in traditional courts. These may include community service, substance abuse treatment mandates, orders to job readiness or G.E.D. classes, or other sanctions involving treatment or social services. Community courts can provide defendants with voluntary referrals for job training, housing assistance, or other services. The wide availability of these services and the attempt to match sentences to the social service needs expressed by defendants may elicit more of a sense among defendants that the court is responsive to their individual situations. Finally, community courts engage communities directly, soliciting input through community advisory boards and providing opportunities for volunteer work and joint planning between citizens and justice officials.

Since most community courts deal with misdemeanor defendants who would otherwise receive relatively short jail sentences, fines, or sentences involving no real conditions at all, threats of long-term punishment are not a realistic option for securing compliance with court mandates or inducing future law-abiding behavior. As a result, community courts have a strong incentive to promote voluntary compliance with court mandates, secured by enhancing defendant trust in the court's legitimacy. Whether community courts succeed in their efforts remains an empirical question, never before examined. The results of such an evaluation are important not just for community courts, but for conventional criminal courts, which might look to adopt successful strategies from experimental community courts.

To review, this study asks:

- Do defendant perceptions of fairness differ between community courts and traditional criminal courts?
- What factors influence defendant perceptions of fairness in both courts? Factors to be examined include perceptions of individual criminal justice agency representatives (judge, prosecutor, defense attorney, and court officers), specific dimensions of fairness (communication, how defendants felt they were treated, and helpfulness), objective aspects of case processing (such as whether the case resulted in a conviction or dismissal), and defendant background characteristics (e.g., race, sex, and socioeconomic status).[1]

Literature Review

Perceptions of Fairness in the Courts

Previous research on defendant perceptions of their court experience has defined two types of fairness, procedural and distributive. Procedural justice concerns the fairness of the court procedures and interpersonal treatment, while distributive justice concerns the fairness of the case outcome. Surprisingly, research in criminology suggests that litigants are more likely to form their opinions of the court based on procedural rather than distributive fairness, although both play some role (Casper, Tyler, and Fisher 1988; Tyler and Huo 2002; Sunshine and Tyler 2003). Similarly, studies of management have found that employees who believe that employers have treated them fairly are more likely to be loyal and accepting of decisions, even when those decisions negatively affect them (Brockner, Tyler, and Cooper-Schneider 1992; Brockner, Siegel, Daly, Tyler, and Martin 1997; Mueller and Landsman 2004; Schaunbroek, May, and Brown 1994). The precedence of procedural justice over distributive justice and other factors is an important but counter-intuitive finding, as it suggests that even when litigants experience an objectively negative outcome (e.g., a conviction or loss in a custody dispute) they can form or retain high opinions of the court as an institution if they are treated fairly.

Further, the opinions that defendants form of the courts as an institution can have concrete behavioral effects. There is significant evidence suggesting that when citizens perceive justice system agencies to be fair, they are more likely to comply with the law, legal authorities, and court mandates (Tyler and Huo 2002). In studies of mediation, perceptions of fairness affect a litigant's willingness both to accept an arbiter's decision (Lind, Kulik, Ambrose, and de Vera Park 1993) and follow its terms in the long run (Pruitt, Peirce, McGillicuddy, Welton, and Castrianno 1993). Similarly, defendants in domestic violence cases were more likely to obey the law in the future if they believed they were treated fairly by the police; indeed, the fairness of their treatment mattered more than how severely they were punished in predicting their future behavior (Paternoster, Brame, Bachman, and Sherman 1997). Since approximately 20 percent of people involuntarily engaged by police are immediately noncompliant, and many people engaged in illegal behavior are never caught (Mastrofski, Snipes, and Supina 1996), an important way to make communities safer is to increase voluntary law-abiding behavior through enhancing defendants' and citizens' sense of fairness.

In some research, perceptions of fairness are differentiated across several dimensions. Tyler (1990) found that litigants are more likely to be satisfied with their court experience overall and to comply with court orders when perceiving that (1) their voice was heard by decision-makers, (2) they were treated with respect, and (3) decision-makers were neutral and trustworthy. The quality of communication appears to be an especially important dimension. Research has found that in multiple contexts, including courts, individuals allowed to have an expressive voice are more likely to believe that they have been treated fairly, particularly if the outcome of a decision was detrimental to their self-interest (Price, Lavelle, Henley, Cocchiara, and Buchanan 2004; Korsgaard and Roberson 1995; Tyler 1990; Bies and Shapiro 1988; Lind, Kurtz, Musante, Walker, and Thibaut 1980).

Factors over which the court has little or no control can also affect defendant perceptions of the courts and, indirectly, their likelihood of re-offending. Defendants' pre-existing societal orientations toward the legitimacy of the courts and their trust in the motives of criminal justice actors can affect their perceptions as well (Tyler and Huo 2002). Favorable societal orientations such as identification with one's community, respect for the law, and trust in others all act to encourage citizens to comply with the law voluntarily (Tyler and Huo 2002).

In addition, defendants' personal background (race, class, and gender) can affect perceptions of the court's fairness. Generally speaking, individuals who identify as a race or ethnicity other than white have more negative perceptions (Rottman 2000; Tyler and Huo 2002; Tyler and Wakslak 2004). Members of racial and ethnic minority groups generally come into the courtroom with lower expectations; they report less trust in other people, less trust in the legitimacy of the court, less identification with the community and country, and more negative experiences with legal authorities (Tyler and Huo 2002; Tyler and Wakslak 2004). For example, 70 percent of black respondents in a national survey of courts stated that as a group they believe they are treated "somewhat" or "far" worse than Hispanic or white respondents. The same study also found that black respondents were less likely to believe that court personnel are helpful and courteous, that juries are representative of the community, or that courts are "in touch" with what is going on in their communities (Rottman 2000). In another study, black respondents were twice as likely to believe that court outcomes are "seldom" or "never" fair as they were to believe that they are "always" or "usually" fair (Rottman, Hansen, Mott, and Grimes 2003).[2]

Once in the courtroom, minority defendants report worse treatment, more negative outcomes, lower perceptions of the quality of the court's decision-making process, and less trust in the motives of court actors. After the case is decided, these negative perceptions translate into less satisfaction with the court overall and less acceptance of the court's decision, all of which in turn lower compliance (Tyler and Huo 2002; Rottman et al. 2003). Particularly for courts that work with predominantly minority communities, such as the ones included in this study, the effects of defendant background on perceptions of the court are important for staff to understand.

The Community Court Model

Community courts share with traditional courts the goals of ensuring community safety while protecting the due process rights of defendants. However, community courts differ from traditional courts in their approach to these goals, and community courts add other goals reflecting their mission to address local needs and priorities. In particular, community courts are designed both to help defendants solve the problems that underlie their criminal behavior and to hold them accountable for the specific incidents that brought them to court; they consult with local stakeholders to set and accomplish priorities; they are proactive in preventing crime rather than merely responding once crime has occurred; they bring criminal justice agencies (courts, prosecutors, defense attorneys, and police) into close coordination to address community issues; and they strive to create an atmosphere that is conductive to engaging communities, defendants, and other litigants (see Feinblatt and Berman 1997; Kralstein 2005).

With specific regard to the defendant experience, the community court model offers increased sentencing options, such as substance abuse treatment and community service mandates, rather than relying on more traditional sentences such as short jail stays, "time served" sentences, or fines. Studies of the Midtown Community Court found that the effect of the court's approach to sentencing was to reduce the use of short-term jail sentences on one end of the spectrum while, on the other, reducing the use of "walks," which consist of sentences such as "time served" or conditional discharges that lack further conditions (Hakuta 2006; Sviridoff, Rottman, and Weidner 2001). Community courts also provide a wide range of social services on site to help defendants combat problems such as joblessness, addiction, or lack of education. They also address concerns that courts have become revolving doors in which "the process is the punishment"—all too many defendants leave court following a brief but unpleasant experience only to return on similar charges with no effort having been made to address either their underlying problems or the effects of their anti-social behavior on the community (Feeley 1992).

There is some evidence that community courts have produced palpable effects on citizen perceptions of the criminal justice system. Residents and merchants surveyed in the neighborhoods served by the Red Hook Community Justice Center (the site for the present study) perceived the courts and other criminal justice agencies more positively after the justice center opened (Chapter 10; Frazer 2005). Between 2002 and 2004, positive feelings about the justice center in the community increased from 57 percent to 78 percent (Frazer 2005). Separate studies of three different community courts (Red Hook, Hartford, and Hennepin County) all reported positive defendant perceptions of their court experience (Justice Education Center 2002; Moore 2004; Weidner and Davis 2000). Yet, in the absence of a "comparison group," it is impossible to know whether these studies of defendant perceptions were reporting findings that differed from what would have been detected in a traditional court setting.

The 30 community courts currently operating in the United States are a part of the larger problem-solving justice movement, an association of court-based innovations that "seek to use the authority of courts to address the underlying problems of individual litigants, the structural problems of the justice system, and the social problems of communities" (Berman 2000: 78). These problem-solving justice projects include specialized drug courts, mental health courts, domestic violence courts, community courts, and a wave of newer models. These projects all have in common a focus on producing tangible outcomes for defendants, victims, and communities (e.g., reducing recidivism, increasing community safety, rehabilitating defendants, or linking crime victims with needed services). In some cases, these projects achieve their goals through the use of therapeutic interventions. The legal theory of therapeutic jurisprudence treats legal proceedings as events with emotional and behavioral consequences as well as bureaucratic and adjudicative functions. In practice, therapeutic jurisprudence uses psycho-medical knowledge and techniques for addressing criminal justice problems; drug courts and mental health courts are the most obvious examples of the application of these techniques (Farole, Puffett, Rempel, and Byrne 2004; Wexler and Winick 1996).

Several studies suggest that defendants handled in drug courts, the most widespread problem-solving model, may be especially likely to believe that they were treated fairly and respectfully (Podkopacz, Eckberg, and Zehm 2004) and to believe that the courts are fair and legitimate institutions (Farole and Cissner 2005). Several qualitative studies of drug courts also point to the judge as the most central figure in determining the overall experience that defendants report (Farole and Cissner 2005; Goldkamp, White, and Robinson 2001; Porter 2000, 2001). However, as with community courts, the existing literature on drug and other problem-solving court models does not involve rigorous quantitative comparisons of the perceptions of fairness held by problem-solving court defendants versus similar defendants handled in a traditional court setting.[3]

Research Hypotheses

Based on the preceding literature, we propose the following nine hypotheses concerning the predictors of procedural fairness among criminal defendants:

The Community Court Model

1. Community court defendants will rate the fairness of their court experience higher than those whose cases were processed in traditional courts.

Specific Criminal Justice Actors

2. The judge will be the most influential court actor in determining ratings of fairness. Defendants who rate positively how they were treated by the judge will be particularly likely to rate positively the overall fairness of their court experience.

Communication

3. Communication will be the most important dimension in determining ratings of fairness. Defendants who rate positively how well court actors communicated with them will be particularly likely to rate positively the overall fairness of their court experience.

Objective Aspects of Case Processing

Although previous research suggests that outcome favorability (whether litigants won their case) may not be as important as how they were treated during the court process, objective case outcomes are still likely to influence perceptions of fairness to a degree (Tyler and Huo 2002).

4. Defendants with an ongoing relationship with the court (ones who have appeared multiple times on the same case) will rate the fairness of their court experience higher than those who were just arraigned (appearing for the first time). While it may annoy some defendants to return to court multiple times for one case, those with ongoing appearances may develop more favorable perceptions, because they will have the opportunity to form relationships with court actors and become familiar with how the court functions. This hypothesis is also consistent with the findings of several qualitative studies that when drug court participants form a relationship with the judge, they have more positive attitudes towards program participation and greater motivation to recover (Farole and Cissner 2005; Farole, Puffett, Rempel and Byrne 2004; Goldkamp et al. 2001).

Table 1: Comparison of Red Hook and the Traditional Court

	Red Hook	Traditional Court
PLANNING AND IMPLEMENTATION		
Attempt to Make Physical Space Inviting	Yes	No
Collaborative Planning With Community	Yes	No
Located in a Community	Yes	No
Types of Cases	Criminal, housing and family	Criminal only
Onsite Social Services	Several	Few
COURT PROCESS		
Plea Bargaining	Yes	Yes
Adversarial	Yes, but with teamwork approach when appropriate	Yes
Staff Relationship and Interactions with Judge	Extensive	Minimal
Court-based Clinical Staff	Yes	No, except specialized domestic violence and drug treatment parts
SANCTIONS		
Community Service Sanctions	Yes	Yes
Social Service Sanctions	Frequent	Infrequent
Sentences of Time Served	Infrequent	Frequent
Jail	Less often as initial sentence; used after alternative sanctions have failed and in that case more severe	Yes, often initial sentence

5. Defendants assigned to substance abuse treatment will rate the fairness of their court experience higher than those who were not assigned to substance abuse treatment. This assumes that defendants assigned to treatment will appreciate the effort of the court to respond to their individual needs. Also, assignment to drug treatment will presumably be perceived more positively than the alternative, which is often jail.

6. Defendants whose cases were dismissed will rate the fairness of their court experience higher than those whose cases were not dismissed. Having a case dismissed is naturally assumed to elicit more positive retrospective perceptions about the process.

Defendant Background

Defendant background characteristics, while not the focus of the study, were included because of their probable impact on perceptions. Previous research suggests that persons who are black, male, and lower in socioeconomic status may have particularly negative opinions of courts and of the criminal justice system in general (Rottman 2000; Tyler and Huo 2002).

7. Black respondents will rate the fairness of their court experience lower than white respondents; Hispanic respondents will fall in the middle.

8. Males will rate the fairness of their court experience lower than females.

9. Respondents with a lower socioeconomic status will rate the fairness of their court experience lower than those with a higher status.

Methodology

Site Selection

The study was implemented in one community court and one nearby traditional court. Table 1 compares the two courts. The two sites were selected because they were convenient to the researchers, close to one another geographically, and serve similar urban populations.

Launched in June 2000 in a low-income community in southwest Brooklyn, the Red Hook Community Justice Center (Red Hook) was designed to respond to the problems of crime, disorder, substance abuse, economic and geographic isolation, and lack of social services in Red Hook, Brooklyn. Red Hook embodies many of the core elements of the community court model: an enhanced range of dispositional and sentencing options, use of an extensive network of community and social service providers, a focus on defendant accountability (avoiding sentences that lack any real conditions and ensuring compliance with court mandates), ongoing exchange between the court and community, and some use of therapeutic techniques in how the judge converses with defendants and in the availability of substance abuse treatment mandates. Possible mandates include community service, substance abuse treatment, job training, GED placement tests, anger management classes, and treatment readiness groups (Berman and Fox 2005).

Based on community input during the planning stages, Red Hook was designed not only to address criminal matters but to solve a range of local problems, including quality-of-life crime as well as family conflicts, landlord-tenant disputes, and juvenile delinquency. For this reason, Red Hook is a multi-jurisdictional community court handling cases from criminal, family, and housing court. A single, permanently assigned judge hears a broad range of the community's cases in one courtroom. He has maintained a collegial relationship with defense attorneys (nearly all of whom are employed by the Legal Aid society) and prosecutors alike. All of the court actors work collaboratively with social workers and other clinical staff to identify appropriate social services for adult defendants, juvenile delinquents, and other litigants. The cases come from three police precincts, which surround the court and extend into nearby neighborhoods. Only misdemeanors and the lowest level of felonies are heard in Red Hook's criminal court; higher level felonies are seen at the centralized Brooklyn Criminal Court. The judge in Red Hook sees 35 to 40 criminal cases per day.

The Red Hook Justice Center is a particularly appropriate site for a study of defendant perceptions of fairness in a community court because it is generally seen as a national leader in the community court movement. The justice center receives hundreds of visitors each year, and several other community courts are replicating the "Red Hook experiment." Red Hook has been examined through both internal research and external study (see for example, Malkin 2005; Moore 2004; Frazer 2005). After the Red Hook Community Justice Center opened, the public's fear of crime dropped and public confidence in local justice system agencies more than doubled, suggesting that the community court has had positive effects on neighborhood perceptions of the legitimacy of the court system (Chapter 10).

The traditional court was chosen because it is geographically proximate to Red Hook. Located in downtown Brooklyn, it serves as a centralized countywide criminal court. It has specialized drug treatment and domestic violence court parts, but outside of these parts it looks like many other traditional, high-volume courts. Courtroom operations emphasize due process, speed, and efficiency, but there is less focus on implementing long-term solutions designed to address the sources of criminal behavior. Use of social service sentences is rare. The traditional court does not engage in planning with the community, nor does it assess public opinion about the court or community safety. The traditional court sees an average of 1,200 to 1,400 misdemeanors per weekday across 16 courtrooms, with a different judge presiding in each courtroom and different judges for arraignments and other stages of a case. This massive volume obviously constrains the attention that the traditional court can realistically devote to each case, and a lack of clinical staff in the courthouse constrains the ability to link defendants with services.

The different goals of the two courts are reflected in their differing structures and practices and the physical layout of the courthouses and courtrooms. The traditional court is a multistory building with many courtrooms and judges. It has separate rooms for arraignments and subsequent trial parts as well as a separate domestic violence court and a drug court. The courtrooms are dark, despite large windows, some of which have bars on them. The floors are scuffed and often dirty. There are 12 metal detectors at the entrance to the building. The presence of social workers in the courtroom is rare, and there are many prosecutors and many different defense attorneys, some private and some from either of two public defender agencies.

The Red Hook courthouse, by contrast, is located in a remodeled parochial school, and the architecture was designed to be friendly and inviting to the community. The courtroom is smaller than the courtrooms used for criminal misdemeanors in the traditional court and is light and airy. The judge's raised platform is not as high as in a traditional courtroom, and he often asks defendants and their families to approach him. Court-mandated and voluntary social services are available within the building. Although the building does have a metal detector, there are only two or three court officers assisting defendants during all but the busiest times, making the courthouse friendlier and far less intimidating.

During the period of study, both courts provided substance abuse treatment to some offenders. At the Red Hook center, defendants were clinically assessed by social workers and might subsequently be recommended for treatment. In the traditional court, among those arrested on misdemeanor charges, only defendants with 10 or more prior misdemeanor convictions were considered for treatment. In both courts, defendants who were found eligible had the ability to plead guilty voluntarily and be mandated to substance abuse treatment as an alternative to proceeding in the usual fashion. In Red Hook, treatment defendants were seen by the same judge as other defendants, while in the traditional court they were seen in a separate courtroom by a specially trained drug court judge.

Data Sources and Sampling

Data for this study came from two sources. The first was a survey, administered verbally in English or Spanish by researchers and research assistants during the summer of 2005. Defendants were approached as they left the courtroom after their appearance in court. Survey participants were given a free public transportation ticket (MetroCard) as a small incentive. The total number of surveys completed was 398, with 202 (51 percent) conducted at Red Hook and 196 (49 percent) conducted at the traditional court. The survey, which totaled 65 questions, included the following topics:

Demographic Background (predictor variables): These included race, sex, age, education, language spoken at home, and housing status (i.e., living in public housing or not).

What Happened in Court (intermediate variables 1): These variables included whether or not the defendant had just been arraigned (i.e., was it the defendant's first appearance on the current case), whether the defendant had just pled guilty or pled guilty at a previous court appearance on the same case, whether the case was dismissed (including adjournments in contemplation of dismissal (ACDs), dismissals that occur after certain conditions are met, including law abiding behavior), and whether the defendant had been mandated to substance abuse treatment.

Interpersonal Treatment in Court (intermediate variables 2): This section included questions about defendant opinions of various court actors (including the judge, prosecutor, defense attorney, and court officers), previous experiences in court, and perceptions of court fairness. Opinions of court actors concerned three types of judgments: perceptions of effective communication (e.g., "The judge listened to you" or "The court officers answered your questions, if you had any"), perceptions of treatment (e.g., "The court officers treated you with respect"), and perceptions of helpfulness (e.g., "Your lawyer was very interested in helping you").

Global Fairness (outcome variable): These questions were not intended to assess perceptions of individuals or specific events in court, but rather an overall sense that the experience in court was fair or unfair (e.g., "Your case today was handled fairly by the court" or "You were treated the way you deserved in court today").

Fairness, in this case, is conceptualized more holistically than in the procedural justice literature, as this study found all four of the questions about fairness, including the one that sought to measure distributive rather than procedural fairness, to be highly intercorrelated.[4] All opinion questions were measured on a five-point Likert scale, with one representing strongly disagree and five representing strongly agree.

To sample effectively, surveys were administered at the Red Hook Community Justice Center first. Only criminal cases arraigned as misdemeanors were sampled. All cases appeared in the same courtroom and before the same judge, but their stage of case processing varied. Key stages included an arraignment, subsequent appearance, and compliance hearing on a substance abuse treatment, anger management, or domestic violence program mandate. The sampling plan for the traditional court was designed to match the distributions of case types found in the actual surveying at Red Hook (e.g., approximately the same percentages of cases just arraigned, returning for subsequent appearances, and mandated to a program). To attain a matching distribution of parts surveyed, defendants at the traditional court were surveyed as they left four separate types of court parts: arraignment parts, all-purpose post-arraignment parts, a drug treatment part, and a domestic violence part.

The second source of data involved structured observations of each court, in which a checklist was used to record the behavior of the judge with regard to the defendants. Observations were made of 142 court appearances, 51 percent in Red Hook and 49 percent in the traditional court. Ethnographic field notes were also taken during courtroom observation, in order to provide detailed descriptions of the observed behavior of the judge. Observations were not made concurrently with surveys, but rather were begun after data analysis of the surveys revealed the importance of the judge and the location context in predicting defendant opinions of their experiences. The observation instrument was pilot tested with 14 measures of the judge's behavior that were thought to enhance defendant perceptions of fairness. The initial instrument was too complicated for reliable data collection and the indicators were subsequently reduced to seven. The final list of behaviors observed included:

- Spoke directly to the defendant
- Praised the defendant
- Admonished the defendant
- Requested further information about the case (usually from social workers or attorneys)
- Asked probing questions (ones with substantive answers, rather than procedural questions or questions that required only a yes or no answer)
- Discussed the defendant's future
- Discussed the defendant's past[5]

In order to ensure the validity of these observations, a second researcher observed 25 of the same court appearances used in the final analysis of the observational data. The second researcher agreed with the primary researcher in 94 percent of the observational items.

Survey Data Analysis Strategy

Initial data analysis included examination of the frequencies, means, and standard deviations of individual survey items, as well as examinations of analysis of variance (ANOVA) and correlations between items. Many of the responses to the items measuring defendant perceptions of fairness were interrelated. To tease apart the underlying concepts, we used factor analysis to combine variables into single factors. By looking at multiple, intercorrelated items as a single factor, the effects of the underlying concept can be detected, whereas if each item were examined individually, there would appear to be no effect on the outcome of interest due to high intercorrelation between these items.

Factor analysis revealed four different concepts of interpersonal treatment: attitudes towards the judge (e.g., "The judge treated you fairly"), communication within the courtroom (e.g., "Your lawyer listened to you"), treatment in the courtroom (e.g., "The prosecutor treated you with respect"), and overall fairness of the court experience (e.g., "Your case today was handled fairly by the court").

Multiple forms of analysis were conducted in order to describe and explain the predictors of defendant ratings of fairness. Frequencies, means, and t-tests established the trends in the data, while ordinary least squares regressions were used for prediction. Further, because of the high intercorrelation between the variables of interest and the importance of detecting indirect effects not immediately obvious in regressions, path analyses were also used. Path analysis, unlike regression analysis, reveals

Table 2: Demographics of Community Court and Traditional Court

	Community Court	Traditional Court	Total
NUMBER OF RESPONDENTS	202	193	398
RACE/ETHNICITY			
Black	33%***	68%	50%
Hispanic	52%***	18%	35%
White	10%	7%	9%
Asian	1%	1%	4%
Other	4%	6%	5%
GENDER			
Male	85%*	75%	80%
Female	15%*	25%	20%
EDUCATION			
No HS Degree or GED	50%	38%	44%
HS Degree or GED Only	26%***	44%	34%
Some College	16%*	9%	13%
Associate's Degree	3%	5%	4%
Bachelor's Degree	5%	3%	4%
SOCIOECONOMIC STATUS			
Lives in Public Housing	25%	27%	24%
Employed Part-time	10%	32%	8%
Employed Full-time	40%+	14%	14%
Speaks English at Home	68%***	84%	76%
IN COURT FOR:			
Arraignment/First Court Appearance	52%	51%	51%
Progress Report/Subsequent Court Appearance	11%**	4%	7%
Other (e.g. Other subsequent court appearance)	37%	45%	42%
OUTCOME			
Pled Guilty	24%	20%	22%
Dismissed	43%	36%	39%
Pending	33%	44%	39%
MANDATED TO DRUG TREATMENT	29%**	18%	23%

+ p<.10 *p<.05 *p<.01 ***p<.001

the indirect effects of variables that may initially seem to have no detectable relationship to the outcome of interest. However, in order to do this, assumptions must be made about the order in which the variables affect one another. One must begin with a non-recursive pair of variables. A study generally needs 20 times as many observations as there are variables in the path. The path cannot contain feedback loops (it must go only in one direction, assumed to be causal). In this case, demographics were ordered first, court location was second, court proceedings and mandates were third, and intermediate procedural justice dimensions such as communication and ratings of specific court actors (e.g., judge, prosecutor) directly preceded the outcome variable, overall ratings of fairness. It was hypothesized that demographic effects would all be indirect, court proceeding and case outcome effects would be indirect, and procedural justice effects would be directly related to overall ratings of fairness.

Results

The community court had a significant, positive impact on defendant perceptions of fairness. In addition, across both courts, how defendants perceived the judge was the most important predictor of how they perceived the overall fairness of the court. Perceptions related to communication (court actors clearly explained the proceedings, answered questions, and listened to what the defendants had to say) also strongly predicted perceptions of overall fairness. In other words, the results of this study were largely consistent with expectations, with a few notable exceptions.

The following sub-sections describe the sample characteristics, test the predictors of defendant perceptions, and explain several important differences between the predictors of fairness in the community court and the traditional court.

Sample Characteristics

As shown in Table 2, the final sample (398 defendants) was racially diverse. In both locations, nonwhite respondents dominated the sample (85 percent). In Red Hook, there were more Hispanics (52 percent versus 18 percent), and in the traditional

Figure 1: Respondent Perceptions of Court Actors at Red Hook and the Traditional Court

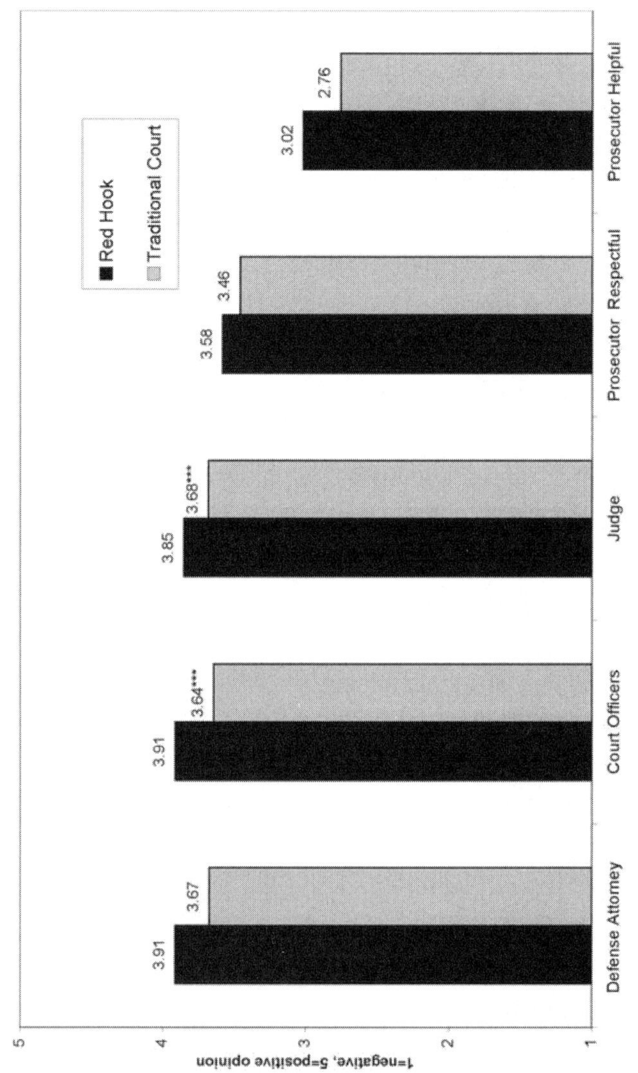

+ p<.10 *p<.05 **p<.01 ***p<.001
Note: District Attorney, Court Officers and Judge are factors created from multiple variables. See Appendix 2.

court, there were more black respondents (68 percent versus 33 percent). In total, 50 percent of the defendants surveyed were black, 35 percent were Hispanic, nine percent were white, four percent were Asian, and five percent identified themselves as some other race.

Overall, 80 percent of the defendants surveyed were male; a slightly larger percentage was male in Red Hook (85 percent) than in the traditional court (75 percent). Red Hook defendants were less likely to have a high school or GED degree (50 percent versus 62 percent), while defendants at the traditional court were less likely to be employed full-time (14 percent versus 40 percent). Also, 24 percent of the sample lived in public housing, with no significant difference between Red Hook and the traditional court. Finally, Red Hook defendants were less likely to speak English at home, perhaps related to their greater likelihood of Hispanic origins (68 percent versus 84 percent).

With regards to the courtroom proceedings, close to half the sample (51 percent) had just been arraigned. Also, 22 percent percent had pled guilty while 39 percent had their case dismissed (the outcome of the case was still pending for the remaining 39 percent). At Red Hook, defendants were significantly more likely to have just had a compliance hearing on a previous program mandate, usually for substance abuse treatment (11 percent versus four percent). Also, defendants at Red Hook were significantly more likely to have been mandated to substance abuse treatment (29 percent versus 18 percent), either during the court appearance that took place immediately prior to the research interview or during a previous court appearance.

Perceptions of Key Court Actors

In both courts, defendants were, on the whole, satisfied with the way that they were treated by the judge, prosecutor, defense attorney, and court officers. Defendants, however, were consistently

Table 3: Predicting Ratings of Court Actors and Court Concepts

Dependent variable name	Fairness Factor	Judge Factor	Court Officers Showed Respect	Prosecutor Was Helpful	Prosecutor Showed Respect	Defense Atty. Showed Respect	Communi-cation Factor	Overall Treatment Factor
Sample Size	356	328	361	356	350	358	332	349
Red Hook Court	0.193***	0.143**	0.149**	0.083	0.005	0.000	0.046	0.137*
Male	0.059	-0.043	-0.008	-0.159**	-0.101+	0.036	-0.024	-.041
Race								
Black	0.083	0.068	0.018	-0.168*	-0.058	-0.070	0.059	-.021
Hispanic	0.081	0.052	0.047	-0.078	0.125	0.019	0.057	.017
No HS Degree or GED	0.059	-0.048	0.012	-0.021	0.001	-.0146**	-0.056	-0.088
Court Proceedings								
Assigned to Drug Treatment	0.142**	0.210***	0.083	0.122*	0.088+	0.059	0.195***	0.010+
Just Arraigned	0.157**	0.153**	0.034	0.085	0.166**	0.144**	0.159**	0.155**
Adjusted R-Squared	0.062	0.054	0.019	0.054	0.049	0.027	0.033	0.036

+ p<.10 *p<.05 *p<.01 ***p<.001

All regression coefficients are standardized partial correlation coefficients.

Figure 2: Respondent Perceptions of Fairness, Treatment and Communication at Red Hook and the Traditional Court

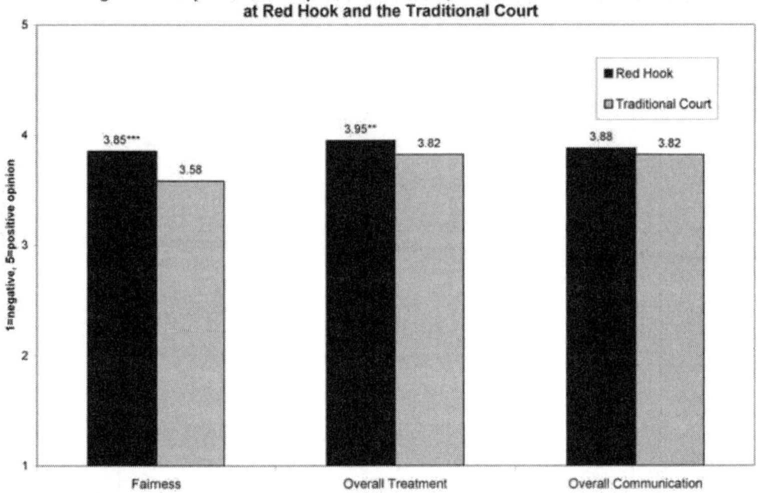

+p<.10 *p<.05 **p<.01 ***p<.001
Note: These concepts are measured using factors created from multiple variables. See Appendix 2.

more satisfied with each of these actors at Red Hook than at the traditional court (with some of the differences reaching statistical significance and others suggestive, see Figure 1). For example, in Red Hook, 93 percent agreed or strongly agreed that the judge treated them fairly, while in the traditional court, 85 percent agreed or strongly agreed with this statement ($p < .001$). Similarly, in Red Hook, 94 percent agreed or strongly agreed that their lawyer treated them with respect (versus 91 percent in the traditional court) and 89 percent agreed or strongly agreed that their lawyer treated them fairly (versus 85 percent in the traditional court) ($p <.001$). Defendants in Red Hook were almost as satisfied with the court officers as with their defense attorneys, as 92 percent agreed or strongly agreed that the court officers treated them with respect, but in the traditional court, this figure dipped significantly to 77 percent ($p < .001$). Not surprisingly, defendants were least satisfied with their treatment by the prosecutor, although well over half continued to express positive perceptions. At Red Hook, 73 percent agreed or strongly agreed that the prosecutor treated them with respect, while in the traditional court, 65

Table 4: Predicting Fairness from Demographic Variables, Court Proceedings and Procedural Justice Variables

	Model 1	Model 2	Model 3	Model 4	Model 5	Model 6	Model 7	Model 8
Sample Size	356	322	348	351	345	344	325	340
Court Factors								
Judge Factor		0.693***						
Defense Attorney Showed Respect			0.310***					
Court Officers Showed Respect				0.336***				
Prosecutor Was Helpful					0.326***			
Prosecutor Showed Respect						0.303***		
Communication Factor							0.573***	
Treatment Factor								0.561***
Red Hook Court	0.193***	0.100**	0.0186***	0.138**	0.169**	0.189***	0.175***	0.101*
Male	0.059	-0.046	-0.050	-0.067	-0.024	-.025	-0.051	-0.044
Race/Ethnicity								
Black	0.083	0.030	0.088	0.055	0.127	0.124	0.039	0.062
Hispanic	0.081	0.042	0.093	0.070	0.110	0.070	0.043	0.074
No High School Degree or GED	0.059	-0.030	0.001	-0.068	-0.069	-0.067	-0.026	-0.007
Court Procedings								
Assigned to Drug Treatment	0.142**	-0.006	0.117*	0.114*	0.097+	0.113*	0.024	0.081+
Just Arraigned	0.157**	0.036	0.113*	0.141**	0.127*	0.096+	0.058	0.063
Adj. R-squared	0.062	0.508	0.191	0.168	0.159	0.144	0.372	0.354

+ p<.10 *p<.05 *p<.01 ***p<.001

All regression coefficients are standardized partial correlation coefficients.

percent agreed or strongly agreed with this statement ($p<.01$). Rather than these percentages, Figure 1 presents the mean index scores drawn from multiple question items concerning each court actor, but the results are analogous in substance.

Perceptions of Overall Fairness, Treatment, and Communication

Given that defendants were generally satisfied with their treatment by individual court actors, it is not surprising that they also largely agreed that their experience had been fair overall, that they had been treated well, and that communication had been effective. As shown in Figure 2, although defendants were largely satisfied across both sites, they were significantly more satisfied in Red Hook with respect to fairness ($p < .001$) and treatment ($p < .01$).

Predictors of Defendant Perceptions

Further analysis focused on why some defendants were more satisfied than others, disaggregating the effects of court location (Red Hook or traditional court), demographic background, stage of the court process, and any mandates received (e.g., to substance abuse treatment). Table 3 presents the results of a series of ordinary least squares regressions, each predicting perceptions related to a different aspect of fairness—overall fairness, judge, prosecutor, defense attorney, court officers, communication, and treatment. Based on the results for overall fairness (Table 3, first column), appearing at Red Hook was the largest predictor ($p < .001$), and court location similarly predicted more positive perceptions of the judge, court officers, and treatment in court. The only other independent variables significantly predicting more positive perceptions across multiple regression models were: (a) assignment to substance abuse treatment, and (b) having just been arraigned prior to the research interview. (The meaning of this last finding is that defendants were more likely to perceive their experience positively if they had just emerged from their

Figure 3: Final Path Predicting Fairness

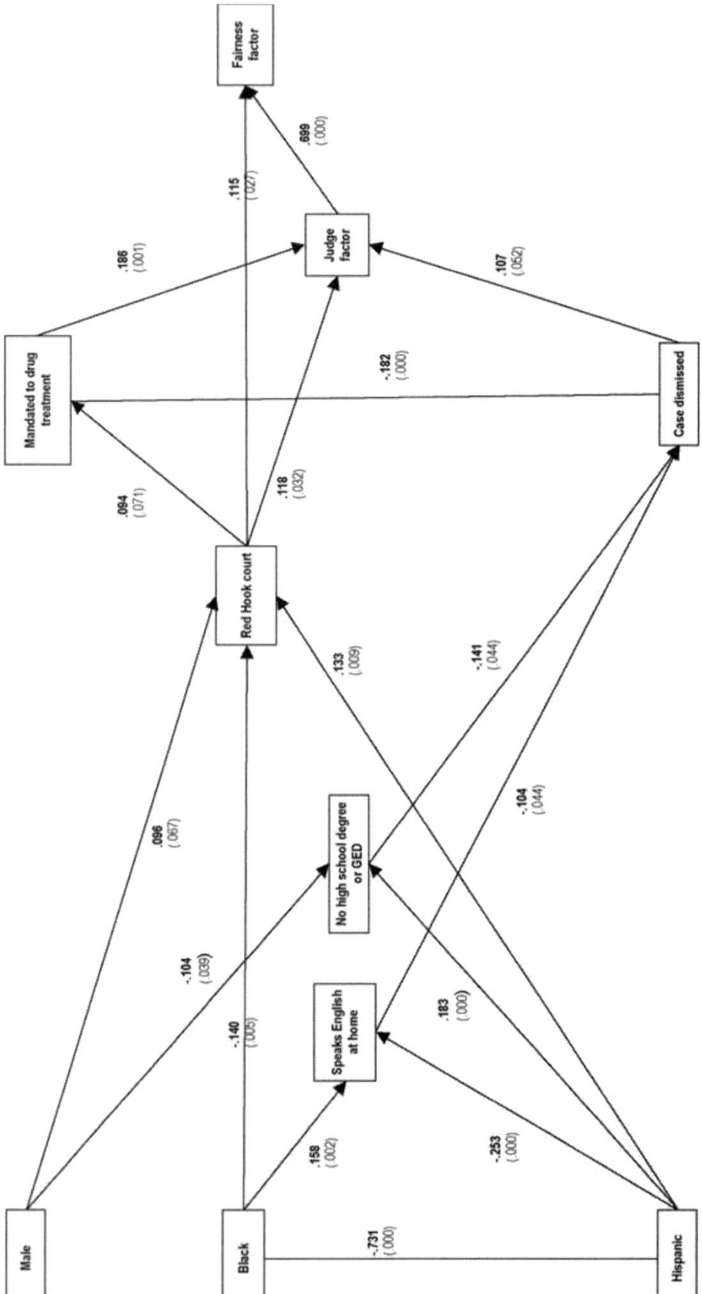

first court appearance, the arraignment, than if they had already had multiple appearances.)

Also important to understand in discerning how defendants form their perceptions is which precursors of fairness are most closely linked to overall perceptions. Therefore, ordinary least squares regressions were conducted predicting perceptions of overall fairness. Variables measuring defendant opinions of specific court actors (judge, prosecutor, defense attorney, and court officers) and court concepts (communication and treatment) are highly related to one another (e.g., defendants who rated the judge highly also tended to rate each other actor highly), so each regression includes only one court actor among its independent variables. By comparing each of the seven models, the strength of the resulting coefficients (which measure the strength of the relationship between the independent variable and the outcome variable) and R-squared statistics (which measure the degree to which the independent variables as a group explain the outcome variable) could then be compared to reveal which factors appeared more strongly linked to overall perceptions (see Table 4, Models 2-8). For comparison purposes, the first model in Table 4 (Model 1) does not include any of the precursors of fairness but merely shows the impact of other background characteristics (e.g., demographic background, stage of case processing, and court mandates).

The results indicate that the best regression model, the one which explained the most variation, included a factor measuring satisfaction with the judge (Table 4, Model 2). This model explained more than 50 percent of defendants' ratings of overall fairness (R-squared =.508), compared with only six percent explained by the initial model (1). The models that included perceptions of other court actors (Models 3–6) explain between 14 percent and 19 percent of the variation in defendant perceptions, the models that included perceptions respectively of communication and interpersonal treatment (Models 7-8) explain from 35 percent to 37 percent—a substantial amount but, again, less than what was explained when including the judge factor instead.

Also of note, throughout all eight models reported in Table 4, being seen in Red Hook remained a significant independent predictor of perceptions; those who had their cases processed there rather than the traditional court were consistently and significantly more satisfied with the overall fairness of their experience. This provides evidence that even when controlling for a variety of other variables—including the immediate precursors of fairness—the community court still had a positive, independent effect on overall perceptions.

The Importance of Effective Communication

The results shown in Table 4 suggest that the effectiveness of communication by all court actors is almost as important as the behavior of the judge in predicting perceptions of overall fairness. The regression including communication (Model 7) explains 37 percent of the variation in the perceptions of overall fairness (compared with 51 percent explained by the regression including perceptions of the judge). Communication was examined separately from (respectful and fair) interpersonal treatment and from perceptions tied to each type of court actor individually,

Figure 4: Path to Fairness in Red Hook

(additional control for Black, Hispanic and High School/GED attainment)

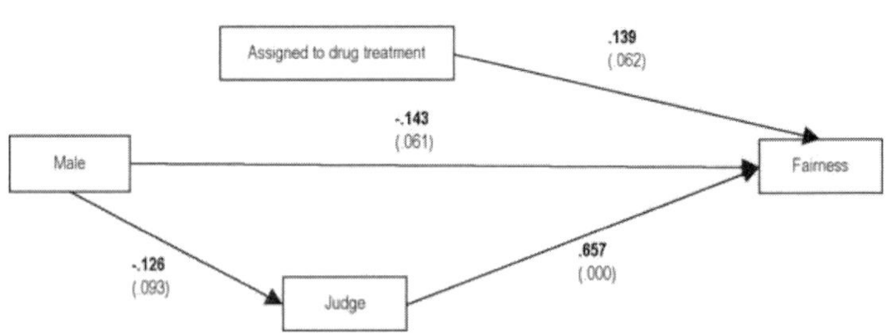

because defendants may be treated well by specific individuals but still feel unclear about what has happened in court or believe that they have been unable to express their opinions and be heard.[6] As can be seen by comparing Model 7 with the other models in Table 4, slightly more than the factor measuring impressions of overall treatment, and much more than any measure of defendant perceptions about various court actors—with the distinct exception of the judge—the factor measuring communication best predicted perceptions of overall fairness. This points to the logical conclusion that any proceeding that is not well understood and does not include an opportunity for the defendant to be heard is less likely to be perceived as fair.

Path Analysis

In order to better understand the underlying dynamics behind defendant ratings of overall fairness, a path analysis was built to detect both the direct and indirect effects of court location, demographic variables, court outcomes, and perceptions of individual court actors. Variables were included according to the rules set out in the methodology section; they are presented left to right in temporal and logical order. Arrows indicate the direction of hypothesized causality; straight vertical lines indicate variables that are related to one another but have no causal relationship. As in a regression equation, the size of the numbers in the path analysis indicates the strength of the relationship between the two variables in question (the numbers below indicate the degree of statistical significance).

The path analysis, shown in Figure 3, does not precisely mirror the ordinary least squares regressions but does confirm their main findings. Defendant perceptions of the judge were overwhelmingly the most important predictors of their ratings of the overall fairness of the court. Whether the case was processed in Red Hook or the traditional court also significantly predicts

Figure 5: Path to Fairness in the Traditional Court

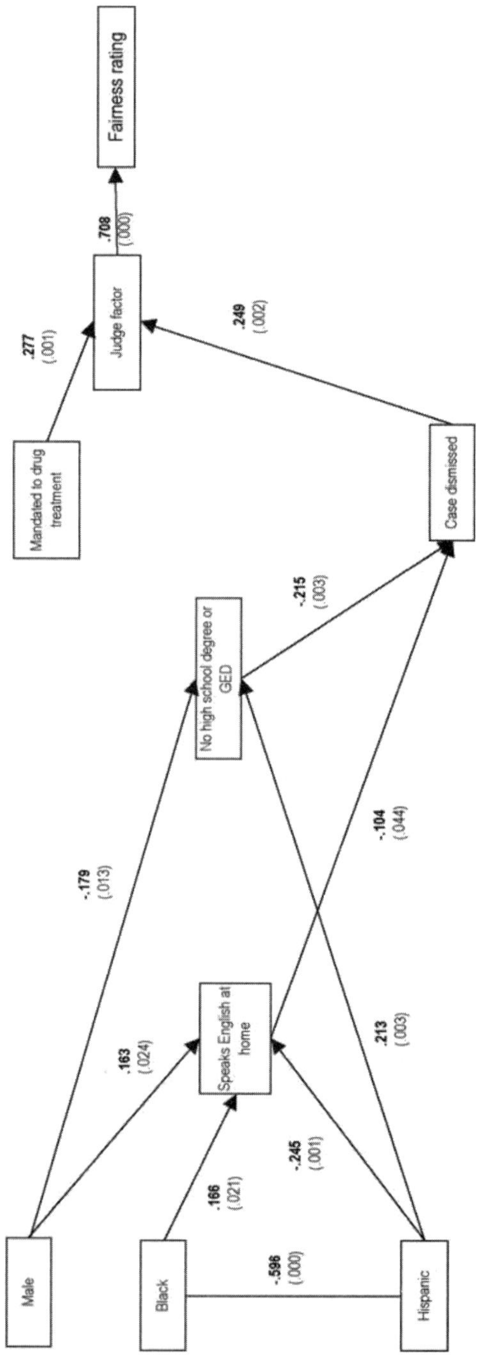

defendant perceptions of fairness. Indirectly, being mandated to drug treatment and having had the case dismissed positively affects ratings of fairness, because each positively affects ratings of the judge.

None of the demographic variables were directly correlated with either opinions of the judge or overall fairness. Both race and sex were distributed unevenly between the two courts, with male and Hispanic defendants more likely to have had their cases processed in Red Hook and black defendants more likely to have had a case processed in the traditional court. Both speaking English at home and having no high school or GED degree were negatively related to defendants having cases dismissed, which in turn led to lower ratings of the judge.

When the sample was split by location two different pictures emerged. In Red Hook (see Figure 4), sex was the only demographic variable that mattered in affecting perceptions of fairness; women perceived the court to be fairer. By contrast, at the traditional court (see Figure 5), race, sex, educational background, and language spoken at home all affected defendant perceptions, although the paths were indirect. Also, in Red Hook, assignment to substance abuse treatment was the only court process factor that mattered to defendants as they rated the fairness of their experiences, while in the traditional court, the objective court outcome (whether the case was dismissed) also mattered to defendants. In general, at the traditional court, a large number of factors affected perceptions of fairness, directly or indirectly, whereas at Red Hook, the path is far simpler because the Red Hook defendants are more homogenous, as well as more consistently positive, in their perceptions.

Structured Court Observation: How Red Hook and the Traditional Court Differ in Practice

The observed behavior of the judges at the two locations provides

Figure 6: Judges' Behaviors in Red Hook and the Traditional Court

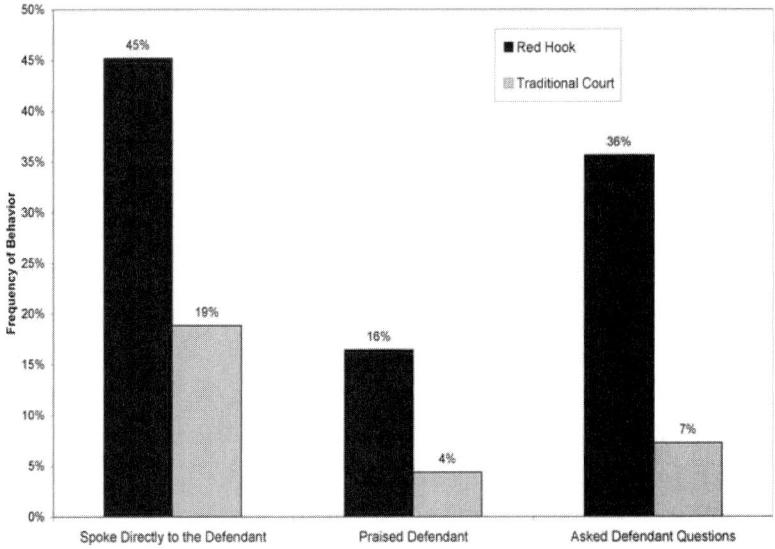

some insight into defendants' higher ratings of the judge and of the overall fairness of the community court. One hundred and forty-two court appearances were observed, 72 in Red Hook and 70 in the traditional court. As shown in Figure 6, in Red Hook, the judge spoke directly to the defendant in 45 percent of the observed appearances, while at the traditional court this occurred in only 19 percent of the appearances. Also, the judge praised the defendant in 16 percent of the observed appearances in Red Hook while at the traditional court this occurred in only four percent of the appearances. One would expect that defendants appreciate being spoken to directly and that they appreciate praise for improvements in their behavior or life situation. For example, the judge in Red Hook often praised defendants in long-term substance abuse treatment if they had repeatedly tested negative. Upon graduation from treatment, he generally shook the hand of the defendant, asked about future plans, and praised the defendant, acknowledging how difficult it is to complete treatment. Further, the judge in Red Hook invariably greeted defendants as the court appearances began, while this was rare in the traditional court. The judge in Red Hook often asked about the defendant's family life and personal circumstances, focusing on the context of whatever had brought the defendant to the court and any challenges to lawful behavior that remained. Just before the winter holidays began, the judge asked nearly all defendants who were in substance abuse or alcohol treatment how they planned to stay sober over the holidays and whether or not they could expect support from their families. With defendants in long-term treatment, which required multiple check-ins with the court over the course of 90 days to one year, the judge remembered and asked about difficult personal circumstances such as illness in the family or difficulty securing employment; and he also often offered referrals that would help defendants to prepare for and find employment. This never occurred during the observed appearances of the traditional court.

The interactions between the judge and other court staff were also far more collegial in the community court than the traditional court. One of the judges observed in the traditional court repeatedly admonished the defense attorneys and prosecutors for not being ready for their cases. Other judges were terse when speaking to court staff, if not overtly annoyed or hostile. The judge in Red Hook was rarely observed admonishing staff, and in the two cases where this did occur, the criticism was delivered gently. Besides the judge, both the prosecutors and defense attorneys at Red Hook often spoke with social workers who appeared in court with clients, while this practice was not observed in the traditional court.

It is important to note that within the traditional court, the drug treatment court part was an exception to the general lack of interaction between judges and defendants. Not surprisingly, defendants were more likely to be satisfied with their experiences in the drug treatment part of the traditional court than in other parts (see Figure 5). In terms of the judge's interactions and defendants' positive perceptions of their experiences, the treatment part of the traditional court was generally more similar to Red Hook then to other traditional court parts.

Discussion

Impact of the Community Court Model

Red Hook's culture and institutional practices are a means to attain its goal of providing long-term solutions to neighborhood quality-of-life problems. Changing a defendant's behavior is difficult, especially when avoiding criminal behavior requires a serious shift in lifestyle or livelihood. Community courts are premised at least in part on the belief that defendants undergoing this kind of change need a supportive structure to improve their chances of success. This structure may in turn affect their long-term willingness to comply with the law.

As expected, defendants at the Red Hook Community Justice Center were significantly more likely to perceive their experiences as fair than defendants at the traditional court, even controlling for differences in their backgrounds, stage of case processing, and mandates. Hypothesis 1 was fully supported. This suggests that community courts are effective at improving the criminal justice system's image in the eyes of defendants. Further, the results indicate that defendants do not perceive Red Hook more positively merely because they have more positive impressions of the specific individuals that are encountered there (the judge, attorneys, and court officers)—although this is certainly part of what is happening. Rather, as demonstrated by the path analysis, even when controlling for intermediate procedural justice concepts (communication and overall treatment) or perceptions of specific court actors (e.g., the judge or defense attorney), Red Hook still exerts a significant independent effect on perceptions of overall fairness. This suggests that the factors distinguishing Red Hook from traditional courts, such as the collaborative culture, friendly architectural design, and efforts to provide services, may affect defendant perceptions independently of their treatment by specific actors and of the types of mandates they receive.

In addition to the more positive ratings of specific court actors and, independently, of overall fairness at Red Hook, the lower variance and dearth of significant demographic or court outcome variables that also predict perceptions of fairness in the Red Hook-only sample suggests that positive perceptions are more consistent at Red Hook. By contrast, the higher variance and statistical significance of race, court stage, court outcome, and court mandate variables in the traditional court-only sample suggests that both the defendant background and what happens in court mediates the perceptions of that court's overall fairness.[7] Although court actors cannot change defendant cultural backgrounds or expectations, they appear to be accommodating and attenuating these differences more effectively at Red Hook than at the traditional court.

Impact of the Judge

Hypothesis 2, that the judge would be the most important court actor in predicting ratings of fairness, was fully supported. The judge was the most important court actor in determining perceptions of fairness. Previous research also points to the vital role of the judge in the success of problem-solving and community-based courts (Farole and Cissner 2005; Goldkamp et al. 2001; Marlowe, Festinger, and Lee 2004). Perceptions of other court actors may affect defendant perceptions as well, but the judge plays by far the dominant role in court proceedings, perhaps because the judge is a particularly powerful and salient symbol of the law.

And yet, due measurement error and the "halo effect," in which respondents are unable or unwilling to distinguish between the different behaviors of individual actors within an institution, relying instead on their overall impressions of one of the actors, the analyses that emphasize the importance of the judge may somewhat overstate this role.[8] The judge is a symbol of the court and particularly a symbol of its impartiality, situated as he or she is on a raised bench above the courtroom, between two lawyers with clear biases toward and against the defendants. The large predictive power of defendant perceptions of the judge on ratings of overall fairness may be about the judge, but it may also be a reflection of defendant impressions of the other court actors, the courthouse itself, or some combination of all of these factors together. Similarly, positive impressions of the judge may be reflected in defendants' satisfaction with the other court actors. This is one possible cause of the high correlation between the ratings of each of the court actors in both courts.

Impact of Communication

Slightly more than good treatment (respectful, helpful, fair), effective communication by all of the various court actors indexed together caused perceptions of the overall fairness of the court to rise. Hypothesis 3 was supported. This suggests that if courts are interested in enhancing defendants' sense that courtrooms are just and fair, they might focus on improving communication. Without expending significantly greater resources or hiring more staff, both traditional and community courts can take steps to provide clear and effective explanations about what is going on in the courtroom. Since the interpersonal treatment factor also significantly predicted perceptions of overall fairness, efforts by all court actors to maintain a respectful and even-handed demeanor in their interactions in front of defendants can also make a positive difference.

The Impact of Court Mandates, Case Outcomes, and Defendant Backgrounds

In keeping with previous research on both drug courts and procedural justice, what factually happened to defendants in court had a small but significant effect on perceptions of the court's overall fairness (Farole and Cissner 2005; Podkopacz, Eckberg, and Zehm 2004; Tyler and Huo 2002). Although the judge, communication, and treatment factors more strongly predicted overall fairness ratings, the favorability of the case outcome (e.g., dismissed or convicted) and the nature of the court's mandates (e.g., to substance abuse treatment) were also important—especially for the traditional court respondents. Specifically, in the final path (Figure 3), both having had their case dismissed and assignment to treatment predicted more positive ratings of the judge, which in turn predicted more positive ratings of overall fairness. In short, hypotheses 5 and 6 were supported, although the correlations were not large. At Red Hook (Figure 4) there is no effect from having a case dismissed, suggesting that the community court model may be able to inculcate more positive feelings towards the court even in defendants who are found guilty. Hypothesis 4, that defendants who have an ongoing relationship with the judge would have more positive perceptions, was not supported.

In both courts, being mandated to drug treatment had a strong, positive effect on opinions of the judge and, indirectly, on perceptions of fairness. Defendants seen in Red Hook were more likely to receive drug treatment mandates; although it is possible that this is due to sampling differences, it is more likely that Red Hook uses drug treatment as a mandate more often than the traditional court given both Red Hook's commitment to the use of alternatives to incarceration and the traditional court's stringent criteria for drug court eligibility. Further, defendants mandated to drug treatment receive additional help in solving related problems (such as lack of health insurance, lack of job training, or family issues). They also receive greater interpersonal support. As noted earlier, the judge at the community court takes note of their successes and failures during regularly scheduled compliance hearings. The additional services and support they receive no doubt enhance defendants' sense that the court process and outcomes are fair.

Although drug treatment itself no doubt directly enhances defendant perceptions of fairness because it is a choice defendants make in order to avoid jail or other traditional sanctions, being mandated to drug treatment is also a route to being connected to many other social service opportunities. Since neither mandated nor voluntary social service use was measured in the survey, the effects of the social services themselves on perceptions of fairness cannot be gauged. However, if drug treatment mandates are understood as a proxy for social service use, this study strongly suggests that enhanced social services have a positive effect on defendant perceptions of the fairness of the court.

The path analyses also provide partial support for the hypotheses about the effects of defendants' backgrounds on their perceptions of the overall fairness of the court. Hypothesis 7, that black respondents will give the lowest fairness ratings of all racial/ethnic groups, followed by Hispanic respondents, was therefore only partially supported; it was not supported at all in Red Hook, and only the expectation that black defendants would give the lowest ratings of any racial/ethnic group was supported in the traditional court. Hypothesis 8, that males will give lower fairness ratings than females, was fully supported. Hypothesis 9, that respondents with a lower socioeconomic status as measured by living in public housing and not having a GED will have lower ratings of communication and fairness, was partially supported. As with race and ethnicity, when the sample was split, this finding applied only to the traditional court-only sample. Second, while not having a GED negatively predicted both communication and overall fairness, living in public housing was not a significant predictor in any direction and in any court when other factors were statistically controlled.

In the final path (Figure 3), race, sex, and socioeconomic status affect perceptions of fairness but only do so indirectly. This provides support for previous findings suggesting that what criminal justice agencies do is overwhelmingly more important than these background factors in shaping perceptions of fairness (e.g. Tyler and Huo 2002). Figures 4 (Red Hook) and 5 (Traditional Court) show that while black defendants in the traditional court have lower opinions of the court's fairness and Hispanic defendants have higher opinions, these effects are absent in Red Hook. Similarly, speaking English at home and having a high school degree have no effect in Red Hook but have significant indirect effects on defendant perceptions of fairness in the traditional court.

The differences between the two paths have important implications for understanding community courts. There is significant evidence to suggest that in the U.S. population, black citizens have lower opinions of the criminal justice system and are less confident than others in the neutrality and legitimacy of the courts (Rottman 2000; Tyler and Huo 2002). If community courts neutralize this effect, they make an important contribution to improving the legitimacy of the court in the eyes of a population disproportionately affected by the criminal justice system.

Study Qualifications and Recommendations for Future Research

This study suggests that further investigation is necessary to improve our understanding of how treatment in different types of courts can enhance or detract from defendant perceptions of fairness. The impact of these perceptions on future compliance with court-imposed sanctions and with the law in general also merits attention—although as discussed above, previous research strongly suggests that positive perceptions increase the likelihood of future compliance. This study alone is limited in its external validity, because it draws upon data from only one community court and one traditional court. Although this study included a variety of measures of defendant perceptions of the court as well as objective measures of their background and case outcomes, it has a few substantive limitations as well. For one, defendants were not asked about their perceptions of criminal justice agencies such as the police who are not involved directly in courtroom proceedings. Second, the study employs a cross-sectional design rather than asking defendants about their expectations and plans before and then again after they appear in court. If defendants were asked about their opinions of the court both before and after appearing, researchers could separate the effects of defendants' underlying societal orientations (such as their pre-existing attitudes towards the court and the criminal justice system), expectations of how they will be treated by various court actors, and prior experiences with the criminal justice system from the effects of how they were actually treated during their current court case. If such a longitudinal design were coupled with courtroom observation of the case of each defendant surveyed, even stronger conclusions could be drawn about the effects of court actors' actual treatment of the defendants on their perceptions.[9] Finally, further research should measure whether defendants intend to comply with sanctions, whether they follow through with their intentions and complete sanctions, and whether or not they comply with the law in the future.

Policy Implications

The results of this study have significant policy implications, including the following:

Community Courts Defendants perceive community courts to be fairer than traditional courts. Community courts, such as the Red Hook Community Justice Center, may be generally better at eliciting positive perceptions because they are designed to serve the individual defendant as well as the surrounding community. Defendants' enhanced opinions of the fairness of the court and the law may in turn encourage defendants not to re-offend. The findings of this study may extend to other problem-solving models (e.g., drug courts and mental health courts), but additional study is needed before confirming such a conclusion.

Traditional Courts Even courts that do not offer the range of services that a community court provides can enhance defendant perceptions of fairness by improving three aspects of their courtroom operations. The quality of interaction and treatment by the judge is crucial. Improved communication, such as allowing defendants to speak and be heard, answering their questions, and ensuring that they understand the process, can also have a positive impact. Good treatment by all court actors (respectful, helpful, and fair) also improves overall perceptions of the court experience. And greater use of long-term substance abuse treatment may further enhance defendant opinions.

The Judge The quality and quantity of the judge's interactions with defendants are crucial in shaping their perceptions. Even within the traditional court, defendants who were more satisfied with the judge were more satisfied with the court's overall fairness. This suggests that in traditional courts, judges who make an effort to connect with defendants (e.g., making eye contact, providing clear explanations of court proceedings and of their decisions, and appearing respectful and impartial) can help to enhance their sense that the court is fair.

Communication Effective communication is also crucial in ensuring that defendants perceive their experiences as fair. Courts, whether traditional or community-based, that work to improve communication can enhance defendant perceptions and, indirectly, increase compliance.

Interpersonal Treatment Even in a traditional court, respectful and fair treatment strongly improves defendant perceptions of the court's fairness. This suggests that court staff in all courts might be attentive to how they interact with defendants. When the judge and other court staff are polite and respectful, defendants are more satisfied. Good treatment can even overcome the effects of an objectively negative court outcome (such as having to return to court or facing a conviction). Traditional courtrooms may be perceived as fairer if they treat all defendants respectfully and politely.

Substance Abuse Treatment In addition to its therapeutic effects, the use of substance abuse treatment as a mandate option for defendants, where appropriate, has the additional benefit of enhancing defendant perceptions that their experiences in court were fair.

Defendant Backgrounds Although defendant background indirectly affects overall perceptions, other factors matter more. Further, even the indirect effects of defendant background were eliminated when examining the results in Red Hook only; neither race, sex, nor educational background affected perceptions of fairness at Red Hook, while at the traditional court they had significant, although indirect, effects. It would appear that as a community court, Red Hook excels in equalizing the differential expectations, prior experiences, and societal orientations of different groups, resulting in a lack of differences based on defendant background in how fair Red Hook's proceedings are perceived to be.

CHAPTER TEN

Views of Safety and Quality of Life: Results of an Annual Survey in Red Hook, Brooklyn

KELLI D. MOORE

The history of the Red Hook community is as tumultuous a story as any New York neighborhood has to tell. Once a vibrant, highly populated shipping community located on the South Brooklyn waterfront, Red Hook fell victim to the development of racially and economically isolating public housing and the violence and misery of a flourishing drug trade amidst diminishing job opportunities. Red Hook's decline was highlighted with the 1992 death of local school principal Patrick Daly. Accidentally killed in a drug-related shoot out, Mr. Daly's death demonstrated the human cost of violence and drugs to a community. In response, the Brooklyn District Attorney's Office, the New York State Court System, and the Center for Court Innovation decided to plan a community court to help improve the quality of justice in one of New York City's oldest neighborhoods.

The planning of the court began in 1994 and from the beginning made use of the voices, experiences, and opinions of the Red Hook residents. Focus groups held in a local library provided the foundation for a grassroots tradition of surveying the actual members of the Red Hook community to assess community needs. In these focus groups residents shared their desires for a better quality of life and their diminished faith in the criminal justice system.

This chapter was originally published in slightly modified form as a white paper in 2004 by the Center for Court Innovation under the same title.

Figure 1: Criminal Justice Approval Ratings: 1997 vs. 2001

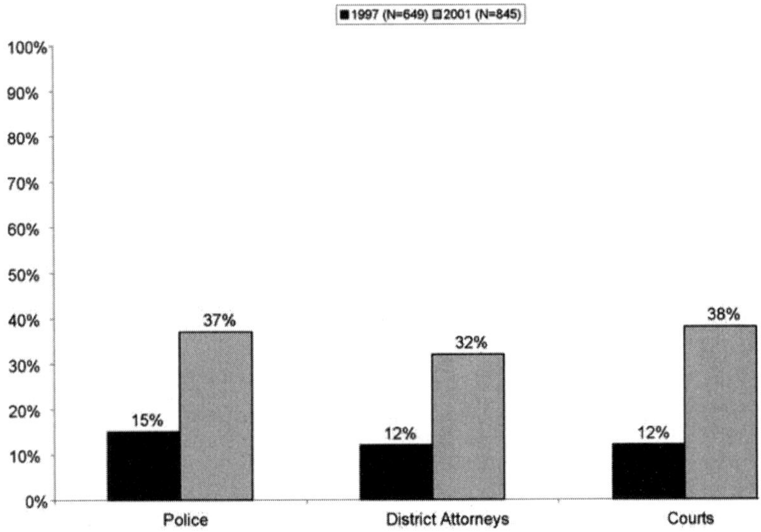

Created in response to these kinds of concerns, the Red Hook Community Justice Center opened its doors in April 2000. As a community court, the justice center handles violations, misdemeanors, and low-level felonies, and links offenders to community and social services with the purpose of providing swift justice, constructive sentencing, and assistance with the very problems that led offenders to the court. Social services coordinated by the justice center include drug and alcohol treatment, batterer programs, job development, and counseling. These services are available free of charge to offenders and non-offenders alike.

The spirit of the focus groups continues in an annual community survey known as "Operation Data." The survey was designed by the Red Hook Community Justice Center as a tool for community members to voice their opinions and concerns about the neighborhood on a regular basis. In October 2001, the 50 members of the Red Hook Public Safety Corps, the justice center's on-site AmeriCorps community service program, administered the Operation Data survey for the sixth consecutive year.

The 2001 survey focuses on residents' perceptions of neighborhood public safety and quality of life, existing community resources, and the criminal justice system. The majority of the surveys were completed in Red Hook, and for the third year in a row the members spread out to the surrounding neighborhoods of Carroll Gardens/Cobble Hill, Gowanus/Wyckoff, Park Slope, and Sunset Park to provide a more diverse sample and allow for neighborhood comparisons.

Wherever possible, the 2001 data was compared to 1999 data in order to demonstrate changes in perceptions of safety, neighborhood problems, and quality of life before and after the opening of the Red Hook Community Justice Center.

Key Findings

Main findings from 2001 include:

- Overall perceptions of safety (day and nighttime) at public locations have increased;
- Self-reports of victimization have decreased by almost half though Red Hook residents continue to report twice as many assaults as non-Red Hook residents;
- Perceptions of neighborhood problems have not changed in Red Hook; for the fifth year in a row, drug selling and drug use were cited as the biggest problems;
- Criminal justice agency approval ratings are consistently below 40 percent in Red Hook but have more than doubled since 1997; and
- Respondent characteristics like living in Red Hook (versus the other neighborhoods surveyed), living in public housing, and being black were associated with more negative perceptions of neighborhood problems, perceptions of safety, and criminal justice agency approval ratings.

Survey Methodology

The 2001 Operation Data survey includes 187 questions covering perceptions of a wide range of community issues as well as basic demographic characteristics of each respondent. Most questions have been repeated from year to year to determine whether perceptions change over time. Assigned to teams of five to seven people, the interviewers covered all major geographic areas in Red Hook. The survey was administered door-to-door in Red Hook's public housing projects, private residences, and local businesses. Members also reached out to community groups and social organizations on weekends and evenings to catch those potential survey respondents who work during the day. The survey was conducted in English and Spanish. The interviewers completed 865 surveys.

In addition to canvassing Red Hook, the Public Safety Corps administered 304 additional surveys in surrounding neighborhoods for the purpose of gathering data that could be compared to Red Hook. The following Brooklyn neighborhoods provided comparative data: Gowanus/Wyckoff, Park Slope, Carroll Gardens/Cobble Hill, and Sunset Park.

All told, 1,169 surveys were completed. For analyses concerning perceptions of quality of life, neighborhood problems, and opinions of the criminal justice system, certain neighborhoods were grouped together based on shared historical influences (e.g., industry, ethnic make-up).

Demographics

Respondents living or working in Red Hook represented 76 percent of the sample. Eighty-five percent of Red Hook respondents were residents while 13 percent were merchants or workers. On average, respondents have lived in Red Hook for 19 years, and 62 percent live in the Red Hook Public Houses. The Red Hook respondents are mostly black (42 percent) and Latino (33 per-

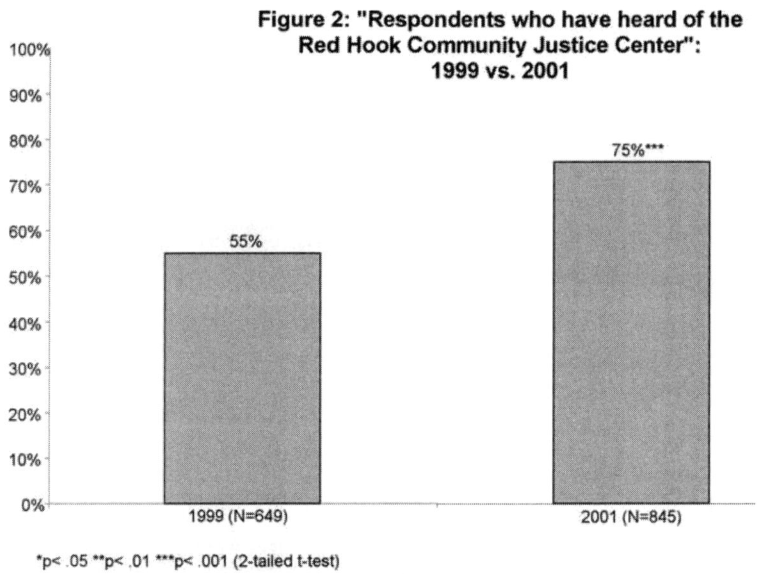

cent), with white survey respondents comprising 18 percent of the sample. Persons living or working in Sunset Park, Gowanus/ Wyckoff, Park Slope, or Carroll Gardens/Cobble Hill together represent 24 percent of the sample. Seventy-two percent of non-Red Hook respondents are residents while 25 percent are merchants or workers in the neighborhood.

Criminal Justice Agency Approval Ratings

In 1997, before the opening of the justice center, the Operation Data surveyors asked the community to rate its level of approval of the criminal justice system. Respondents were asked how positively they felt about the police, prosecutors, and the courts. That year, positive opinions about the criminal justice system did not reach higher than 15 percent for any of these criminal justice agencies.

In 2001, just one year after the Red Hook Community Justice Center opened its doors, positive views of the criminal justice system more than doubled (Figure 1). This does not mean the justice

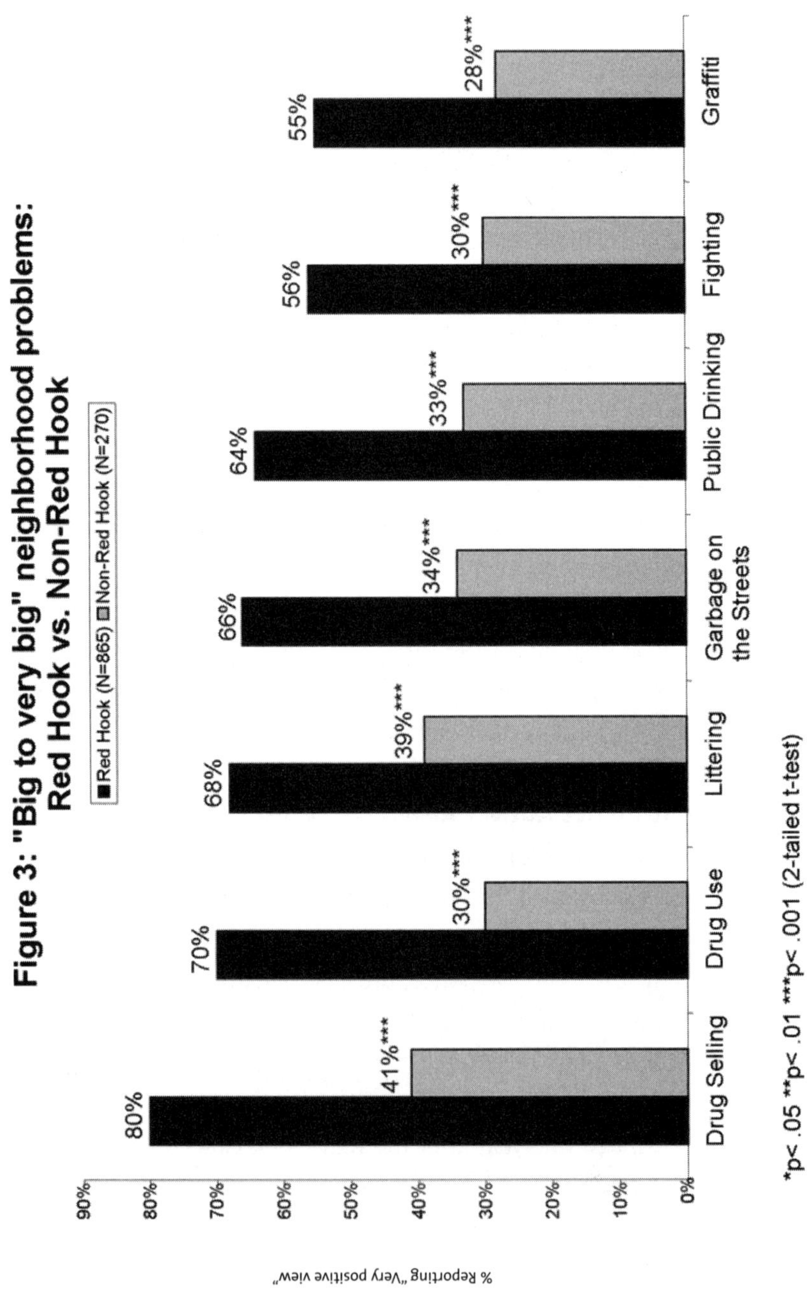

Figure 3: "Big to very big" neighborhood problems: Red Hook vs. Non-Red Hook

Figure 4: Perceived Youth Problems in the Community: 1999 vs 2001

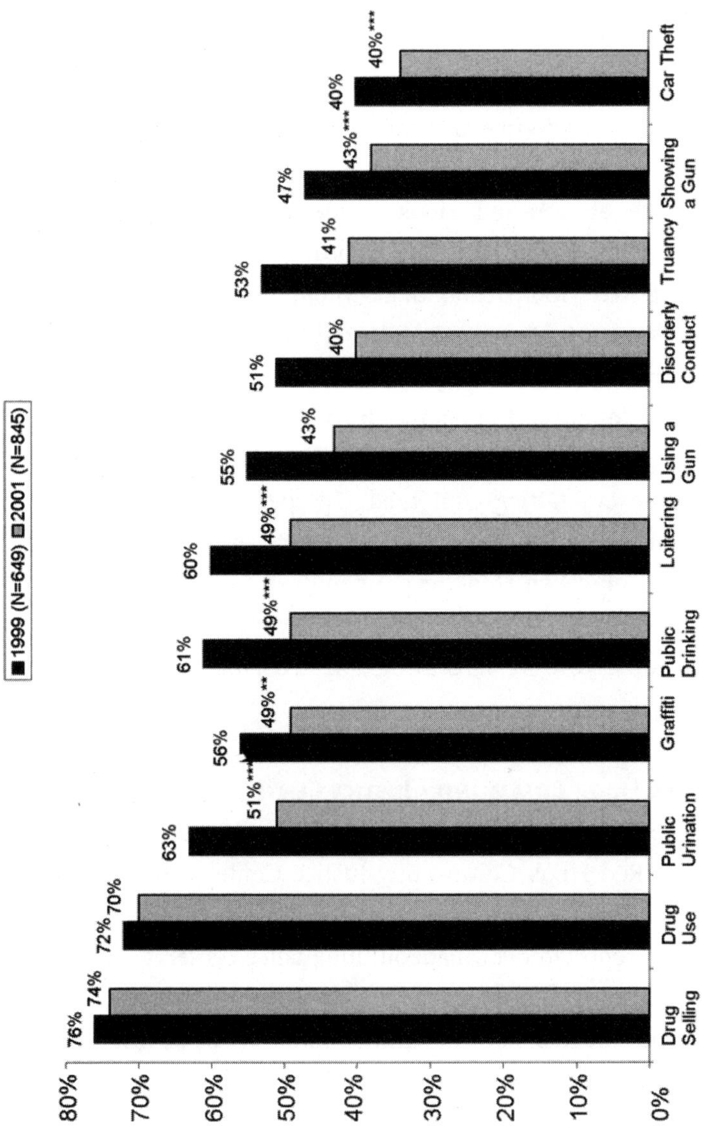

*p< .05 **p< .01 ***p< .001 (2-tailed t-test)

center was solely responsible for the change; other social and economic developments in the community may have contributed to this transformation. It is also important to note that the ratings remain under 40 percent for all three criminal justice agencies.

Significantly, positive views of the criminal justice system (police, prosecutors, and courts) were positively correlated to using the services offered by the justice center. That is, survey respondents who had used services at the justice center were more likely to rate criminal justice agencies favorably.

Comparing Red Hook views of the criminal justice system to those of non-Red Hook residents suggests that Red Hook gained in criminal justice approval ratings. Fifty-six percent of non-Red Hook respondents thought that the police response was good to excellent, compared to 42 percent reported by Red Hook respondents. Both groups were evenly matched in their views of the court system. Thirty-eight percent of non-Red Hook respondents felt somewhat to very positive about the District Attorney's Office, compared to 32 percent of Red Hook respondents. Continuing to show gains in court approval ratings, 39 percent of Red Hook respondents felt somewhat to very positive about the relationship between the courts and their community, compared to 41 percent of non-Red Hook respondents reporting.

Red Hook Community Justice Center

In 2001, 75 percent of respondents reported that they heard of the Red Hook Community Justice Center (See Figure 2). This represents a significant increase from 1999, when only 55 percent reported hearing about the justice center.

The 2001 data suggest a relationship between knowledge about the justice center and opinions about neighborhood satisfaction and civic engagement. People who knew about the justice center were more likely to know their neighbors very well and less likely to report being victimized or worrying about being robbed, assaulted, or a victim of a home break-in. Knowledge about the justice center was also positively correlated with feeling safe in public locations at night.

Quality of Life

Fifty-eight percent of respondents felt somewhat to very satisfied with Red Hook as a place to live and work. This is statistically identical to 1999, when 57 percent felt somewhat to very satisfied with the neighborhood. In contrast, seventy percent from the surrounding neighborhoods surveyed reported feeling somewhat to very satisfied with their neighborhood as a place to live and work. It appears that Red Hook's perception of neighborhood satisfaction continues to lag behind that of other neighborhoods.

Neighborhood Problems

For the fifth year in a row, Red Hook respondents cited drug selling and drug use as the biggest problems—80 percent and 70 percent respectively rated them as "big" or "very big" (results shown in Figure 3). Those from surrounding neighborhoods reported about half the number of "very big problems" that affect quality of life.

Linear regression models indicate that participating in tenant patrol was associated with higher ratings of neighborhood problems. Interestingly, these same people were also likely to give higher ratings of neighborhood satisfaction. This data may suggest that when residents have serious concerns about their neighborhood and join an initiative that addresses those concerns it can positively affect their opinion of the community.

Youth Problems in the Neighborhood

In 2001, respondents felt that problems with youth crime were less serious than in previous years. Youth drug selling and drug use, however, remained high at 74 percent and 70 percent respectively. As indicated in Figure 4, these top two youth problems did not changed significantly from 1999, when 76 percent thought youth drug selling was a big problem and 72 percent thought youth drug use was a big problem.

Victimization

Significant decreases occurred in self-reports of victimization in 2001. Self-reports of victimization dropped by almost a half from 1999 to 2001. However, Red Hook respondents reported almost twice as many rapes, stabbings, and shootings as their non-Red Hook counterparts.

Personal Safety

In 2001, respondents reported a significant overall increase in the level of safety they felt at various locations in the community. More people responded that they felt "very safe" in or on the streets, home, lobbies, stairways, elevators, and subways as opposed to merely "safe." As shown in Figure 5, each of these locations saw a six percent to 21 percent increase in the number of people that reported them as "safe" to "very safe" during the evening. These locations remained safer during the day and less safe during the evening. Like the nighttime levels of safety, on average, the daytime levels almost doubled in 2001 compared to 1999. Again, some caution is advised in interpreting these apparent trends.

Safety precautions, like avoiding certain buildings, not traveling alone, staying in at night, and carrying a weapon, decreased significantly. Taking these precautions was negatively correlated with feeling safe at public locations around the neighborhood. Respondents who live in the Red Hook Houses reported slightly higher levels of precautions taken for safety and worried about

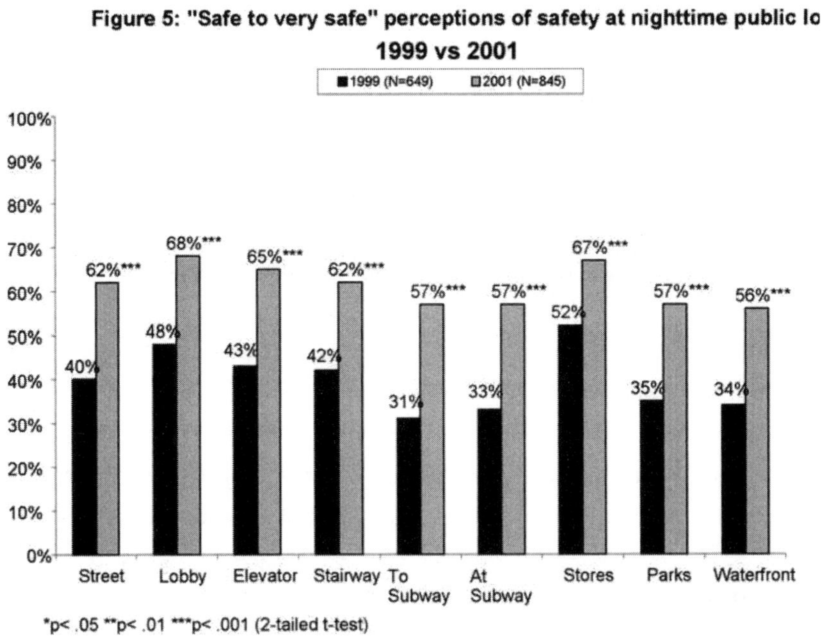

home break-ins, robberies, and assaults as much as other Red Hook respondents.

Predictors of Respondent Perceptions

Six major variables emerged as predictors of neighborhood satisfaction, levels of perceived safety, reports of neighborhood problems, and views of criminal justice agencies. These variables were:

- Residing in public housing;
- Residing in a low-income neighborhood (Red Hook, Gowanus/Wyckoff, and Sunset Park);
- Participation in tenant patrol;
- Racial/ethnic identification;
- Heard of the Red Hook Community Justice Center; and
- Previous case processed at the Red Hook Community Justice Center.

Respondents identifying as black and/or Latino were more likely to hold negative views about criminal justice agencies. Respondents who previously had a case processed at the Red Hook Community Justice Center held similarly negative views about criminal justice agencies, a result that is not surprising for any court-involved population. Public housing residents and residents of low-income neighborhoods gave lower ratings of neighborhood satisfaction, more serious reports of neighborhood problems, and fewer reports of perceived neighborhood safety. Conversely, respondents familiar with the justice center gave higher ratings of neighborhood satisfaction than those not familiar with the work and services offered at the justice center.

Summary

Two years after the Operation Data 1999 survey was completed, the Red Hook community reports an overall improvement in perceptions of public safety, neighborhood problems, and criminal justice agency approval ratings. However, further analyses suggest that blacks, Latinos and residents of public housing are less likely to have improved feelings about these neighborhood factors. The data suggests that race/ethnicity and public housing may serve as proxies for social isolation. The public housing community and black and Latino respondents seem to put the overall improvements into a greater perspective.

Other Problem-Solving Justice Experiments

Recent years have seen an explosion of new problem-solving models, including family and juvenile drug courts, mental health courts, reentry courts, DUI/DWI courts, youth courts, and others. Beyond the development of new specialized court models, a growing number of policymakers have expressed an interest in the application of problem-solving practices more broadly throughout state court systems. This effort responds to the criticism that problem-solving experiments often take the form of "boutique courts," small-scale forums in which a narrow group of litigants receive special, intensive attention. One possible means of addressing this concern is to expand eligibility and institute centralized screening mechanisms designed to ensure that larger numbers of litigants are identified as problem-solving court candidates. Another approach is to practice problem solving outside the specialized court setting, making treatment options, intensive judicial supervision, and other elements of the problem-solving model available throughout the courthouse. The chapters in this section present research on two of the newer problem-solving court models (mental health and reentry courts) and explore the opportunities and barriers to engaging in problem solving outside of specialized courts.

Mental health courts, an adaptation of the drug court model to a mentally ill population, are currently among the fastest growing criminal justice experiments in the country. There are already believed to be more than 120 mental health courts nationwide, compared to just a handful in 2000. Since these courts are relatively new, a research literature is only beginning to emerge. In Chapter Eleven, Kelly O'Keefe presents an in-depth evaluation of the Brooklyn Mental Health Court, one of the first such programs in the country to serve felony defendants. The results include positive preliminary findings, including reduced hospitalization, substance abuse, and re-arrest rates among participants in the mental health court.

Prisoner reentry is another subject of expanding national interest. The past decade has seen many initiatives seeking to assist released prisoners with the varied challenges of community reintegration and crime-free life—unemployment, lack of education and job skills, lack of housing, family problems, and substance abuse. Chapter Twelve is an evaluation of one such initiative, the Harlem Reentry Court. In it, Donald J. Farole Jr. documents the program's accomplishments and challenges in serving returning prisoners. The evaluation also includes a quasi-experimental study of the project's impacts on parole revocation and reconviction rates.

Finally, in Chapter Thirteen, Donald J. Farole Jr., Nora K. Puffett, and Michael Rempel report the results of a study conducted with the California Administrative Office of the Courts that examined how problem-solving techniques might be practiced more broadly throughout state court systems. The study reports the results of focus groups with prosecutors, defense attorneys, probation officers, treatment professionals, and representatives of statewide organizations. It seeks to answer a set of provocative questions: should problem solving be expanded beyond specialized "problem-solving courts"? What barriers might be confronted? What practical changes would need to be implemented in and outside of the courthouse to make it operationally feasible?

CHAPTER ELEVEN

The Brooklyn Mental Health Court: Implementation and Outcomes

KELLY O'KEEFE

The recent emergence of mental health courts in the U.S. has been a response to what many judges, prosecutors, attorneys, and providers know from experience—people with mental illness have not fared well under traditional case processing, and the result has been a "revolving door" between the criminal justice system and the community (Denkla and Berman 2001). Indeed, research shows that persons with mental illness are significantly overrepresented in jails and prisons. Approximately five percent of the U.S. population has a serious mental illness. The U.S. Department of Justice reports, however, that this figure becomes a much higher 16 percent among those housed in jail or prison (Ditton 1999). Further, the average length of stay in jail or prison tends to be longer among those with a mental illness than among the general inmate population; in New York City, inmates with such an illness average 215 days in jail, compared with 42 days for the entire jail population (Council of State Governments 2005).

In an effort to improve the criminal justice system's response to mentally ill offenders, mental health courts began appearing in 1997, and by the end of the 1990s there were eight well established courts (Goldkamp and Irons-Guynn 2000; and Griffin, Steadman, and Petrila 2002). The first mental health courts

This research was supported by a grant from the New York State Office of Mental Health. Opinions and interpretations in this chapter are those of the author and do not necessarily represent the official position or policies of the New York State Office of Mental Health.

demonstrated considerable diversity, but over the years, a general definition has emerged. Steadman, Davidson, and Brown (2001) define mental health courts as those that: 1) are criminal courts, 2) have separate dockets exclusive to persons with mental illness, 3) divert defendants from jail and/or prison into community-based mental health treatment, and 4) judicially monitor mental health treatment and potentially impose sanctions for noncompliance. Approximately 100 mental health courts meeting the above definition had emerged in the U.S. as of February 2005 (The Mental Health Court Survey 2006).

This article presents a process and outcome evaluation of the Brooklyn Mental Health Court during its first 28 months of operations from March 2002 to June 2004. The Brooklyn program is of particular interest; when it opened the court was one of the first and largest mental health courts in the country serving felony level defendants. This article documents the court's planning and implementation process and highlights important issues and lessons to consider when applying the model elsewhere. The outcome evaluation highlights key participant outcomes (program retention, recidivism, psychosocial functioning, and housing stability) and areas for future research. The evaluation is based on interviews with stakeholders, attendance at clinical team meetings, structured court observation, participant interviews, and analysis of quantitative data.

Overview of the Evaluation Literature

Meaningful evaluations of mental health court are just beginning to emerge, leaving the field with little empirical evidence to determine whether or not these innovative courts work. An evaluation of the Broward County mental health court found that the percentage of participants engaged in treatment increased from 36 percent in the eight months prior to their first mental health court appearance to 53 percent during the eight months following that appearance, whereas a "comparison group" undergoing regular case processing did not show any change between equivalent periods (29 percent to 28 percent). All research subjects faced misdemeanor charges (Boothroyd, Poythress, McGaha, and Petrila 2003).

An evaluation of the Kings County, Washington, mental health court found that participants had lower recidivism rates during a post- compared with a pre-enrollment period—although it is not tested how this change might have compared with similar defendants not enrolled in the mental health court (Trupin and Richards 2003). This same evaluation looked at a second Seattle municipal mental health court program and found that the number of days spent in jail decreased during a post-enrollment period while it increased over an equivalent period for a comparison group that was referred to the mental health court but opted not to participate. As in Broward County, these defendants also faced misdemeanor charges only.

Of particular interest due to its strong research design, an evaluation of the mental health court in Santa Barbara, California, randomly assigned 235 defendants to either the mental health court or to standard case processing and tracked outcomes over a two-year follow-up period (Cosden, Ellens, Schneell, and Yamini-Diouf 2005). The study found that a majority of the defendants in both study groups spent less time in jail and showed improved psychosocial functioning when comparing post- with pre-enrollment periods of time. Improvements in psychosocial functioning and quality-of-life measures were somewhat greater for mental health court participants, although none of these differences were statistically significant. Of note, many defendants in the comparison group received intensive mental health services through normal case processing options available through the Santa Barbara court; therefore, although the study comprised a randomized trial, those randomly assigned to the comparison group did not truly provide for a sharply differentiated "no treatment" comparison.

Another randomized trial was conducted in Butte County, California. There defendants were randomly assigned to either an Enhanced Treatment or Treatment-as-Usual group. A main component of the Enhanced Treatment group was a mental health court. Results showed lower rates of recidivism for the 50 Enhanced Treatment participants compared to the 43 Treatment-as-Usual participants. Also, Enhanced Treatment participants demonstrated statistically significant improvements in participant functioning and symptomatology (Bess 2004).

Finally, a study of the Clark County mental health court in Vancouver, Washington, showed reduced recidivism among mental health court participants post- compared with pre-enrollment, although this study lacked a non-mental health court comparison group (Herinckx, Swart, Ama, Dolezal, and King 2005).

In sum, the evaluation literature has produced a small number of studies, some with promising results, but many with methodological or other limitations. For instance, many of the available evaluations focus on courts treating misdemeanor offenders, while the current "second generation" of mental health courts focuses more on offenders facing more serious felony charges (Redlich, Steadman, Monahan, Petrila, and Griffin 2005). The evaluation of the Brooklyn Mental Health Court seeks to contribute to the knowledge in the field by studying a program primarily for felony offenders and examining both its process and outcomes.

Planning

The Brooklyn Mental Health Court was conceived as a demonstration project that would serve as a model to be replicated by other jurisdictions if proven successful. Keeping this in mind, the planners created goals for the court at the beginning of the planning process. The goals reflected the larger problem-solving court movement and were tailored to serve defendants with mental illness:

- Improve the court system's ability to identify, assess, evaluate, and monitor offenders with mental illness;
- Use the authority of the court to:
    - Link offenders with mental illness to appropriate mental health treatment services and supports;
    - Ensure that participants receive high quality community-based services;
    - Engage participants in treatment; and
    - Hold participants accountable for their actions;
- Create better understanding and effective linkages between the criminal justice and the mental health systems; and
- Improve public safety by reducing the recidivism of offenders with mental illness.

Key Challenges

Despite broad agreement among the courts, prosecutors, the defense bar, and other stakeholders on the program's overarching goals, several fundamental challenges needed to be addressed during planning to determine the scope of the mental health court and its target population. These are likely to be faced by other mental health courts and, as such, may be instructive (see Fisler 2005).

Mental Health Eligibility

Mental health courts throughout the nation require that defendants be diagnosed with a mental illness, but defining "mental illness" can be problematic. In line with the definition used for New York state mental health services, it was decided that eligible defendants must have a "serious and persistent mental illness" for which there is a known treatment: schizophrenia, bipolar disorder, major depression, or schizoaffective disorder. The implication of using this criteria was that many fewer defendants would be eligible than if the court were open to all mental health disorders, such as personality disorders, mental retardation/developmental disabilities, or traumatic brain injury.

Criminal Justice Eligibility

At the time the Brooklyn Mental Health Court was in the planning and early implementation stage, the majority of the mental health courts in existence were accepting misdemeanor offenders only. Through individual meetings with all relevant stakeholders, a plan emerged that the court would start with non-violent felony cases and consider chronic misdemeanor cases once the court was well established. The reasoning is outlined below.

> *Past Experience* Stakeholders were comfortable with the idea of the Brooklyn Mental Health Court accepting felony-level defendants through their experiences with other felony-level problem-solving courts in Brooklyn. Mental health clinicians and advocates said that engaging defendants in long-term treatment and judicial court monitoring had benefits that would not be seen with misdemeanor defendants who rarely faced long jail sentences.
>
> *Proportionality* Stakeholders agreed that a defendant's involvement in the Brooklyn Mental Health Court should not be longer than the sentence that would have been received under regular case processing. Given that misdemeanor offenders in New York City spend very little time in jail, the Brooklyn Mental Health Court was more appropriate for felony and specific, chronic misdemeanor defendants.

> *Logistics* Creating and implementing individualized treatment plans can take a great deal of time. Many misdemeanor defendants could be expected to receive a "time served" sentence before an assessment and community-based placement could even be completed.

After Brooklyn Mental Health Court operations began, the court then had to confront the question of whether defendants arrested for *violent* charges would be eligible. This question is addressed below.

Public Safety/Managing Risk

The judge and the Kings County District Attorney's Office put public safety at the top of their list of priorities when planning the mental health court. In the beginning, the District Attorney's office wanted to see significant numbers of defendants placed in restricted housing similar to residential or in-patient therapeutic communities for substance abusers. This proved unrealistic due to a general shortage of supportive housing in New York City and because restrictive housing is often in conflict with the mental health system's mission to promote independent living. A compromise was reached: the District Attorney's office would have ultimate veto power over the terms of each treatment plan. A related issue revolved around managing risk and predicting violent behavior. Stakeholders discussed how to assess an offender's risk of violence and ability to function in the community. The stakeholders determined that a thorough clinical assessment conducted by a clinical social worker and psychiatrist, individualized treatment plans, and the discretion for unilateral rejection of a referral by the Brooklyn Mental Health Court judge or the prosecutor would be used to ensure public safety.

Coercion to Enroll

The defense bar and some mental health advocates expressed concern regarding coercion in the court. Would defendants take a plea they didn't really understand? Would participants be forced to take medication? Would mental health providers be forced to jeopardize their relationships with their clients through reporting regularly to the court? What types of sanctions could be used? The defense bar expressed the need to be able to explain sanctions/clinical responses and rewards to clients. The project director collaborated with the District Attorney's Office, the judge, mental health providers, and other stakeholders to develop a list of possible sanctions/clinical responses and rewards. (As discussed below, the Brooklyn Mental Health Court opted not to adhere to a formal schedule delineating exactly which sanctions or rewards would be administered in response to specific behaviors.) The project director also created program participation guidelines and a formal Brooklyn Mental Health Court contract, both of which were to be reviewed by the defense attorney and defendant prior to taking a plea. The program participation guidelines explained the program, expectations, sanctions/clinical responses, and rewards. The contract outlined the rights and responsibilities of the defendant and the judge and was signed by the judge and defendant at the time of plea. Finally, the court developed consent forms, which the defendant would sign to release the court staff and mental health providers to share information.

Coercion to Accept Medication

The New York State Mental Hygiene Legal Services and other stakeholders voiced concern regarding the participant's right to refuse medication. Mental Hygiene Legal Services feared that treatment providers would use the mental health court to coerce participants into taking medication rather than seeking a civil court order to medicate over the participant's objection. In response, the Brooklyn Mental Health Court addressed the issue of medication compliance in its program participation guidelines, contract, and treatment mandate. The guidelines stated that, as a participant in the court, the defendant must agree to take the medication prescribed by his psychiatrist and speak to the treating psychiatrist or a Brooklyn Mental Health Court clinical team member if problems arose with medication. The guidelines stated that noncompliance with medication could result in a sanction. However, the participant would be given the opportunity to explain his situation or reasons for noncompliance prior to a sanction being imposed. A representative from Mental Hygiene Legal Services observed court proceedings regularly for the first four to six months to ensure that participants' civil rights were protected in terms of medication compliance and to offer advice on civil mental hygiene procedures, as needed.

Priority Access to Emergency Placement Beds

The Brooklyn Mental Health Court project director and clinical director worked with the New York State Office of Mental Health throughout the planning process and well into the second year of court operations to establish a mechanism by which participants would have priority access to emergency placement beds. The New York State Office of Mental Health tried to work with two partner agencies to find a creative way to set up one emergency placement bed for participants in an existing facility. These efforts proved unsuccessful. The Brooklyn Mental Health Court never obtained priority access to any type of housing. As a consequence, the data presented below will show significant median waiting times for participants awaiting supportive or residential housing.

Program Implementation

The Brooklyn Mental Health Court Team

The project team consists of a project director, clinical director, dedicated judge, resource coordinator, dedicated assistant district attorney, designated defense attorneys, and clinical team members. The clinical team has offices housed in the courthouse and consists of a social worker, two full-time and one-part-time forensic coordinators, and a consulting psychiatrist. The full-time social worker's primary responsibility is conducting psychosocial evaluations of defendants. She also takes on the role of a forensic coordinator for female clients, when necessary. Forensic coordinators have a wide range of responsibilities that include but are not limited to arranging placement in the community, monitoring compliance, acting as a liaison between community providers and the court, and coordinating services for participants when community-based case management services are unavailable or inadequate.

The Screening Process: Referrals, Assessment, and Volume

One of the goals of the Brooklyn Mental Health Court is to improve the court's ability to identify and assess offenders with mental illness. Brooklyn stakeholders had extensive experience with felony level drug courts and domestic violence courts, for which the referral process was standardized through automatic identification of eligible charges or through a universal screening of non-violent felony offenders for addiction/drug court eligibility. There is no universal screening for mental illness or Brooklyn Mental Health Court eligibility and there is no single charge to identify potentially eligible defendants. Although there is uniformity in eligibility procedures, the process contains a number of subjective elements due to the complexity of issues presented by offenders with mental illness. The referral process includes, in many cases, a discussion between the defense and the prosecutor.

The Brooklyn Mental Health Court received a total of 262 referrals during the implementation period of March 2002 to June 2004 (28 months). As Table 1 demonstrates, defense attorneys account for the largest percentage of referrals. Cases calendared after mental health competency proceedings make up the second largest source of referrals. (These defendants were found fit to stand trial but often faced serious mental health issues nonetheless.) Note that a significantly greater percentage of men are referred from the competency proceedings (34 percent) than women (14 percent).

In order to enroll in the court, participants must be found eligible on both mental health and criminal justice grounds. A defendant must have a serious and persistent mental illness for which there is a known treatment (schizophrenia, schizoaffective disorder, bipolar disorder, and major depression). The court's clinical director makes the final clinical eligibility determination. Concerning criminal justice eligibility, for the first several months, only non-violent felonies were eligible. As the court gained confidence and experience, the list of acceptable charges expanded to include some violent felonies and misdemeanors (the expansion of charges will be discussed below).

Eligibility of Violent Charges

In stakeholder interviews during the pilot phase, defense attorneys predicted low caseloads since defendants with violent charges would be excluded. One defense attorney stated that she respected the prosecutor's and the judge's commitment to protecting public safety but that the majority of her mentally ill clients were charged with violent crimes and deserved further investigation to examine the details of the case and whether mental illness played a role in their behavior.

Table 1. Referral Source (March 2002 - June 2004)

	Male		Female		Total	
	#	%	#	%	#	%
Referral Source						
Competency Proceedings	67	34%	8	14%	75	30%
Defense Attorney	84	42%	31	53%	115	44%
District Attorney	18	9%	9	15%	27	10%
Other Problem Solving Courts	7	4%	5	8%	12	5%
Other Judge Referrals	22	11%	5	8%	27	10%
Other	2	1%	1	2%	3	1%
Total	200	100%	59	100%	259	100%

As the court grew in experience and size, criminal justice eligibility expanded to include violent charges on a case-by-case basis. Starting from the second quarter of court operations through the end of the evaluation period, the data shows a general increase in acceptance of defendants charged with violent crimes as full-fledged participants. The ADA stated, "As we became more comfortable with the process and saw genuine success, we were ready to consider different charges." Overall, 39 percent of the 106 total participants enrolled through June 2004 were charged with violent offenses, and 46 percent of those enrolled in the most recent year (July 2003–June 2004) were charged with violent offenses.

Clinical Assessment

A thorough clinical assessment is completed in two parts. First, a psychosocial evaluation is conducted by one of the two clinical social workers. Second, a consulting psychiatrist conducts a psychiatric evaluation. The clinical social worker and psychiatrist each write a narrative report that provides a detailed description of each candidate, including the current mental illness, substance abuse history, family history, and other individual factors. For those who are likely to be found eligible, a treatment plan is developed. Each plan outlines a service utilization regimen consisting of mental health treatment, case management, supported housing services, substance abuse treatment (residential and outpatient), or integrated treatment for people with co-occurring mental illness and substance abuse. The clinical team then generates ideas for possible placement with appropriate community-based providers. Forensic coordinators start the time-consuming placement process. Applications to community-based providers are faxed and mailed. Forensic coordinators repeat this process as many times as necessary in order to find appropriate placements for each defendant.

Securing housing for a person with mental illness is a major challenge. The clinical team works with the providers and family members to return detained participants to pre-arrest housing, either with a community-based provider or family members, if clinically appropriate and agreeable to the court. Clinical team members also find housing in residential therapeutic communities and supported housing.

The aforementioned assessment process is far more comprehensive and labor intensive than the typical process in the country's specialized drug courts. To create some limits in terms of an acceptable time frame for this process, the court set up an internal objective to determine eligibility for each referral within 21 days. The eligibility determination date is when the psychiatric and psychosocial evaluations are distributed to all parties. Overall, the median number of days from first court appearance to eligibility determination is 21 days and the mean is 31 days, which demonstrates that the court procedures instituted for determining eligibility are meeting the stated objective.

Eligibility Summary

Of the 262 referrals received from March 2002 to June 2004, a total of 130 (50 percent) were found eligible. Of those, 106 (82 percent) enrolled as participants. Women were slightly more likely to be found eligible (58 percent) than men (47 percent).

Participation Process

Even though a defendant must enter a plea of guilty in order to participate in the Brooklyn Mental Health Court, the court is considered voluntary since the defendant can choose instead to return to regular case processing. The specific terms of the plea must be agreed upon by the judge, prosecutor, and defense attorney. First-time felony offenders must agree to a treatment mandate of 12 to 18 months and predicate felony offenders (those who have a prior felony conviction) to a mandate of 18 to 24 months. Misdemeanor offenders must agree to a treatment mandate of exactly 12 months.

Days to Plea Date

One indicator of case processing efficiency is the number of days from the date of first court appearance to plea date, which marks the formalization of Brooklyn Mental Health Court participant status. Of the 106 participants observed in Table 2, the median number of days to plea date is 60, the mean is 81, and the range is zero to 343 days.

Significantly, the mean number of days for those who remained in pre-arrest housing (community-based housing obtained prior to arrest) is 58 days compared to 116 for those waiting for supportive housing. The difference underscores that scarce housing resources for the mentally ill create significant delays to placement that participants typically spend detained in the local jail.

Monitoring

Judicial monitoring is a crucial component of the court. During the candidacy stage, a defendant appears before the judge approximately once a month so the judge can receive updates to the treatment plan and monitor the defendant's mental health status. All fully enrolled participants appear in court every two weeks for

Table 2. Days to Plea Date by Housing Type

	N	Median	Mean	Range
Defendant remained in pre-arrest housing[1]	48	45	58	0-252
Defendant placed in supportive housing[2]	25	105	116	28-343
Defendant placed in residential drug treatment	28	73	91	14-238
Other	5	75	75	70-75
Overall/Total	**106**	**56**	**81**	**0-343**

[1] Majority returned to family/friends or independent living. A few returned to supportive housing.

[2] Placed in an N.Y.S. Office of Mental Health residence, mental health program shelter or residence with mental health services onsite.

the first three months and then monthly, unless otherwise specified by the judge. More frequent court appearances may result from noncompliance or because the judge feels extra monitoring will encourage compliance.

In addition, the clinical team monitors defendants from the initial interview to graduation or termination. During the candidacy stage, the clinical team meets with each defendant a minimum of once a month to keep abreast of his or her mental health status, reinforce their relationship with the client, and assist with placement. Once a defendant becomes a participant, the mental health team meets with the participant after each court appearance and contacts community-based providers to obtain accurate updates on a weekly basis.

Phases of Participation (I – IV)

Each participant must pass through four phases before graduating. Unlike in drug court or other specialized courts that have specific behavioral requirements and time markers for each phase, the phases in the mental health court mark overall progress in treatment. Certificates, awarded at the end of each phase, are intended to encourage participants to continue their treatment and to maintain compliance rather than marking specific accomplishments such as being drug-free for 60 days.

Phase I :	Adjustment in treatment
Phase II:	Engagement in treatment
Phase III:	Progress in treatment
Phase IV:	Continued progress and preparing to graduate

Graduation and Failure

In order to graduate, participants are supposed to comply with their treatment mandate and not commit any new offenses. In practice, a new offense is not automatic grounds for termination. If a participant commits a new offense, the judge will consider the nature and severity of the crime, the participant's previous compliance, and the participant's motivation to remain compliant. The judge will speak with the prosecutor and the clinical director prior to making a decision.

Upon graduation, misdemeanor and first-time non-violent felony offenders have their plea vacated and all charges dismissed. Predicate felons and first-time violent felony offenders see their guilty plea vacated and their felony charge downgraded to a misdemeanor. Violent felony offenders receive a probation sentence, which remains in effect post-graduation. If a participant fails to comply with the mandate, the participant receives a pre-negotiated sentence determined at the time of plea. (In practice, 32 percent of participants have had a pre-negotiated alternative sentence of one year in jail and the remaining 68 percent have had alternative sentences that would require time in prison, which means a minimum term of one year—and longer for some participants. As of June 30, 2004, seven participants had been terminated. All seven participants were sentenced to the exact prison alternative determined at the time of the plea.)

Rewards and Clinical Responses/Sanctions

The terms "reward" and "sanction/clinical response" were purposely never defined in court documents but there was a loose understanding that a reward would be used to acknowledge a participant's compliance and continued success; a sanction would be implemented as a punishment or consequence for noncompliance; and a clinical response would be a modification in a treatment plan because of noncompliance—but with the goal of encouraging future compliance, not of "punishment." These terms were not formally defined for two reasons: 1) a sanction for one participant may be viewed as a reward for another, and 2) the team did not want a participant to view a modification to his or her treatment plan as punishment. Regardless of the term being used, the goal is always to motivate compliance and engage the participant in the court process.

Three illustrative examples follow:

- The judge tells the participant he must come to the courtroom and observe court every day of the week until further notification.
- A participant has been compliant except for one instance of testing positive for drugs two months earlier. The participant requests permission to travel to see a family member. The judge denies the request since he and the clinical director believe the participant isn't ready and needs to be engaged longer in treatment.
- A participant is in a residential drug treatment program. She gets into a fight at the program and is forced to leave without any warning. The clinical team fears she will relapse and decompensate if she remains in the community while looking for a new placement. The judge remands her to jail until a placement with a residential treatment provider can be found. The judge and the clinical team explain to the participant why they are remanding her to jail.

For many participants, the first example is clearly a sanction. However, there are some participants who would view coming to court as a reward since it would provide them with additional opportunities to speak with the judge. The second example could either be a sanction or clinical response depending on the circumstances, and the third example is clearly a clinical response even though at first glance jail would traditionally be considered a sanction.

Sanctions and clinical responses have not been captured systematically by the Brooklyn Mental Health Court team. One reason is that it is difficult to track something that is clearly not uniform and requires interpretation from the clinical team or the judge. A second reason is that the technology application used by the court does not have the ability to track compliance in the form of sanctions/clinical responses. Since so little is known about how mental health courts use sanctions/clinical responses or rewards, in the future it would be beneficial to define more clearly the terms and track usage to explore if they impact compliance or program success.

Courtroom Experience

The Brooklyn Mental Health Court is an unusual court. The audience fills up with participants and family members. Sidebar conversations take place between clinical team members and attorneys. Attorneys and clinical team members move in and out many times throughout the course of the morning to speak to participants and candidates in the hallway. Bench conferences and the sharing of artwork or creative writing by participants are common occurrences. Yet what may at first appear chaotic to an outsider is, in fact, a well organized court that seems to suit the needs of Brooklyn Mental Health Court members and participants.

Qualitative court observations were conducted from March 2002 to April 2003. Structured, quantitative court observations were conducted on a monthly basis from March 2003 to June 2004, as presented in Table 3. Qualitative observations revealed that basic processes such as the distribution of forms or awarding phase certificates were refined during the court's first sessions. The first few months also saw the judge conferencing frequently with the Brooklyn Mental Health Court psychiatrist and clinical director for clarification on mental health issues or services offered by local providers. As the calendar grew and all parties became more comfortable, candidates and participants started speaking more often, appearing in court when their attorneys could not be present, and waving at the judge from the audience. The judge began to expand clinical responses/sanctions beyond reprimands to include making a participant come to court daily and refusing a pass to see family on the weekend.

Observation notes highlight that the judge is willing to address and be addressed by defendants in unconventional ways within the limits of maintaining order and public safety. He will make eye contact with anxious defendants or wave to family members. For example, one participant asked the judge to shake his hand with a specific hand and accept a gift with the other hand. The judge complied with the request but was still very clear that he expected the participant to remain in compliance with the court's mandate.

Table 3 represents the court experience quantitatively and shows a great deal of consistency in courtroom behavior and procedures. Participation is defined as instances when a party spoke in court other than to state their name or provide basic information for the record. The data shows that when a candidate (not yet enrolled) is appearing in court all parties actively participate, including the defendant. Discussions during the candidacy stage

Table 3. Court Observation

	Candidates N	Participants N	Overall N
Appearances Coded[1]	40	78	118
Duration[2]	2	2	2
Participation			
Judge	100%	100%	10%
Clinical Team Member	30%	12%	17%
Assistant District Attorney	55%	8%	24%
Defense Attorney[3]	80%	80%	81%
Defendant[4]	40%	90%	73%
Judge's Communication			
Direct Converstation	68%	96%	91%
Eye Contact	69%	94%	90%
Probing Conversation	6%	64%	54%
Approached Bench w/ Def.	31%	63%	57%
Shook Hands w/ Def.	60%	46%	47%
Approached Bench w/o Def.	20%	4%	12%
Clinical Response/Award/Sanction			
Good Report Mentioned/Positive Feedback	n/a	63%	63%
Negative Report Mentioned/Negative Feedback	n/a	23%	23%
Warrant	n/a	1%	1%
Certificate Awarded	n/a	10%	10%
Other			
Family Member Present	5%	13%	10%
Artwork/Special Skill Performed	3%	7%	5%

[1] Appearances coded March 2004 - June 2004. [2] Median hearing length rounded to the minute.
[3] Defense Attorney not present candidate (15%) and participant (19%).
[4] Defendant not present candidate (15%) and participant (6%).

often center on the progress and timeline for the clinical evaluation, which requires input from all parties.

Participation after a defendant becomes a formal participant is remarkably different and is limited largely to the judge, defense attorney, and participant. Communication focuses on the progress report, next steps, and an exchange between the judge and the participant. The clinical director and the ADA remain silent unless there is a specific issue to address.

The structured court observations highlight signature patterns and behaviors of the Brooklyn Mental Health Court judge for engaging defendants while managing the busy calendar. Common techniques include direct conversation, eye contact, and probing questions in open court. Direct conversation is defined as questions posed directly to the candidate or participant along the lines of "How are you today?" or "Tell me, how's it going?" and probing questions are defined as questions about the defendant's life, treatment, or overall well-being such as "Are you still drawing?" or "What is it that you don't like about it (the program)?" The judge makes direct conversation and eye contact with approximately 90 percent of those appearing before him. He asks probing questions to 64 percent of the participants and six percent of the candidates. One participant said, "He remembered that my mom was sick. That made me feel good." And another participant said, "He respects me. He asked me questions." In the course of direct conversation or probing questions, the judge often refers to the progress reports submitted by the clinical team. The judge uses the reports as a basis for his comments, such as, "It looks like you are doing well," or, after reviewing a document with poor ratings, "What's going on?"

In addition to communicating openly in court, the judge uses bench conferences as another way to communicate with both participants and candidates. What started out as a one-time event turned into a regular and effective method to engage Brooklyn Mental Health Court participants. The judge says:

> *I didn't do it with any plan in mind. This one guy was nervous and the only way to get him to talk was to bring him up to the bench... to engage human to human... I think it is effective because people have been given short shrift their entire life... if they can be engaged then they can have faith in themselves and hope for the future."*

In 57 percent of observed appearances, the defendant approached the bench, and during those appearances, the judge either shook hands or touched the hand of 47 percent of the defendants during the bench conference. In 12 percent of the cases, bench conferences took place without the defendant present to discuss sensitive matters the judge deemed inappropriate for open court.

It should be noted that the judge's ability to engage the participant and candidate in direct conversation is facilitated by a technology application on the computer at the judge's bench. This application allows the judge to record comments and notes while hearing cases. These notes provide an excellent source of information for the judge when seeing defendants from month to month. He often makes notes about progress in treatment, family members who have been ill, and other milestones in the participants' lives. The judge says these notes assist him in monitoring the defendant's compliance and substantively engaging the defendant. The judge stated, "[Technology] is one of my greatest public safety tools."

The Participant Perspective

Participants enrolled during the period of March 2002 to June 2004 were asked to partake in an interview at their one-year anniversary date. Of the 37 participants eligible to complete the interview, 31 agreed to it, three refused, and three were either warranted, sentenced, or hospitalized and thus unavailable. The goal of the interviews was to better understand the Brooklyn Mental Health Court experience from the perspective of the participant and to ask for constructive criticism. The interview instrument included measures of perceived coercion and perceived procedural justice. Additional items focused on the Brooklyn Mental Health Court experience such as court appearances, phase certificates, and the role of the Brooklyn Mental Health Court team.

Perceived Coercion

Questions about coercion in the literature about mental health courts include whether or not legally imposed treatment affects clients' perceptions of coercion and whether court monitoring impacts participants' compliance or perceptions of coercion (Rain et al. 2003).

The court is considered voluntary because defendants have a choice of whether to enter a plea of guilty in the Brooklyn Mental Health Court or appear before another judge for regular case processing. However, questions about coercion persist. Participants were asked to complete a modified version of the MacArthur Perceived Coercion Scale to explore the idea of coercion and how it related to their overall experience in the court. The scale was modified in an evaluation conducted of the Broward County Mental Health Court (Poythress et al. 2002), which used the scoring mechanism developed by Gardner, Hoge, and Bennett (1993). The scale measures four items: influence, control, choice, and freedom. The scores range from 0 (low) to 5 (high).

Participants were often confused and required the interviewer to repeat questions multiple times. However, it was clear that participants were not concerned with coercion and were often confused as to why the questions were being asked. Participants would interrupt and say "I like Judge D'Emic" or "I'm here. I like it." Participants were interviewed after being in the Brooklyn Mental Health Court for one year and may not have been able to recall their decision making a full year earlier. Brooklyn Mental Health Court stakeholders did not want to have participants interviewed at time of program entry since the court was still new and had yet to establish concrete procedures for taking a plea. A stronger design would have been to interview participants when taking their plea and then again one year later to determine if their perceptions of coercion changed over time and if their understanding of the instrument would have been clearer at the time of plea.

The scores ranged from 0 to 4.53 and the mean score was .84 (standard deviation 1.29). The low score indicates that participants perceived themselves to have a high level of independent

Table 4. Perceived Coercion Scale

1.	Was it your decision to keep your case in the mental health court...? (Entirely what you wanted...entirely what other people wanted)
2.	How much control did you have over whether you would keep your case in the mental health court or have your case go to another judge? (Very much...None/Not at all)
3.	Overall, would you say that you chose to keep your case in the mental health court, or that someone else made you keep your case in the mental health court? (Yes, No)
4.	How free did you feel to do what you wanted about keeping your case in the mental health c ourt or going back to a regular court? (Very much...None/Not at all)

decision making, control, choice, and freedom. In short, participants did not feel coerced into the Brooklyn Mental Health Court, or at least did not feel coerced after having spent a year in treatment monitored by the judge and clinical team. These results are comparable to those from the Broward County Mental Health Court evaluation, which found a mean score of .69 (standard deviation 1.30). Although it is interesting to show how the Brooklyn Mental Health Court scores in relation to another mental health court, it should be noted that there are significant differences between the courts. For example, at the time of the evaluation the Broward County Mental Health Court accepted only misdemeanor cases, and participants completed coercion measures immediately after their first mental health court hearing.

Perceived Procedural Justice

Research shows that people care about having a voice and being treated with dignity in the court process, regardless of the outcome (Sydeman, Cascardi, Poythress, and Rittenband 1997; Tyler 1990). Procedural justice measures the participant's subjective experience of case processing. Stakeholders were interested in knowing whether participants felt they were treated fairly in the

Brooklyn Mental Health Court and if they felt their voices were heard.

The instrument used to measure procedural justice was the same as the one used for the Broward County Mental Health Court, although modified slightly to fit the timeline of the Brooklyn Mental Health Court (see Table 5). The origin of the Broward County Mental Health Court scale is Cascardi, Poythress, and Hall (2000). The original scale asks a set of questions about the judge and a set of questions about the defense attorney. Since the Brooklyn Mental Health Court is a court-based program, this evaluation only asked questions pertaining to the judge. The instrument consists of five items and participants rated each item from 1 (not at all) to 7 (definitely).

The results in Table 5 demonstrate a high level of participant satisfaction with Brooklyn Mental Health Court case processing and judicial monitoring. The high scores reinforce the positive comments regarding the judge provided by the participants during the interviews. Participants raved about the judge's listening skills, his knack for remembering personal details of their lives, and his ability to respect them in a way often missing in other court proceedings. One participant said, "I've been to a lot of courtrooms in my life, and I've never met a judge like him. He respects me. I'm sick. That means a lot to me to be respected now." Another participant said, "I've got no complaints. He asks about me, my husband, and my son. Sometimes I asked for something and he said no. He's the boss, so it's okay."

Attitudes about the Court Team Members and Specific Program Elements

In addition to the questions about coercion and procedural justice, the participants completed 12 items with a scale ranging from 1 (strongly agree) to 5 (strongly disagree). The 12 items focused on participants' feelings toward key stakeholders (clinical

Table 5. Perceived Procedural Justice

		Mean (S.D)
1.	While your case has been in the mental health court, have you had enough opportunity to tell the judge what you think he needed to hear about your personal and legal situation?	6.22 (1.48)
2.	While your case has been in the mental health court, has the judge seemed genuinely interested in you as a person?	6.78 (.698)
3.	While your case has been in the mental health court, has the judge treated you respectfully?	6.93 (.267)
4.	While your case has been in the mental health c ourt, has the judge treated you fairly?	6.96 (.192)
5.	Overall, are you satisfied with how the judge has treated you and dealt with your case?	6.78 (.641)

team, defense attorney, judge), court processes (phase certificates, judicial court monitoring) and whether the participant would recommend the court to someone else. Overall, Table 6 demonstrates a very high level of satisfaction with court stakeholders and court processes.

Participants agreed that frequent judicial monitoring helps them to continue with their treatment, as does receiving the phase certificates. Even though participants realized that the frequent visits with the judge were helpful and positive, they were fairly unified in their dislike of sitting and waiting for their turn to appear before the judge (M=2.48). Participants were often hesitant to give negative feedback and would qualify this answer with statements, such as "I like the judge but I hate waiting," or "I have to make up the time on the weekend but it's okay."

Participants agreed or strongly agreed with the statement, "I would recommend the Brooklyn Mental Health Court to someone else." When asking for suggestions and feedback, participants returned to this statement frequently. One participant commented, "It's great you're giving me a chance. Others need

Table 6. Mental Health Court Program Feedback Questions

		Mean 1 (strongly agree) 5 (strongly disagree)
1.	The phase certificate encouraged me to continue with my treatment.	1.63
2.	Coming to court on a regular basis encourages me to continue with my treatment.	1.85
3.	I like sitting and watching others appear before the judge.	2.48
4.	I find it helpful to meet with the clinical team when I come to court.	1.59
5.	I would recommend the Brooklyn Mental Health Court to someone else.	1.52

chances, too." Another said, "You should make all those other courts like this one."

Participant Outcomes

Who is the Brooklyn Mental Health Court serving? What are their outcomes? And who benefits most from the Brooklyn Mental Health Court? This section seeks to answer these questions by presenting:

- Intake data such as demographics, socioeconomic status, criminal justice background, and mental health characteristics for all participants enrolled before June 2004.
- Participant progress in the mental health court as of June 2004, including a comparison of those participants who graduated and participants who were terminated.
- Analysis of outcome data before and after entrance into the Brooklyn Mental Health Court for the first 37 participants in terms of homelessness, hospitalizations, recidivism, substance abuse, and psychosocial functioning.

Participant Profile

Table 7 presents descriptive data gathered at intake for all 106 participants enrolled by June 2004. Overall, the participants are mostly African-American, male, single, and have poor education and work histories. The majority has been hospitalized for psychiatric reasons at least once in their lives; however, only a few were in mental health treatment at time of arrest.

- *Race and Ethnicity* African Americans make up 51 percent of participants, white defendants 21 percent, Hispanics 25 percent (regardless of race), and "other" four percent.
- *Homelessness* Fifteen percent of participants were homeless in the year preceding arrest.
- *Diagnosis* About 75 percent of participants were diagnosed with bipolar disorder, major depression, or schizophrenia. Schizoaffective disorder and other diagnoses make up the final quarter. In addition, 48 percent of participants suffered from co-occurring disorders.
- *Psychiatric Hospitalizations* Sixty-nine percent of participants reported being hospitalized at least once in their lives for psychiatric reasons; 32 percent reported that they had been hospitalized for psychiatric reasons in the 12 months prior to arrest.
- *Charges* Eighty-five percent of participants were charged with a felony, of which 37 percent were charged with a violent crime.
- *Treatment Mandate* The majority of participants (60 percent) received a 12- to 18-month mandate.

Retention and Recidivism

Table 8 shows that as of June 30, 2004, 72 percent of the enrolled participants were in good standing and five percent were still active but had either been remanded/sanctioned or had warrant-

Table 7. Participant Profile

	All Participants (N 106) # %
DEMOGRAPHICS	
Median age at entry	34
Race/Ethnicity	
Black/African-American	51%
White/Caucasian	21%
Hispanic/Latino	25%
Asian/Pacific Islander/Other	4%
Single (never married)	74%
SOCIOECONOMIC STATUS	
High school degree/GED (minimum)	42%
Living Arrangements	
Alone/Family/Others	80%
Community Residence	4%
Single Site Supported	4%
Psychiatric In-Patient	3%
Homeless	8%
Homeless in past 12 months	15%
Days homeless in past 12 months	107
Longest Employment (years)	2
Employed Full-Time / Part-Time	13%
MENTAL HEALTH FACTORS	
Diagnosis	
Bipolar	28%
Major Depression	25%
Schizophrenia	26%
Schizoaffective	14%
Other	7%
Co-Occurring Disorders (Yes)	48%
Hospitalized for psychiatric reasons ever (Yes)	70%
Receiving mental health treatment at time of arrest (Yes)	30%
Number of psychiatric hospitalizations in 12 months (average)	0.58
Days hospitalized in past 12 months (average)[1]	34
CRIMINAL JUSTICE FACTORS	
Charges	
Felony	85%
Drug Sales/Drug Possession	16%
Crimes against property	28%
Crimes against people (violent)	37%
Crimes against people (non-violent)	18%
Other	2%
Length of Treatment	
9 to 12 months/12 months	14%
12 to 18 months[2]	60%
18 to 24 months[3]	26%

[1] Includes only those with psychiatric hospitalizations in past 12 months.

[2] Includes one sentence for 12 to 24 months.

[3] Includes one sentence for 30 to 36 months.

ed. A total of 18 participants had graduated and five had been terminated. Of the 37 participants that had been enrolled at least one year as of June 30, 2004, 38 percent had open cases, 46 percent had graduated, 13 percent were terminated, and three percent were warranted. This indicates a one-year retention rate of 84 percent.

Of these first 37 participants, 17 graduated and five were terminated as of June 30, 2004.

The median number of months to graduation is listed below:

- 9- to 12-month mandates: Median number of months to graduation was 12 (N=3).
- 12- to 18-month mandates: Median number of months to graduation was 12 (N=9).
- 18- to 24-month mandates: Median number of months to graduation was 19 (N=5).

These results signal that actual times to graduation closely approximate the formal minimum times that are told to participants when they enter the program. Also, terminated participants averaged 16 months from plea date to termination date. Three of the five terminated participants were warranted for very lengthy periods of time prior to being sentenced.

Psychosocial Outcomes—Pre- Vs. Post-Participation

This section examines participant outcomes for the 37 participants enrolled as of June 30, 2003. The data compares the first 12 months as a participant to the 12 months preceding entry into the Brooklyn Mental Health Court or 12 months preceding arrest for those detained at the time of intake (see Table 9). In the discussion below, "participants" refers to the 37 participants included in the preliminary outcome study. Staff completed forms at baseline

Table 8. Program Status as of September 30, 2004

	N	%
1. Open	76	72%
2. Graduated	18	17%
3. Remanded/Serving Jail Sanction	4	3%
4. Warranted	1	1%
5. Terminated/Sentenced	7	7%
Total	**106**	**100%**

and again at 12-month follow-up. Questions were not asked directly to the participants.

The reader should note that, while suggestive, the results presented in this section do not comprise an impact evaluation, since participant outcomes are not compared with those of other defendants who never entered into the Brooklyn Mental Health Court. (An impact evaluation of the Brooklyn Mental Health Court is forthcoming in 2008.)

Recidivism

Over three-quarters of Brooklyn Mental Health Court participants (78 percent) had been arrested at least once as adults prior to the incident that qualified them for the Brooklyn Mental Health Court. In addition to the Brooklyn Mental Health Court qualifying arrest, 27 percent had been arrested at least once in the 12 months prior to enrolling. During the first 12 months of participation, a total of six participants (16 percent) committed a new offense. Charges included criminal possession of marijuana, grand larceny, criminal possession of stolen property, loitering for purposes of prostitution, and criminal possession of a dangerous weapon. While suggestive, this reduction in recidivism is non-significant.

In all cases, the new arrest was not automatic grounds for sentencing. Of the six participants who re-offended during their first year of participation, two eventually graduated, three were sentenced after lengthy warrants, and one was administratively ter-

Table 9. Participant Outcomes

	Intake	Follow-Up
Recidivism	27%	16%
Homelessness		
Homelessness in the past 12 months	16%	11%
Number of days homeless	60	35
Hospitalizations		
Psychiatric hospitalizations in the past 12 months	50%	19%**
Number of psychiatric hospitalizations in the past 12 months[1]	0.58	0.27
Psychiatric emergency room visits in the past 12 months	44%	25%*
Frequency and current level of alcohol use		
Not at all in the past 6 months (frequency)	0.19	0.56**
Abstinent (current level)	0.38	0.82***
Frequency and current level of drug use		
Not at all in the past 6 months	0.15	0.61***
Abstinent	0.30	0.90***

[1] Includes only those participants who had been hospitalized in the past 12 months.
+p<.10, *p<.05, **p<.01 ,***p<.001

minated because of complications due to pending federal charges.

Homelessness

The percentage of participants who experienced homelessness and the median number of days homeless decreased while participants were enrolled in the Brooklyn Mental Health Court. A total of 16 percent of participants reported being homeless in the 12 months preceding their enrollment, compared to 11 percent who reported experiencing homelessness during their first 12 months as a participant. The median number of days homeless decreased from 60 days pre-participation to 35 days homeless during the first year of participation. These differences were also not significant.

Hospitalization

Psychiatric hospitalizations occur for different reasons depending on individual circumstances. A hospital stay may mean a participant is not fully engaged in treatment or that a participant's treatment needs are not fully met. Regardless of the reason, psychiatric hospitalizations are not necessarily a sign of failure or viewed negatively by providers or court staff. Table 9 shows a significant decrease in the percentage of participants who were hospitalized for psychiatric treatment from 50 percent to 19 percent when comparing the 12 months preceding enrollment with the first 12 months as a participant. Of those who had psychiatric hospitalizations, the number of days hospitalized remained fairly constant and the average number of psychiatric hospitalizations decreased slightly from .58 at intake to .27 at follow-up.

Drug and Alcohol Use

Clinical staff were asked to report on participants' drug use and alcohol use at intake and 12 months following intake. Overall, participants showed dramatic decreases in drug and alcohol use. From intake to follow-up, the data shows a significant decrease in the percentage reporting use of alcohol or drugs "one or more times in the past week" and a significant increase in the percentage reporting use "not at all in the past six months." When looking at the current level of alcohol and drug use, similar gains are evident. A significantly higher number of participants were reportedly abstinent at follow-up for alcohol and drug use than at intake. Also, the percentage of participants who reported their current level of drug and alcohol use as "dependence" decreased significantly.

Psychosocial Functioning

One way to measure participant outcomes is to measure changes in their overall psychosocial functioning. Accordingly, the clinical director and clinical social worker completed the Health of the Nation Outcome Scale (HoNOS) at intake and 12-month follow-up (The Royal College of Psychiatrists' Research Unit 2002). The instrument was designed by The Royal College of Psychiatrists and has been tested for reliability and validity. It is designed to be used by clinicians, researchers, and providers repeatedly over

Table 10. Health of the Nation Outcome Scale

		Intake	Follow-Up
1.	Overactive, aggressive, disruptive, or agitated behavior	.39	.39
2.	Non-accidental self-injury	.00	.00
3.	Problem drinking or drug taking	.44	.39
4.	Cognitive problems	.94	.21***
5.	Physical illness or disability problems	.38	.29
6.	Problems with hallucinations or delusions	.15	.29
7.	Problems with depressed moods	1.59	.79***
8.	Other mental and behavioral problems	.73	1.03
9.	Problems with relationships	1.41	1.26
10.	Problems with activities for daily living	1.21	1.03
11.	Problems with living conditions	1.53	1.00**
12.	Problems with occupations and activities	2.09	1.24***

+p<.10, *p<.05, **p<.01 ,***p<.001

time. The scores for individual scales are to be compared to one another to determine the impact of the interventions, and to create a picture of the client's overall functioning. The HoNOS is comprised of 12 scales that measure a wide range of health and social domains (psychiatric symptoms, physical health, functioning, relationships, and housing). Each scale is scored from 0 (no problem) to 4 (severe to very severe problem).

Overall, as shown in Table 10, participants improved their psychosocial functioning on nearly every scale. Participants showed statistically significant improvement for the scales measuring problems with cognition, depressed moods, living conditions, and occupations and activities.

The HoNOS does show a slight, non-significant increase in problems with hallucinations/delusions and other mental and behavioral problems. It is clear that this increase can be attributed to two outlier participants. One was in the process of adjusting his medication and another often experienced paranoia as the time for her next injection drew near.

Table 11. Service Utilization at Baseline

	Female		Male		Total	
	#	%	#	%	#	%
Case Management	7	70%	19	70%	26	70%
Supported Housing	2	70%	2	70%	4	11%
Mental Health Treatment	6	60%	21	78%	27	73%
MICA Treatment	4	40%	6	22%	10	27%
Substance Abuse Treatment (Outpatient)	4	40%	2	7%	6	16%
Substance Abuse Treatment (Residential)	0	0%	10	37%	10	27%
MICA Housing	2	20%	5	19%	7	19%
Vocational Rehab/Education	0	0%	2	7%	2	5%
ACT Team	0	0%	1	4%	1	3%
Total (current participants)	**10**		**27**		**37**	

Service Utilization

Clinical team members were charged with tracking participant service utilization: name of providers, type of providers, start date of service, and end date of service. The Brooklyn Mental Health Court database did not capture the specific activities or treatments provided. For example, the database tracked that a participant was placed in residential substance abuse treatment but did not capture if the person was in group therapy or when the person moved from one phase of treatment to the next.

Due to limitations in available treatment modalities, the clinical team must often be creative when drafting a treatment plan, and the result is "wrap-around" services for participants involving multiple providers and multiple services. The first cadre of participants had a median number of three providers simultaneously. Table 11 shows the types of services received at baseline by the first 37 participants during their first year as Brooklyn Mental Health Court participants. The data shows that 73 percent were receiving mental health services. The remaining participants (27 percent) were receiving some level of mental health treatment through a community-based provider, such as residential drug treatment or outpatient day treatment. The chart also shows that 70 percent of participants were linked with New York State Office of Mental Health's Intensive Case Management (ICM) services.

Conclusion

During the first 28 months of operations, the Brooklyn Mental Health Court generally achieved its goals of improving the court system's ability to identify, assess, and monitor offenders with mental illness and of using the authority of the court to link offenders with mental illness to appropriate mental health treatment services.

Brooklyn Mental Health Court stakeholders and team members also confronted several important challenges. Some were overcome with creativity and diligence, while others persist to this day. Since many of these challenges are likely to be faced by other mental health courts across the country, reviewing them may be instructive. They include:

- *Clinical Eligibility* The Brooklyn Mental Health Court opted to limit eligibility to defendants with "serious and persistent mental illness for which there is a known treatment" (schizoaffective, schizophrenia, major depression, and bipolar disorder).
- *Criminal Justice Eligibility* Unlike most of the mental health courts that had previously opened, the Brooklyn Mental Health Court opted to work primarily with felony defendants, whose greater legal exposure allowed them to be mandated to the longer periods of treatment that their illnesses required.
- *Eligibility of Violent Defendants* Although defendants arrested on violent charges were at first excluded, this policy became more flexible over time, as it became clear that mental illness was sometimes an underlying factor leading to violent crimes; more than one third of participants to date have entered with a violent charge.
- *Coercion* Brooklyn Mental Health Court team addressed concerns surrounding coercion in several ways.

Enrollment in the court is voluntary, and the program participation guidelines and program contract clearly spell out the rights and responsibilities of the defendant and the judge. Medication compliance, on the other hand, is required. However, participants receive opportunities to discuss medication with team members and the judge, and interviews suggest that participants did not feel coerced.

- *Community-based Services* Given the limited slots available, the Brooklyn Mental Health Court clinical team continues to face the daily challenge of placing participants in appropriate mental health treatment and housing services, sometimes leading to delays in placement and a frequent need to place participants in "wrap-around" services with multiple providers at the same time.
- *Referral Process* The referral process is not automated and may be a contributing factor to lower-than-planned volume. Team members must explore ways to streamline this process, making it speedier and easier for defense attorneys and others to understand and navigate.
- *Sanctions, Rewards, and Clinical Responses* The Brooklyn Mental Health Court began implementation with purposefully vague definitions of sanctions, rewards, and clinical responses. As the court moves forward, there may be value in documenting these court elements in order to better articulate and formalize the model.

Despite these barriers, many of the evaluation's key findings are exceptionally promising. Participants interviewed about their experience perceived themselves to have a high level of independent decision making, control, choice, and freedom. Participants also demonstrated a high level of satisfaction with their case processing and judicial monitoring. Courtroom observation showed a judge interacting with participants regularly and using individualized techniques to engage participants.

Also, the participants included in the outcome evaluation showed significant improvements in several outcome measures and a tendency toward improvement in nearly all other measures, even when the effect sizes were not statistically significant. The measures under examination include criminal recidivism as well as homelessness, substance use, hospitalizations, and psychosocial functioning. The encouraging outcome results, coupled with an unusually high one-year program retention rate of 84 percent, suggest that the Brooklyn Mental Health Court had a meaningful positive effect on its participants. Future research may expand upon these results and provide more insight regarding whether, how, and for whom mental health courts work.

CHAPTER TWELVE

The Harlem Parole Reentry Court: Implementation and Preliminary Impacts

DONALD J. FAROLE JR.

The success of adult drug courts has encouraged innovators and practitioners to adapt the drug court model to other areas in which criminal justice oversight and supervision can play a role in problem-solving. Prisoner reentry, the process by which offenders are released from prison, jail, or a detention facility and returned to their communities, is one such area. In 1999, the Office of Justice Programs of the U.S. Department of Justice developed a Reentry Court Initiative to test the feasibility and effectiveness of a collaborative, court-based approach to managing offender reentry, with the ultimate goals of reducing recidivism and prison return rates and supporting offender reintegration into the community.

This chapter presents a process and preliminary impact evaluation of one of the Reentry Court Initiative's nine sites, the Harlem Parole Reentry Court. The Harlem Parole Reentry Court began operations in June 2001 as a pilot demonstration project at the Harlem Community Justice Center, located in the East

---

This chapter is adapted from the executive summary of a research report originally published in 2003. The research was supported under an award from the Bureau of Justice Assistance, U.S. Department of Justice. Opinions and interpretations are those of the author and do not necessarily represent the official position of the U.S. Department of Justice. The New York State Division of Criminal Justice Services provided criminal history and recidivism data for the evaluation, and the New York State Division of Parole provided parole data. The author is solely responsible for the methodology and results obtained with this data.

Harlem neighborhood of New York City. The Reentry Court was developed by the New York State Division of Parole, the Center for Court Innovation, and the New York State Division of Criminal Justice Services, with technical assistance from the Office of Justice Programs.

The Reentry Court reflects growing national concern about prisoner reentry. Nationwide, more than 600,000 individuals are released from state or federal prison each year. Upon release, ex-offenders face significant barriers to obtaining employment, housing, medical care, and other basic needs, factors that affect their ability to reunite with their families, reintegrate into their communities, and lead law-abiding, productive lives. Indeed, within three years, 68 percent are rearrested and nearly half returned to jail or prison for either a new crime or parole violation. The prisoner reentry challenge has potentially profound implications not only for ex-offenders and their families but also for public safety and the economic and social health of states and communities.

This chapter focuses on the Harlem Reentry Court's first 20 months of operations (June 2001–January 2003). During this time, the Reentry Court targeted a population of nonviolent adult felony offenders convicted on drug charges (possession and sales) and with a post-release residence in one of three precincts in the East Harlem area.

Key Elements

Key elements of the Harlem Reentry Court model include:

- *Assessment and planning* Identification of candidates prior to release; needs assessments and planning prior to release; involvement of the offender, community corrections, and other key partners.

- *Active oversight* Regular court appearances beginning immediately after release involving the ex-offender, Reentry Court staff, and family or other informal support mechanisms.
- *Coordination of support services* Identification of necessary resources including substance abuse treatment providers, job training programs, private employers, family members, housing services, and other community- and faith-based organizations, with a case management approach accountable to the court.
- *Graduated sanctions and incentives* Use of a predetermined range of sanctions in response to violation of supervision conditions that can be administered swiftly, predictably, and universally; and the use of incentives to recognize program milestones.
- *Neighborhood focus* A narrowly defined geographic area covering three police precincts (23rd, 25th, and 28th) in East and Central Harlem; access to on-site services available at the Harlem Community Justice Center.

The first 20 months of the Harlem Reentry Court saw many accomplishments but also numerous challenges and implementation barriers. Despite the challenges, the Reentry Court demonstration provides support for the viability of a collaborative, team-based model of supervision and treatment services in New York.

Implementing the Harlem Reentry Court

The Reentry Court put in place a collaborative, team-based model that improves communications between parole and treatment agencies. There is coordination and sharing of information between supervision and service providers that cannot occur in traditional parole supervision, which has neither team meetings nor case managers to facilitate communications with service providers. As a result, parolees appear to receive greater access to needed services (substance abuse treatment, job training, transitional housing, etc.) and more coordinated service delivery using a case management approach. Enhanced communication facilitates intensified parole supervision and allows the team to identify substance use/relapse at an early stage. Program implementation was facilitated by building upon the Division of Parole's existing relationships with service providers and the Harlem Community Justice Center's roots in the community.

However, the Reentry Court faced significant implementation challenges, due principally to difficulties locating and enrolling participants during early program operations. While the Reentry Court's caseload has nearly doubled since the outset of the project, only 45 participants were enrolled during the first year (short of the goal of 96) and participants were not identified until shortly before release from prison, which limited time for pre-release planning and services. In addition, the Reentry Court struggled to define staff roles and responsibilities, both across and within agencies, in the context of a collaborative team-based model. A particular challenge has been to make substantial changes to supervision practices to accommodate a model that seeks to combine proactive supervision with treatment. The Reentry Court also struggled to develop ties to community organizations to provide needed services, most notably transitional housing.

Through January 31, 2003, the Reentry Court had enrolled 61 parolees. These participants, though nonviolent, were (like the majority of the parolee population) at high risk of recidivism—none were first-time offenders, all had at least two felony convictions, and most were released from prison with an array of problems, including a history of substance abuse, limited employment prospects, and limited education. Participants made regular appearances, beginning the day of release from prison, before the Reentry Court's administrative law judge, who implemented graduated sanctions and rewards in an effort to promote compliance with the treatment and supervision plan. Twenty-two parolees successfully completed the three program phases, graduated, and entered program aftercare, during which time they continued to report to Reentry Court parole officers and receive services at the Harlem Community Justice Center. For these first participants, successful progress in the program does not appear to be correlated with many observed characteristics (although heroin users were somewhat less likely to graduate). Qualitative evidence suggests, however, that the motivation to succeed—perhaps positively correlated with age—may affect participants' prospects in the Reentry Court regimen.

Given that the program enrolled a high-risk population, it is not surprising that many participants have had continued criminal justice involvement. Criminal justice records indicate that, within one year of release from prison, 36 percent were rearrested, with 22 percent reconvicted for a misdemeanor or felony while under the Reentry Court's supervision. In addition, during their time in the Reentry Court's supervision, most participants resumed drug use at least once, and many did so repeatedly. These outcomes are testament to the difficulty this population faces reintegrating into a community most have been removed from for considerable amounts of time while incarcerated. They are also testament to a challenge the Reentry Court has faced and will continue to face in the future—to react promptly to technical infractions through the use of intermediate interventions designed to avoid problems escalating to the point of revocation.

Lessons

The early days of Harlem Reentry Court implementation highlight a number of lessons about managing prisoner reentry into the community. As such, these lessons provide valuable guidance for the future development of programs and policies:

Effective joint problem solving requires building the structures and relationships to sustain ongoing collaboration between supervision agents and service providers.

The Harlem Reentry Court functions best when the parole officers, case managers, and service providers are proactive in sharing information and using that information to develop supervision and treatment strategies to reduce risk factors that contribute to reoffending. Such a collaborative, team-based effort requires all staff to take on non-traditional roles, and that does not always come easily. A key management problem has been to build and sustain a team-based model, particularly when personnel change. Strong local leadership, clearly defined staff roles and responsibilities (perhaps through written memoranda of understanding), and ongoing staff training in team building and case management techniques are all essential to these efforts.

Identifying eligible offenders as early as possible prior to release from prison is critical in reentry management and requires coordinated efforts between correctional and supervision agencies.

Identifying eligible offenders in a state correctional system with 72 facilities as potential feeders is a challenge. While the Harlem Reentry Court's caseload has grown at a significantly faster pace in recent months, candidates continue to be identified with difficulty and only shortly before their scheduled release. Efforts to support successful reintegration benefit greatly when offenders are identified as early as possible prior to release, allowing maximal time to assess the offenders' needs and to begin to build the linkages to needed services (treatment, job training, housing, etc.) Early identification of eligible offenders, particularly when it does not occur at the time of sentencing, requires institutional support from both correctional and supervision agencies. Ideally, the process would be integrated with existing mechanisms already in place in order to avoid duplication of efforts.

Interventions designed to build offender motivation and readiness to change may be critical to offender success, particularly in a mandatory reentry program.
A continuing challenge for the Harlem Reentry Court is to prepare parolees for the program, a particularly thorny challenge since parolees are mandated to participate as a condition of release and given little advance notice of their selection. The Reentry Court regimen is stricter than traditional parole, with parolees held to higher behavioral standards and monitored more closely. In programs such as this, where participation is a mandatory condition of parole for selected offenders, there is less certainty that offenders will enter the program with the level of motivation and commitment to a crime- and drug-free lifestyle than they might have if participation was voluntary. Many program participants and project staff cite readiness to change as key to success. The Harlem Reentry Court highlights the need to cultivate readiness as early as possible—ideally prior to release from prison—through interventions designed to build motivation.

The Preliminary Impact of the Harlem Reentry Court

A preliminary impact evaluation examined one-year rates of reconviction and return to prison—for either a new felony conviction or technical violation of parole—among the first 45 Reentry Court participants. The analysis relies on a quasi-experi-

One-Year Recidivism Rates

	Reentry Court (N=45)	Comparison Group (N=90)
Reincarcerated within 1 Year Post-Release	22%	14%
New Felony Conviction	7%	3%
Technical Violation	15%	11%
Any New Conviction within 1 Year Post-Release	22%	30%
Any New Felony Conviction	9%	13%
Any New Misdemeanor Conviction	13%	18%
Any Drug Conviction	20%	16%
Any Non-Drug Conviction	4%	20%*

*$p < .05$ (two-tailed test)

mental design in which Reentry Court participants are compared to a matched sample of 90 parolees, highly alike on key characteristics, who were released onto parole supervision in northern Manhattan during the same one-year time period (June 1, 2001–June 1, 2002) as program participants included in the analysis. The preliminary evaluation offers a snapshot of the first 20 months of implementation, rather than a definitive analysis of the Reentry Court's operations and long-term impacts.

Key recidivism measures are presented in the table above. Overall, reconviction rates were not significantly—although they were somewhat—reduced. However, the results indicate a significant reduction in convictions on non-drug-related offenses within one year of release from prison. Reduced reconviction on non-drug-related offenses appears to reflect the Reentry Court's increased attention and scrutiny. It is unclear why similar reductions were not detected in drug-related convictions, although this may possibly reflect the long-standing and less tractable substance-abuse problems that some of the parolees face.

The results also indicate no reduction in overall rates of return to prison after one year. Indeed, the reincarceration rate for Reentry Court participants is somewhat, although not significantly, higher than the comparison group. Parolees in both groups are more likely to have been returned for a technical violation than a new felony conviction, with no difference emerging between the two groups on this measure either. Research suggests that intensive supervision alone will not reduce recidivism, and indeed may increase return to prison on technical violations, but that the integration of treatment with intensive supervision might lead to reduced recidivism.

These findings, once again, are preliminary—the small number of Reentry Court participants available for analysis considerably limits the ability to detect program impact or draw meaningful conclusions. The results are also best understood in light of the significant implementation challenges cited above. Participants in this analysis were enrolled in the Reentry Court during the early implementation period. It is not possible to make firm conclusions about the effectiveness of the Reentry Court model until it has had a chance to work with more participants. Nonetheless, this report highlights the challenges of working with a high-risk offender population that is prone to recidivism and the difficulties of implementing an innovative criminal justice partnership involving multiple players and significant changes to standard operating practice.

Future Changes to the Harlem Parole Reentry Court

Since the study period ended in January 2003, the Harlem Reentry Court has undergone several programmatic changes. Due largely to budgetary difficulties facing all state agencies, the maximum caseload of Reentry Court parole officers has increased and the administrative law judge is now available to the court one day, rather than two, per week. The program is expected to undergo additional modifications in coming months as it expands to include serious and violent offenders. Finally, in the near future, program participants are likely to spend less overall time under the supervision of the Reentry Court, although at the time of this writing the nature and scope of this change has yet to be fully determined. Although the collective impact of these changes may be considerable, key innovations—a collaborative, community-based model of treatment and supervision, oversight by an administrative law judge, an emphasis on substance abuse treatment and employment—will remain in place. This initial report suggests that there is need for continued study of the Reentry Court model to determine not only whether or not it works, but also what its impacts are across various ex-offender populations and which of its various components is most effective.

CHAPTER THIRTEEN

Towards a New Model of Judicial Innovation: Problem-Solving Justice Without Specialized Courts

DONALD J. FAROLE JR., NORA K. PUFFETT, AND MICHAEL REMPEL

As the preceding chapters make clear, courts across the country have begun to redefine their role in the administration of justice, moving to intervene in individual and social problems like addiction, mental illness, and domestic violence. This has been done primarily through the vehicle of specialized courts such as community courts, drug courts, mental health courts and domestic violence courts. While widely known for their "problem-solving" focus, these specialized courts share other unique elements, including the integration of treatment and social services into the court process, ongoing judicial supervision, a collaborative model of decision making, direct interaction between litigants and the judge, and community outreach.

There is a growing body of research to indicate that problem-solving courts, or "collaborative justice" courts as they are known in California, are successful in addressing at least some of the issues they attempt to confront. In particular, adult drug courts have been demonstrated to significantly reduce recidivism among substance-abusing defendants (see Chapter 1). Yet the limited jurisdiction and eligibility restrictions of these courts often

---

This chapter is based on a research report published in 2005 by the Judicial Council of California, Administrative Office of the Courts and underwritten by the California Administrative Office of the Courts. Any opinions and interpretations are those of the authors or, where attributed, of the focus group and interview participants. They do not necessarily represent official positions of the California Administrative Office of the Courts.

prevent them from reaching more than a small percentage of the defendants and litigants who might benefit from them (see Schafer and Zweig 2004). Thus innovators in the field have begun to explore how to institutionalize and expand problem-solving innovations to reach greater numbers and varieties of defendants, litigants, and cases—whether through the proliferation of specialized courts or the application of their core principles and practices throughout conventional court settings.

A 2000 resolution of the Conference of Chief Justices and Conference of State Court Administrators, which was reaffirmed in 2004, would seem to endorse the latter approach. Both resolutions advocated for "Encourag[ing], where appropriate, the broad integration over the next decade of the principles and methods of problem-solving courts into the administration of justice to improve court processes and outcomes while preserving the rule of law, and meeting the needs and expectations of litigants, victims, and the community" (CCJ and COSCA 2004).

In light of these resolutions, the California Administrative Office of the Courts and the Center for Court Innovation in New York initiated a research partnership to address the nature and feasibility of expanding problem-solving justice beyond the specialized court setting. In a first phase of research, we conducted focus groups and interviews with 35 problem-solving court judges in California and New York (Farole, Puffett, Rempel, and Byrne 2004). The participating judges were cautiously optimistic about the opportunities to expand the practice of problem solving, at least on a limited basis, in courts of general jurisdiction. Practices such as adopting a problem-solving orientation, engaging in interaction with defendants and other litigants, and conducting ongoing supervision of treatment cases were deemed feasible and appropriate in many general court contexts. Participants noted numerous barriers as well. Chief among those were the limited time and resources in general courts and philosophical opposition or lack of education among colleagues on the bench and in judicial leadership positions. Opposition from attorneys, probation officers, and others was also cited as a barrier.

This article presents the results of a second phase of research, in which focus groups were conducted with representatives of other stakeholder groups: attorneys (prosecutors, public defenders, and the private defense bar), probation officers, treatment and service providers, and statewide organizations (see complete research report in Farole, Puffett, and Rempel 2005). Motivating this phase of the research was the recognition—confirmed by judges in phase one—that problem-solving courts are created through the cooperative efforts of multiple agencies; hence, taking problem-solving practices to scale would inevitably require the support and commitment of justice system and social service partners.

Research Methodology

The exploratory nature of this study made focus groups the most appropriate methodology. While focus groups may draw on participants who are not representative of the general population of stakeholders, thereby limiting the ability to generalize from the findings, they can yield a wealth of information on attitudes, opinions, and suggestions on topics about which little is known.

There were a total of 24 participants in four focus group sessions, all held in California. Attempts were made to recruit participants that were familiar with the issues of interest and represented a mix of urban, suburban, and rural jurisdictions. All participants had current or past direct involvement with one or more problem-solving courts. For the attorney sessions, we attempted to recruit prosecutors, defenders, and civil attorneys representing a mix of line, supervisory, and managerial staff. For the treatment/service providers and probation session, we attempted to recruit a mix of line, supervisory, and managerial staff from probation, and representatives from several treatment and social service providers. For the statewide organizations session, we attempted to recruit representatives from statewide professional associations representing relevant stakeholders (i.e., public defenders, district attorneys, treatment providers, probation, police, and the California State Association of Counties). Actual participation divided as follows:

- *Attorneys #1*: seven participants in a Southern California (Burbank) session (three public defenders, two prosecutors, one civil law attorney, one community court coordinator);
- *Attorneys #2*: four participants in a Northern California (Sacramento) session (two prosecutors, two public defenders);
- *Treatment, Service Providers, and Probation*: eight participants in a Southern California (Burbank) session (four probation and four treatment or service provider representatives); and
- *Statewide Organizations*: five participants in a Northern California (Sacramento) session (including one representative each from statewide associations representing public defenders, probation officers, treatment professionals, police chiefs, and the California State Association of Counties).

The 24 participants also brought to the table experience with various problem-solving court models. Approximately half had some experience with adult or juvenile drug courts, one-third with mental health courts, and one-fifth with domestic violence courts. Other models with which participants had experience included youth courts, community courts, homeless courts, elder abuse courts, and driving under the influence (DUI) courts. In fact, many participants had planned or served in more than one type of problem-solving court.

To prepare for the focus groups, the research team conducted interviews with 11 representatives of similar New York stakeholder agencies, gathering background information that would help shape the focus group protocols. In spring 2005, the research team conducted telephone interviews with three court administrators in California to explore in further depth the administrative implications of applying problem-solving practices throughout the courthouse.

After a brief warm-up exercise (concerning the differences between problem-solving courts and conventional courts), participants were asked to read an outline of a hypothetical model in which general courts implement many of the practices and techniques associated with specialized problem-solving courts (see boxed text for the full statement). The description was not necessarily intended to represent a desirable, realistic, or complete model for the administration of justice. Rather, it was designed to stimulate discussion and to tap participants' immediate reactions to the prospect of applying problem-solving principles and practices outside of the specialized court setting.

Emergent Themes and Findings

Stakeholders' initial reactions to the concept of applying problem-solving principles and practices more broadly were mixed. Some participants immediately expressed their support, while many were initially skeptical, due to concerns that such an endeavor might be not only infeasible but also inappropriate. As they engaged in further discussion, however, most of these participants expressed some degree of support for the idea, identifying circumstances and cases in which they favored using problem-solving approaches on general court calendars.

Hypothetical Model of the Administration of Justice

This model of the administration of justice envisions the practices and techniques of problem-solving courts, such as drug courts, mental health courts, and domestic violence courts, applied broadly in mainstream courts throughout the court system. The approach could be applied in all courts—not just specialized courts—with the goal of enhancing courts' ability to address the underlying problems of litigants, victims, and communities.

Under this model, court operations could be characterized by elements such as:

- Problem-solving focus;
- Proactive role for the judge;
- Non-adversarial team approach to decision making;
- Integration of treatment and social services into the court process;
- Ongoing judicial supervision of the treatment process;
- Direct interaction between litigants and the judge; and
- Community outreach.

While the discussion in all focus groups was often theoretical and speculative, as is expected of reactions to a hypothetical construct, three clear themes emerged:

1. Most stakeholders favored the broader application of problem-solving practices in conventional courts, at least under certain circumstances.

2. This general support was tempered by a number of concerns, principally about the feasibility of the broad application of problem-solving approaches and about the appropriateness of such approaches in certain settings.

3. Stakeholders identified a number of steps that could be taken to facilitate the broader application of problem solving, but emphasized proceeding with caution.

1. General Support *Most stakeholders favored the broader application of problem-solving practices in conventional courts, at least under certain circumstances.*

Most focus group participants supported selectively applying problem-solving practices in conventional courts; one attorney commented that this "would be a great direction to move in." Participants noted that this would allow the justice system to address defendants' underlying problems, which is "not only more appropriate, but... [more likely to generate] a long-term solution." Another attorney believed that such an "outcomes-orientation" could help to generate support for change among key players in the justice system. This attorney argued that, for example, if problem-solving approaches can be shown to reduce criminal recidivism, prosecutors might be more likely to support them. And indeed, some participants argued that the efficacy of problem solving has been established, and thus its integration into the broader system should be regarded simply as the dissemination of best practices.

Although very few stakeholders argued that problem-solving should never be applied outside the specialized court setting, there was widespread agreement that some cases "will never be appropriate ... [for] this model." Attorneys were, in general, somewhat more skeptical than other stakeholders, primarily due to concerns that problem-solving approaches within general criminal courts in particular might infringe upon the adversarial process.

Specific Cases and Calendars

In considering which types of cases and court calendars might be more or less appropriate for problem solving, the discussion mirrored that of judges in the previous study (Farole et al. 2004). In criminal matters, participants identified as a deciding factor the presence of an underlying problem that contributes to a defendant's criminal behavior and can be addressed by court intervention. For example, one attorney spoke about problem-solving interventions for the "basic three [problems]: drug addiction, mental illness, and domestic violence." Another attorney suggested that prostitution cases can also be appropriate for treatment and service interventions, and others added DUI cases to the list.

One prosecutor, while agreeing with these positions, stressed that courts must distinguish cases in which addiction, mental illness, or other problems motivate the criminal behavior from cases in which the defendant "is a criminal who also happens to be an addict" (i.e., underlying problems are not criminogenic factors). This participant felt that defendants in the latter category should not be considered for a problem-solving approach.

Most focus group participants seemed to agree that problem-solving solutions are unlikely to be, and should not be, applied to violent crimes (with the possible exception of domestic violence cases). One attorney commented that it "will be way down the road before [problem solving] works for arsonists or violent offenders."

The question of violence aside, one participant in the focus groups (and several involved in individual interviews) believed that felony cases may be more appropriate than misdemeanors for problem-solving solutions that are likely to involve lengthy treatment mandates. This was attributed not only to the fact that felony defendants have a greater legal incentive to comply with a lengthy treatment mandate than misdemeanants (i.e., they face a more significant penalty for failure), but also to the perception that there are greater resources available (e.g., in probation departments) for monitoring felony cases.

In addition to criminal matters, juvenile court, family law, small claims court, and other civil courts were also mentioned by some as quite appropriate for problem-solving practices. Again, some caveats were made, with several participants identifying business litigation in particular as unlikely to be resolved through problem-solving approaches because "a lot of money is at stake."

Current Practice

An additional theme that emerged in all focus groups, but received the most extensive discussion among attorneys, was that practices identified with problem-solving courts, particularly treatment mandates, are in fact already applied in general court calendars, albeit informally and unsystematically:

> *The judges are doing [problem-solving], but they don't have uniformity, they don't have resource organization... So the courts are doing this in a patchwork way.*

> *Some courts simply make... treatment plans informally, make treatment plans part of the conditions of probation, and schedule regular court reviews so that they're overseeing it... The treatment process is very informal. It's not a collaborative court. There aren't partners sitting at the table... It's just the judges' way of doing business... I think that in mainstream courts informally much of this is going on.*

Informal problem-solving approaches were believed to occur more often in smaller jurisdictions, with one participant declaring that "attorneys have been doing this is my small community for almost 20 years... [In a] small town, it begins more as a problem-solving approach to criminal justice" because "everybody knows everybody." Smaller jurisdictions also have fewer players (judges, attorneys, probation officers, etc.) and less frequent changes of assignment, all of which facilitate the development of the working relationships necessary for a problem-solving approach, relationships that may be harder to forge in larger jurisdictions.

When asked for examples of the informal practice of problem solving in general courts, an attorney who works extensively with a specialized mental health court reported "try[ing] to do a little mental health court in every courtroom." On an informal, case-by-case basis, this attorney attempts to educate general calendar judges about clients who require judicial monitoring. And, although "it is not the same warm atmosphere as there would be in a mental health court," these defendants do come back to court for progress reports. The attorney also arranges, again informally, for many higher-risk offenders who are technically ineligible for mental health court (due to past history of violence, sex offender status, etc.) to remain under court monitoring during the probation period by reporting to the master calendar judge.

Another participant from a larger jurisdiction believed that many judges there were quite often imposing treatment mandates in lieu of jail and having certain defendants report back to court for monitoring. However, this participant cautioned that the practice varies widely throughout the courthouse, depending on the philosophy of each individual judge and the availability of resources like probation or case management staff.

2. Barriers *This support was tempered by a number of concerns, principally about the feasibility of the broad application of problem-solving approaches and about the appropriateness of such approaches in certain settings.*

While many participants, in principle, supported the application of problem-solving practices in conventional courts, support was tempered by a number of concerns. Two that were discussed extensively in all sessions were limitations on time and resources, and the need to preserve the adversarial process in general calendar settings. A third group of concerns related to the receptivity, experience, and motivation of justice system stakeholders, particularly judges and attorneys. Several other concerns were raised as well.

Limitations on Time and Resources

Focus group participants spoke at great length about the heavy caseloads in conventional courts and the limited time and resources available to apply problem-solving approaches more broadly. For some, this issue seemed insurmountable:

> *There is just not enough time on a court date to accommodate this, unless you create the increased court staff and the number of judges.*

It'll never happen—putting billions of dollars, and that's what we're talking about here, billions of dollars, into rehabilitation and [reducing] recidivism.

Who's going to pay for it? ... That's the gorilla in the room.

Court Capacity

A number of capacity-related concerns were mentioned. Focus group participants cited the limited time available for assessment and individualized attention to cases, particularly in larger, urban jurisdictions and in high-volume courts:

...Misdemeanor arraignment [is] so busy. There's not enough time for defendants to actually engage with the judge and converse about what your issues are and have the judge provide feedback.

What we can't forget is the caseloads that we are facing. We are constantly going through cases... We have to be practical about it. Because in an ideal world, it would be great to sit down and get to know [every] person and figure out how we can help... maybe ultimately that will decrease the amount of cases and that'll be a really good thing. But we also have to look at the time that we're given.

In the treatment and probation session, participants also noted the lack of case management and assessment staff available in general courts.

Community Service Capacity

In addition to the court's capacity to administer problem-solving practices, focus group participants spoke extensively about the community's capacity to provide necessary treatment and other services, worrying that "If the courts open their doors to anyone who needs a certain kind of treatment... the resources aren't out there." Many noted that residential treatment is especially problematic; as the most costly form of treatment, its availability is limited, and waiting lists are long. The availability of treatment for juveniles, mental health and dual diagnosis services, and job training in many communities was also questioned. Some treatment and service providers also worried that, even in communities with the necessary services, most courts lack the staffing and resources to identify and develop relationships with service providers.

A related barrier regarded the quality of available services. Participants in all focus groups cited an insufficient number of certified treatment programs adhering to best practice guidelines:

> *Our biggest concern is making sure treatment providers are certified and offer the treatment that is necessary.*

> *[Treatment providers] need to be held accountable for using professional level services and evidence-based practices. And they need to be able to document fidelity to those evidence-based practices.*

Probation Capacity

Finally, participants in all focus groups acknowledged that probation is "overloaded and undermanned and under-budgeted." They noted that many probation departments are struggling to maintain even minimal levels of supervision, and doubted that they could provide the additional monitoring and service coordination that might be required in the absence of additional staff. One probation officer speculated that this could create a "conflict between reality and expectations," as probation would be unable to meet the court's requirements.

The Need to Preserve the Adversarial Process

Participants in all focus groups spoke about the need to retain the adversarial process, particularly in criminal court settings. The topic was discussed extensively among attorneys, many of whom considered it just as critical a barrier as limited resources, if not more so:

> *In the end there needs to be a model where people really go at it.*

> *There are some cases where... the crime is the thing, [cases] that simply are not [appropriate] for this process. The courts tend to be, and really should be, adversarial environments.*

This concern was expressed by both prosecutors and defense counsel. The latter noted that it is their responsibility to zealously defend clients and protect their due process rights, and that in some cases this precludes a collaborative approach. One voiced concern that in less adversarial court settings, judges "become advocates and not the arbiters that they ought to be." Judges attempting to take on such a "non-traditional" role might, therefore, expect resistance from the defense bar. One defense attorney, for example, noted that at present, if general calendar judges "even veer towards talking [with the client in open court] about anything regarding the case, I stop them." Problem solving might require more open communication among the parties, but "I don't see that as translating into a regular courtroom."

Prosecutors, for their part, also spoke about the value of an adversarial criminal justice system in enhancing public safety:

> *A prosecutor's job has more to do with the security and the safety of society... [than] the well-being of the client... When we're looking at a problem we're not looking at 'Hey, what's good for this guy?' We're looking at, 'Hey, what's good for the safety of the community?'*

Stakeholder Opposition or Hesitancy

Participants in all groups identified multiple concerns related to the ability and willingness of stakeholders, particularly judges and attorneys, to adopt problem-solving methods outside of a specialized environment. They argued that many stakeholders would oppose the concept outright, while even those who were amenable to it might be dissuaded by perceived institutional disinterest and a lack of relevant knowledge and skills. This latter challenge, some suggested, would be overcome only through education of stakeholders system-wide, and would require significant revision of current training and continuing education programs.

Opposition from the Bench and Bar

Stakeholders worried that judges, prosecutors, and defense counsel would be reluctant to embrace an approach that is so contrary to the traditional adversarial model of litigation:

> *A lot of people will have problems with that. There are judges, there are prosecutors and probably even defenders who think that [problem solving] has no place [in the system... That attitude is] especially obvious when you get into more serious crimes and felonies.*

> *People who participate in problem solving believe in it. And there are many people, most people, in the criminal justice system who are not of that mind.*

Attorneys indicated that many of their colleagues would not endorse the broader application of problem solving. Explained one defense attorney:

> *This is not what [defense attorneys] got into it for. They are there to protect the client's rights. They run the motions and try cases. The head of my office is very supportive of collaborative courts, but in their place. The rest of the office... [believes in] fighting the fight.*

A district attorney agreed that, among prosecutors too, "it's a pretty hard sell." Assigning a prosecutor to a problem-solving court "is like sending them to Siberia," he said. He went on to distinguish among different types of problem-solving courts, arguing that domestic violence court is a "much easier sell" than drug court to most prosecutors, presumably because domestic violence courts place less emphasis on defendant rehabilitation and more on prosecution of the offenders and victim safety.

Professional Incentives

Several focus group participants were skeptical that judges and attorneys, particularly prosecutors, would practice problem solving given the current incentives for advancement and promotion:

> *It's unrealistic in terms of the incentives that exist... judges are not promoted by virtue of supporting collaborative courts... There would need to be a reappraisal of incentives for some of the heavy hitters in the criminal courts, the judges and the D.A.s.*

Various participants mentioned that judges are evaluated and promoted based on such measures as effective docket management and publications, prosecutors on conviction rates. Neither, therefore, has strong professional motivation to support problem solving. Participants also suggested that those district attorneys and judges who are elected may have an additional incentive to avoid collaborative approaches:

> *Elected judges have political considerations—they would not want to be looked [at] as soft on crime, you're letting all the criminals loose, etc.*

> *District attorney[s] in California are political and see very little value in constructing a non-adversarial kind of approach to a criminal offender. They collect their skulls on convictions in state prison.*

However, at least one participant in the treatment stakeholder group suggested that electoral considerations could induce judges and prosecutors to support rather than oppose problem solving if the community demanded it.

Efficacy: "Diluting the Model"

Some focus group participants felt that problem-solving courts work precisely because they take "very small bites of the apple," while larger endeavors might lose their efficacy:

> *The problem-solving system works... because we... focus the attention of all parties... on a particular problem, train them and try to get the resources together. You lose that efficacy once you start trying to make it into a general proposition. And therefore, I believe the more practical [approach] is to continue to do these small boutique courts... We can focus our attention on some of the solvable problems.*

It's a great concept, it's a great idea, but we don't want to become ineffective because we're expanding.

These discussions seemed to reflect a belief held by most stakeholders—not only attorneys—that it may be preferable to allocate limited resources to more intensive interventions in fewer cases, as is currently done in specialized problem-solving courts. Attempting to apply problem-solving solutions to larger numbers of cases on general calendars, some participants feared, could spread resources too thinly. While these themes were raised by only two or three participants in each focus group, they were not disputed by others.

Participants raised related concerns about how effective problem-solving practices would be in general courts, particularly if the practices are applied piecemeal rather than as an integrated whole, the "full model." They noted that general courts lack the reduced caseloads, additional staff, established ties to community-based service providers, and other resources available to specialized problem-solving courts, and worried this would make the interventions less effective. Several stakeholders across focus groups also questioned whether and how the team-based, non-adversarial model, which is "relationship-driven" and requires "trust" among relevant personnel, could be taken to scale:

[In specialized courts,] whether you communicate with a judge or a PO [probation officer] for treatment or a coordinator, you ... have some sort of relationship with them. If we were to take this to scale and you lost that kind of relationship, what would you be losing and what would you need in order to be able to continue functioning? ... How would you interact with a whole courthouse instead of just a courtroom?

3. Next Steps *Stakeholders identified a number of steps that could be taken to facilitate the broader application of problem solving, but emphasized proceeding with caution.*

Having identified a host of potential barriers to the broader application of problem-solving practices throughout the courts, focus group participants proceeded to suggest several steps that could be taken to overcome them. According to one participant:

> *The demand is there, I think from all the key players. Participants, defendants, prosecution, defense, courts, in-service providers alike, they need a venue in which to solve the problems they're facing. And whether it's through the specialty courts we have or expanding it one county at a time, there have to be some mechanisms established to open that door a little bit further.*

An overarching theme was that change should be introduced cautiously and incrementally. For instance, it was proposed that a pilot project be introduced in a small number of counties: "I think you'd have to start like you did with drug court: Do it in some courts; try it out. Figure out what works and what doesn't." One participant recommended selecting one trial court in northern California and one in southern California.

Alternatively, initial efforts might be restricted to particular types of cases and calendars. Participants generally recommended cases for which there are already specialized courts, particularly those involving domestic violence, juvenile delinquency, or a need for substance abuse or mental health treatment. Several noted that the existing problem-solving courts do not reach all potential cases, so there would certainly be room for expansion. Although most problem-solving courts deal with criminal matters, the discussion of appropriate courts and calendars often emphasized the family and dependency arena (juvenile delinquency, abuse and neglect, and matrimonial matters). One reason for this is that the adversarial process is less of a barrier on such calendars: "It's generally a less adversarial court than a criminal court, which is the fundamental key." The phase one research (Farole et al. 2004) evidenced a similar trend, suggesting consensus among stakeholders on this subject.

An important qualification regarding these and other points discussed below is that they tended to reflect the "top of mind" reactions of a small number of focus group participants. While participants rarely objected to their colleagues' comments, they often moved to other topics without responding or elaborating, making it difficult to assess the degree of consensus.

Laying the Groundwork

Training and Education

Participants in all focus groups believed that, before problem solving can be practiced on a wide scale, judges, attorneys, probation officers, and other justice system players would require extensive training and education. Training could introduce these professionals to core problem-solving concepts, change oppositional attitudes, and provide the skills necessary for effective problem-solving practice. Participants suggested that judges could easily be trained during new judge orientation and in other forums attended by more experienced judges. Similar opportunities exist for other justice system personnel:

> *There's a core training for probation officers that's mandated by law. [Problem solving] could be part of a day in court training for probation. District attorneys, public defenders have ongoing training.*

One attorney argued that problem solving needs to be taught even earlier, in law school, if only because "judges have to go to law school." Others recognized that education takes time:

> *It's a generational thing; we're not going to see it in your lifetime. Not in my lifetime either, none of our lifetimes. But if slowly we start introducing the concept to people who are coming up through the system maybe that's a way to build.*

Judicial and Community Leadership

Echoing a central theme from the earlier focus groups, participants believed that judicial leadership was a necessary precondition for any substantial expansion in the reach of problem solving. One participant illustrated the importance of judicial leadership in describing how a local problem-solving court was started:

> *There was a homeless court that a judge expressed interest in getting together, started the preliminary work and then came [up] against some obstacles; finally, got a call from the chief judge: 'Make it happen.' And that provided the impetus within the court to help open that door and establish their homeless court.*

Several of the representatives of statewide organizations added that initiating any expansion of problem solving outside of a specialized court would require the support of the heads of county agencies:

> *This would have to be blessed by the county administrative office. And supported from the county administrative office and the board of supervisors down to the district attorney, who is a political figure, as the courts are... [S]o you're taking all those*

political environments in hand. You'd have to really get the blessing of the entire county.

Participants in several groups suggested that community pressure could influence county leaders. This in turn suggested a need to disseminate information about the problem-solving approach to the public in order to raise awareness and (perhaps) support. One participant illustrated the point with reference to Proposition 36, a ballot initiative approved by California voters to expand treatment opportunities for substance-addicted criminal defendants:

To build any type of investment in this model... one possible way that could occur, your last point being your community outreach. Judges and D.A.s are elected officials and if the community has an interest in these kinds of innovative programs, backed up by outcome research, as we all saw with Prop. 36, the D.A.s and many judges were shocked that the public would support that kind of innovative approach to drug abusers.

Other Steps

Although the subject did not receive a great deal of attention, some participants flagged a need to increase statewide treatment capacity, particularly for residential substance abuse and mental health treatment. Indeed, a study of the implementation of Proposition 36 in California found that the capacity for residential substance abuse treatment is in many counties far less than that for outpatient treatment; and for this reason, the overwhelming majority of treatment mandates under Proposition 36 have been to outpatient services (Longshore et al. 2003). In addition, several participants expressed concern that justice system stakeholders are often unaware of what services and facilities are available.

Finally, participants in two focus groups suggested that new policies might need to be implemented to enable clients to identify their personal problems or service needs without facing adverse legal consequences. Otherwise, it would be difficult for the defense attorney to have a frank discussion with the prosecutor and judge about a criminal defendant's need for treatment. As one participant explained, "[A defense attorney's] concern is, you get into a room and he says, 'Yes, my client did X, Y, and Z, and this is how he did it, and here's what's behind it.' And then if... it goes back to criminal court he's afraid that there may be testimony that his client did X, Y, and Z." In a specialized problem-solving court setting, the key players have typically built up a level of trust, leading everyone to believe that needs assessment-related information will not be used against a client's legal interests: "It has to be a trust issue. And it has to be built over time." However, some participants felt that more formal legislative protections might be necessary if problem solving was expanded to involve greater numbers of judges, prosecutors, and defense attorneys.

In light of this last consideration, some participants felt that the broader practice of problem solving would have greater potential in a smaller county, where existing personal and professional relationships might make judges and attorneys more likely to trust each other with sensitive information, even without the protection of formal agreements:

> *Do they share information [in small courts]? Yes, they do, because... it's relationship-driven. They have the trust and the relationship to say, 'Let's talk about this, we're going to share information. With one goal: what's the best thing for this person. If we decide that we can't make it work and they're going off down this criminal path, there's an understanding that we're not going to use this.' ... Informally, this is happening.*

Operational Changes

The final portion of the focus group protocols in both the justice and treatment/probation sessions was dedicated to questions about operational change at the courthouse level: For those elements of the problem-solving approach that could and should be more broadly applied, how might implementation proceed? This part of the protocol was the most challenging to participants, since it asked them to give close consideration to the implementation of what was only a loosely defined hypothetical model of the administration of justice. Yet, the ensuing discussion did identify a few subjects as critical:

- Early screening and assessment;
- New roles for prosecutors, defense attorneys, and probation;
- Some level of staff specialization;
- Revised protocols for judicial supervision; and
- Courthouse-based case management resources.

Early Screening and Assessment

While differing on how screening and assessment might be conducted, and by whom, participants agreed that it should occur as early as possible, ideally pre-arraignment. Several suggested that the assessment might begin even before a criminal case has reached the court, if police officers were trained to identify defendants with obvious treatment needs. A number of participants believed that the public defender had a critical role in screening the case:

> *I would assume [assessment would begin with] the public defender's contact with the client... the public defender would probably need to be aware of certain questions they need to ask. Maybe have an intake tool. And that way, they can assess*

> *whether or not this individual needs to take advantage of this treatment team, or mental health service providers.*

While no participant disagreed that the public defender was in an ideal position, two caveats were raised. First, this approach would require public defenders to make clinical assessments for which they are not qualified. The prosecutor might therefore view the resulting recommendations with skepticism. One prosecutor felt that the use of some kind of standardized instrument would help to increase a prosecutor's level of trust in what the public defender claimed to have discovered:

> *... [The use of] an intake interview, a psychometric [instrument] ... [would] go on a long way in being able to trust the outcomes and the solutions of the issues. Currently, if somebody [a defense attorney] comes up to me and says, 'Hey, look, this guy's crazy' or 'He's got a drug problem'... [what evidence do I have of] the validity of that issue?*

Second, as previously discussed, for public defenders to share their information freely with the prosecutor and the judge, agreements might need to be forged to protect that information from subsequent use against the client. As one defense attorney noted, "This would all require a safe environment for the client so that there were policies amongst the D.A. and the public defender and the courts that anything the client said would never be used if their case stays on the trial track."

New Roles for Justice System Stakeholders

The common thread running through discussions of individual stakeholders' roles was that they would all have to become more proactive and collaborative. Public defenders and, to a lesser extent, prosecutors would have to embrace the extra-legal roles of identifying problems and treatment needs, and proposing treatment or social service plans. Explained one prosecutor: "We have to start working together right from the get-go" while also expanding the range of activity included in case preparation: "As a prosecutor, you find out things by talking to your victim, by talking to witnesses, by talking to your police officer."

Judges would similarly have to adapt. A proactive judge could promote a problem-solving resolution when the attorneys could not agree to one, or could help finalize an agreement reached through initial discussions held among the attorneys. According to one participant in the statewide organizations session:

> *I would see the D.A. and the public defender... [discussing] this before it gets to the judge, so that there's consensus hopefully when it gets to the judge. And then the judge can ask some questions and say, 'Yes, this can go to this thing [a treatment track], set up a meeting for it,' or 'Heck no, nobody agrees and we go after criminals.'*

Another participant stressed, however, that while the defense attorney might relay a defendant's possible interest in a program, a truly proactive judge could take the lead in moving the parties forward to a final resolution. Commenting on the practice of some judges in this participant's court:

> *Often, the judge is making offers or discussing it, and defense counsel will make a pitch, and the judge will make a decision ... on a felony arraignment calendar [the judge might propose] 'You're here for arraignment, here are the charges, if you're going to plead guilty, here's what I'll offer. Your attorney said you'd be amenable to a program, so here are the terms and conditions, and what's your decision?'*

Continued Specialization

Although the concept of applying problem solving more broadly connotes doing so outside the confines of specialized courts, opinion nonetheless seemed to converge around the necessity of preserving some degree of specialization. This was attributed in part to the implausibility of the majority of judges and attorneys in any given courthouse embracing problem-solving practices in the near future. It was also argued that some level of specialization and centralization may be more efficient for stakeholder agencies. As one defense attorney reflected:

> *I think the collaborative courts work better when the prosecutor, the defense attorney, probation, whoever's involved, are especially assigned... rather than asking your line attorneys to spend 10 percent or 20 percent of their time being collaborative courts attorneys. Or probation officers being collaborative probation officers... These cases, the collaborative cases, are different, and they really work well only when the people working in those courts can devote pretty much all of their time to that particular assignment.*

How might some degree of continued specialization be achieved? Participants in three of the focus groups suggested variations on the idea of a "problem-solving" track encompassing a limited number of courtrooms, judges, and attorneys within a particular courthouse, with "a clear-cut delineation" between the two tracks, "because this will never overtake the criminal justice system adversarial process, nor should it."

> *...The cases in theory can come through any arraignment court or any criminal court in the system. But once they were identified as a drug treatment [case] or a case with mental health issues, an efficient way to do it would be to funnel that to a par-*

ticular judge and to a particular group of attorneys and probation officers who deal with those cases. So they might come in from a variety of locations, but be funneled into a court or a series of courts dealing with those particular issues.

Many participants agreed that the decision of whether cases would be funneled to the proposed "problem-solving" track or continued on a more conventional "guilt or innocence" track would need to be made early—by arraignment or, at the latest, after arraignment but prior to an adjournment to a trial calendar. Two participants in the statewide organizations group both advocated this approach, commenting:

I can see a collaborative approach up to that point. From the time it gets to the system until the time it is determined whether this thing is going to go to trial or not.

If you come in at that stage, between arraignment and the matter of being signed off for trial... we can take it out of the [conventional] track for a moment, put it over here and say let's bring in the social worker, let's bring in probation, let's bring in treatment and see whether or not this guy's amenable to some, some type of [treatment] thing.

Revised Protocols for Judicial Supervision

Although focus group participants observed during the warm-up exercise that judicial supervision was an important component of problem-solving courts, many were skeptical that it could be implemented with the same frequency and intensity on general court calendars. This concern applied especially to high volume courts in large urban areas:

> *The practicality of translating this check-in every week to a felony judge who is doing preliminary hearings in a lower court: impossible, because they don't want to. Their calendars are too heavy... They want to get everything done, they want as little as possible on their calendar, and they are not going to let someone just come in to say 'Hello' every week, which is what they need.*

One suggested alternative was for probation to perform more of the monitoring typically conducted by the dedicated judge in problem-solving courts. However, a probation representative worried about placing more reporting pressures on probation officers and treatment and social service providers, and several other participants were concerned that monitoring might lose its impact if not conducted in court by a judge, which research has shown to be critical to program success. As one attorney opined, "The amount of attention, the checking-in with the judge: that is what is central to the operation of the court and to the success of the participants in the court that I work in, no question about it."

Courthouse-Based Case Management Resources

Several participants felt strongly that having case management and treatment resources available in the courthouse would be invaluable. Such resources could aid judges and attorneys in assessing litigants' problems and in finding appropriate treatment or social services. Further, having resources in the courthouse would also increase the likelihood that defendants actually reach those services. Observed one attorney, "The resources almost have to be in court because the clients get lost if they're told, 'Show up in probation a week from now and treatment center two weeks from now.' They go out into society and disappear."

While no consensus was reached on how to implement on-site case management, participants advances several suggestions.

One was to hire a small number of case managers or counselors who could be available to judges throughout a particular courthouse or perhaps even throughout all courthouses from a particular county. One participant illustrated this idea with reference to an elder abuse case manager in this participant's court:

> *She works throughout [the] county with other courts where there is perhaps a more traditional approach, where there's not a separate [problem-solving] calendar. But she is available because in this instance, these courts are held on separate days. She is available to all the judges and she brings those resources literally to them. That's where I'd put money.*

Another participant suggested that on-site case management should be provided not by the court itself but by dedicated staff from community-based agencies:

> *If you could possibly create a treatment team, where you would have different agencies represented, mental health, employment agencies... housing, just have a variety of service providers present as a treatment team, possibly available to the court. So that way defendants can be identified as eligible to go to this treatment team and... be assessed as to what resources could be made available to him or her to help them better themselves.*

In considering how problem solving might be implemented with only the limited resources now available, participants suggested that courts might need to select only the neediest cases for service mandates or ongoing monitoring. They also thought that, in the absence of a specialized court's dedicated case management staff, defense attorneys and prosecutors might take a more active role in the identification of appropriate cases, as discussed earlier.

Conclusions and Next Steps

Across this study and the previous phase of research considering the judicial perspective, numerous stakeholders offered their perspectives, insights, and experiences about an issue receiving increased attention among justice system professionals in recent years. We conclude by discussing common themes and lessons from the two phases of research now completed, and potential next steps.

Opportunities currently exist to apply problem solving more broadly

Participants in all focus groups recognized the potential, and the need, to integrate principles and methods from problem-solving courts into general calendar settings. Participants recognized that specialized problem-solving courts currently handle only a small fraction of the criminal cases in which defendants' underlying problems (e.g., addiction, mental health issues) contribute to their criminal behavior; therefore, it would be productive to expand problem-solving solutions for these types of cases, so that more of those in need could actually be served. Other types of cases (e.g., juvenile delinquency, civil cases that can be resolved through alternative dispute resolution) and calendars (e.g., family law) are also ripe for broader applications of problem solving. For these reasons, participants urged the courts to continue to explore how problem-solving principles and methods might be productively integrated into general court settings.

Courts should move forward cautiously and incrementally

Participants supported integrating problem-solving methods into the administration of justice but, particularly in the current study, urged court systems to proceed cautiously. An incremental process might begin with only a few trial counties, or might initially restrict the range of cases and calendars to be included.

Participants also urged that careful consideration be given to which practices can and should be integrated into general court practice, given limited resources, the demands of the adversarial process, and existing knowledge of best practices. Finally, participants cautioned against setting unrealistic expectations for what problem solving can accomplish.

Courts should expect to face obstacles
All focus groups identified numerous barriers, but two were most prominent:

> *Limited resources* Problem-solving approaches require a substantial investment of time and resources, both of which are in short supply in the justice system. Particular deficits cited by participants included limited court time for individualized attention and ongoing judicial supervision, a lack of case management and treatment resources, and chronic under-funding of probation.
>
> *Philosophical opposition* Focus group participants felt that many judges, prosecutors, and defense attorneys would oppose problem solving in general courts, particularly to the extent that it contradicts traditional models of adversarial litigation and judicial demeanor.

In addition, the attorneys in the current study (much more so than the judges included in the Phase One research) placed significant emphasis on the need to preserve certain elements of the traditional adversarial process, particularly in criminal courts.

Court systems can take steps to facilitate the broader practice of problem solving

Across the two phases of research, a few concrete steps were commonly suggested:

Education and training Recognizing that many stakeholders are unfamiliar with or opposed to problem-solving methods and principles, all participants cited the need for extensive education and training among judges, attorneys, probation officers, and others. Education should begin as early as law school.

Leadership Focus group participants felt that the judicial and political leadership can promote problem-solving practices by sending the message that these practices are not only permissible but encouraged. The judges included in the phase one research placed the greatest emphasis upon judicial leadership, while the stakeholders included in the current study also discussed the role of leadership emanating from prosecutor offices, public defenders, other county agencies, and the public at large.

Addressing resource constraints While acknowledging the enormous challenge posed by any attempted expansion of resources, participants urged the court system to explore possibilities in this area, including the potential for making more efficient use of the resources now available. Specific suggestions included centralization of service coordination and compliance monitoring within courthouses, development of jurisdiction-wide lists of community service providers, and greater funding of treatment.

In addition, the sessions in the current study were intended to explore implementation issues in greater detail than had been done with the judges in phase one. A few of the more notable recommendations were for public defenders to play an expanded role in identifying cases for a problem-solving approach, and for some level of specialization to be maintained in the courthouse, whereby certain court parts, judges, and attorneys might dedicate at least part of their time to a "problem-solving track," while others would not have to be involved. This type of system would require screening litigants at the earliest possible time, so that they could be routed to the appropriate track near the outset of case processing.

Future Directions

This research project was conducted among multiple justice system and treatment/service provider stakeholders with experience in and familiarity with problem-solving courts. A common message from these stakeholders was that promoting problem solving throughout court systems will depend on the receptivity and participation of judges, attorneys, and others who may not have any problem-solving court experience. A next logical step would therefore be to conduct a systematic survey among general calendar judges and attorneys concerning their knowledge, attitudes, and current practices relating to problem solving, as well as their receptivity to problem-solving training and to changing their practices in the future (such a survey is in fact underway with respect to trial court judges nationwide). Subsequent research might also test the impact of any pilot experiments (in California or elsewhere) aimed at integrating problem-solving practices on to the general bench. National interest is clearly growing in broader applications of problem-solving approaches, but the extent to which this interest can yield to feasible plans for implementation remains to be examined. What this research project makes clear, however, is that at least in principle, the potential exists for problem solving to be practiced both in specialized and conventional court settings.

Contributors

Greg Berman

Greg Berman is the director of the Center for Court Innovation and co-author of *Good Courts: The Case for Problem-Solving Justice* (The New Press, 2005). He co-edited *A Problem-Solving Revolution: Making Change Happen in State Courts* (Center for Court Innovation, 2004). In addition, he has contributed to the American Bar Association's *Judges' Journal* (guest editor), *Law and Policy, New York Sun* (op-ed), *Justice System Journal, New Statesman* (United Kingdom), *Judicature, American Criminal Law Review* and other publications.

Amanda B. Cissner

Amanda B. Cissner is a senior research associate at the Center for Court Innovation. She is currently working on an impact evaluation of the Brooklyn Youthful Offender Domestic Violence Court, a randomized trial of judicial monitoring at the Monroe County (N.Y.) Integrated Domestic Violence Court, and several additional domestic violence-related projects.

Robert C. Davis

Robert C. Davis is a senior research associate at the Rand Corporation. He has directed more than 30 projects on policing, domestic violence, victimization, crime prevention and prosecution for federal and state governments, and private foundations. His interests include police accountability, citizen experiences with the police, reducing repeat victimization, private policing, and victim experiences in the criminal justice system. He is the author of two books on crime prevention and editor of five books on crime prevention and crime victims.

Donald J. Farole Jr.

Donald J. Farole Jr. is a senior research associate at the Center for Court Innovation. Currently, he is principal investigator of a national survey of trial court judges concerning problem-solving justice, and serves as chief data analyst on an ongoing multi-site adult drug court evaluation. He coauthored a statewide evaluation of New York's drug courts. Prior to joining the Center, he conducted research on state appellate courts, publishing several articles and a book, *Interest Groups and Judicial Federalism* (1998). Dr. Farole received his Ph.D. in Political Science from Indiana University.

M. Somjen Frazer

M. Somjen Frazer is a senior research associate at the Center for Court Innovation. She conducts research and evaluation projects at the Red Hook Community Justice Center and serves as a program evaluator for TEACH, an HIV/AIDS and substance abuse prevention program for teenagers. Prior to her work with the Center, she was a Rhodes Scholar at Oxford University, where her research focused on police responses to hate crime.

Chandra Gavin

Chandra Gavin is a senior research analyst at the Center for Applied Research & Technical Assistance, Inc. She was formerly a research associate at the Center for Court Innovation, where she analyzed the predictors of offender compliance at the Bronx Misdemeanor Domestic Violence Court, among other projects.

Dana Kralstein

Dana Kralstein is associate director of research at the Center for Court Innovation. Ms. Kralstein studies drug courts and community courts. She is currently involved in a multi-site adult drug court evaluation; is the principal investigator on a study of the effectiveness of a community justice initiative in Baltimore, Maryland; and supervises researchers at two New York City community courts.

Melissa Labriola

Melissa Labriola is a senior research associate at the Center for Court Innovation. She recently participated in a national study to determine court responses to offender noncompliance with batterer program mandates. She is currently conducting an evaluation of the Queens Misdemeanor Treatment Court and a formative program evaluation of the New York City Coalition Against the Commercial Sexual Exploitation of Children. Ms. Labriola received a Master's Degree in Sociology from George Washington University and is currently pursuing her Ph.D. from the Graduate Center, The City University of New York.

Kelli D. Moore

Kelli D. Moore is a former research associate at the Red Hook Community Justice Center where she researched public health issues, among other topics. She is a graduate of Wellesley College and currently a doctoral student at the University of California, San Diego, Department of Communication. Her research interests include policy reform, deliberative democracy, public space, and aesthetics.

Kelly O'Keefe

Kelly O'Keefe is a senior research associate at the Center for Court Innovation. Ms. O'Keefe is working on an evaluation of an

HIV/AIDS and substance abuse prevention program for teenagers and serves as the chair of the Center's Institutional Review Board. She received her B.A. from Marquette University and a Master's in Public Health from the University of North Carolina at Chapel Hill.

Nora K. Puffett

Nora Puffett is a program analyst at the New York City Department of Health and Mental Hygeine. She was formerly a senior research associate at the Center for Court Innovation, where her work focused primarily on domestic violence courts and problem-solving justice. She recently served as principal investigator on an in-depth process and impact evaluation of one of New York State's new integrated (civil and criminal) domestic violence courts; and collaborated on several focus group studies of the potential to apply the problem-solving court approach more broadly throughout the court system.

Michael Rempel

Michael Rempel is research director at the Center for Court Innovation and is actively involved in projects focusing on drug courts and domestic violence courts. He recently directed a statewide evaluation of New York's adult drug courts. He is currently principal investigator of a national study of domestic violence courts; co-principal investigator of a multi-site evaluation of adult drug courts around the country; and is participating in research on the potential to apply the problem-solving court° approach more broadly throughout the court system.

Robert V. Wolf

Robert V. Wolf is director of communications at the Center for Court Innovation. His work has appeared in numerous publications, including *The Justice System Journal, The Judges' Journal,*

Journal of the Center for Families, Children & the Courts, Crime & Justice International, Texas Journal of Corrections and *Perspectives,* the official journal of the American Probation and Parole Association. He is a co-editor and a contributing author of *A Problem-Solving Revolution: Making Change Happen in State Courts* (2004), published by the Center for Court Innovation.

Notes

Chapter 1: The State of Drug Court Research

1. Concerning a baseline for what retention might look like in the worst performing drug courts, in a study of 11 New York State drug courts, the one with the lowest one year retention rate was found to have a rate of 47 percent (Rempel et al. 2003).

2. Results exceeded the statistical margin of error in five of the six New York State sites. The New York study also found significant reductions in recidivism (in five of six sites) over a one-year post-program period, which involves a period of time beginning after the point of drug court graduation and failure. Two other studies have similarly detected post-program reductions in recidivism (Bavon 2001; Fielding, Tye, Ogawa, Imam, and Long 2002).

3. The differences in use of residential treatment stem partly also from variations in the addiction severity level of participants, but that factor alone cannot explain the magnitude of the differences. Regarding the tremendous variations in the modalities and quality of services available at treatment programs used by drug courts, see also Anspach et al. 2003.

Chapter Two: Seeing Eye to Eye

1. At one court, a second participant session was conducted to test the replicability of the first session's findings.

2. Staff at the third site preferred no honorarium be offered. Payment was of course discussed with the courts in advance.

3. In a study of six New York State drug courts, the median time from arrest to disposition (i.e., acceptance of guilty plea and entry into drug court) averaged just less than 25 days across courts (Rempel et al 2003).
4. Based on our interviews and observations, this drug court does appear to have a distinctive judging style and view of the judicial role.
5. Case management functions are conducted by probation officers in two of the drug courts. In the third, case management was divided between counselors at treatment facilities (for clinical issues) and case managers employed by the court.
6. Staff at this court were concerned when they learned that focus group participants did not believe their attorneys were important. In response, this court edited its participant orientation protocol to include discussion of the structure and functioning of the drug court team, with a segment focused on how defense attorneys advocate for their clients behind the scenes.
7. Note that participants in this court also complained about having little time to talk to their case managers about, among other things, their experiences in the courtroom.
8. Not surprisingly, criticisms was more muted in the session conducted among participants who had either graduated drug court or were about to do so.
9. In contrast to other topics covered in the focus groups, we did not ask drug court staff for their feedback on the courtroom experience. Tthe responses of participants were recounted to staff, but staff accounts of the drug court experience were not elicited. The rationale behind this decision was that participants' experiences in the courtroom are likely a relatively internal process, which may potentially have consequences on outcomes. However, staff perceptions of the drug court experience were thought to be of less consequence.

Chapter Three: Evaluation of the Staten Island Treatment Court

1. The Staten Island Treatment Court was planned and established through a collaboration of the Richmond County (Staten Island) Criminal Court, the Richmond County District Attorney's Office, Treatment Alternatives for Safe Communities (TASC), the office of the Administrative Judge of the New York City Criminal Court, and the law firm of Battiste, Aronowsky, and Suchow (BAS), which provides indigent defense services on Staten Island.
2. We also investigated whether the presence of non-felony drug charges in the participant but not in the comparison sample could represent a meaningful source of bias. We found that this was not the case. Those arrested on non-felony drug charges within the participant sample were neither more nor less likely to re-offend on any of the outcomes measures presented below than were those arrested on felony drug charges; hence the inclusion of these other charges in the participant sample would have no effect on the reported recidivism rates below.
3. The actual variable entered into the Cox regression procedure was the natural logarithm of the number of prior arrests variable; the logarithm function served to make the prior arrest variable less right-skewed (i.e., give relatively less influence to the few defendants with extremely high numbers of prior arrests).

Chapter Five: Specialized Domestic Violence Courts in New York City

1. The interviews conducted for this study preceded the release of a randomized trial of batterer programs used in the Bronx (see this volume, Chapter Six; and Labriola et al. 2005). The study found that the programs did not reduce re-offending rates, either in general or specifically for domestic violence. Since the study's results were widely publicized among this same group of New

York City stakeholders, it may have led some perceptions to change.

Chapter Seven: Confronting Teen Dating Violence

1. The first judge assigned to the Youth Offender Domestic Violence Court, the Honorable Richard Allman, served for the first six months of operations. The second judge, the Honorable Miriam Cyrulnik, took over in June 2004.
2. Since many of these defendants will be granted status as youthful offenders (YOs), many defendants have their cases not only dismissed, but dismissed and sealed, either in lieu of participating in STEPS or after completing STEPS. For those cases that have been dismissed and sealed (N=96), this supplemental data is not available. Likewise, the criminal history included here represents only criminal incidents that were not dismissed and sealed. Therefore, it may underestimate defendants' prior criminal involvement.
3. Each participant signed an informed consent prior to being interviewed. For defendants who were under 18 years of age, a parental consent form was also required. Participants were offered an honorarium of $20, paid at the end of the interview. All research protocols for this project were approved by the Center for Court Innovation's Institutional Review Board.

Chapter Nine: Defendant Perceptions of Fairness at the Red Hook Community Justice Center

1. The factor measuring how defendants felt they were treated by individual court actors is composed of variables measuring defendants' perceptions of how fairly and respectfully the court officers, judge, defense attorney, and prosecutor treated them.
2. In 2004, black men and women were 4.8 times more likely than others to be incarcerated (Harrison and Beck 2005). Also, a meta-analysis of many studies of sentencing patterns revealed

that after taking into account defendant criminal history and current offense severity, minority defendants were generally sentenced more harshly than white defendants (Mitchell and MacKenzie 2004).

3. A forthcoming multi-site study of drug courts will in fact test whether participants are more likely to perceive that they were treated fairly than similar non-participants. It will also test whether perceptions of fairness influence future criminal behavior, drug use, and other outcomes (see Urban Institute, Research Triangle Institute, and Center for Court Innovation 2003). The final results of this study are not anticipated to be available until 2008.

4. Even when each variable was treated separately, fairness was predicted by the variables used in this study in much the same way; using a factor composed of four variables, however, allowed for an improvement in statistical significance and power.

5. Although the judge's praise, admonishment, and discussions of the future and past were generally spoken directly to the defendant, these statements were also counted when the judge spoke about these matters to the court at large, clearly with the intention of the defendant hearing them and understanding that they were directed towards his or her past or future behavior. This occurred most frequently when the judge in Red Hook would state to the entire court, "That's not good," rather than telling the person in question directly, "You did something bad" (or something to the same effect).

6. When variables related to effective communication (questions about the ability of court actors to answer questions clearly and to listen) are factor analyzed, they cluster separately from those related to treatment (questions about respectful, fair, and helpful treatment). See Appendix 2.

7. Levene tests, which detect significant differences in variance (in a similar way to t-tests' ability to detect differences in means)

were significant when the Red Hook and traditional court samples were separated in a top-two box analysis.

8. The "halo effect," first observed in respondents' ratings of different attributes within individuals in social psychology experiments, has since been applied to ratings of teams, companies, and groups (Nisbett and Wilson 1977). See Rottman (2000) for a discussion of the Supreme Court's halo effect on state courts.

9. This in turn may increase researchers' ability to discriminate what aspects of their treatment are most important for which defendants. For example, one might expect that defendants with low expectations of the courts' fairness at the outset might be particularly inclined to change their opinions if they are treated respectfully, or that defendants with previous negative experiences with the police might have more positive perceptions of court officers who surprised them by being exceptionally fair and communicative.

References

Anglin, M. D., Brecht, M, and Maddahian, E. 1989. "Pre-treatment Characteristics and Treatment Performance of Legally Coerced Versus Voluntary Methadone Maintenance Admissions." *Criminology* 27: (3): 537-556.

Anspach, D. F., Collom, V., and Ferguson, A. 2003. "Assessing the Impact of Functional Components of the Drug Court Model on Post-Program Recidivism." Presented at the Annual Conference of the American Society of Criminology, Denver, CO.

Aos, S., Phipps, P., Barnoski, R., and Lieb, R. 2001. *The Comparative Costs and Benefits of Programs to Reduce Crime Version* 4.0. Olympia: Washington State Institute for Public Policy.

Bavon, A. 2001. "The Effect of the Tarrant County Drug Court Project on Recidivism." *Evaluation and Program Planning* 24: 13-22.

Belenko, S. 1998. "Research on Drug Courts: A Critical Review." *National Drug Court Institute Review* 1: 1-42.

Belenko, S. 2001. *Research on Drug Courts: A Critical Review: 2001 Update.* New York, NY: National Center on Addiction and Substance Abuse at Columbia University.

Belknap, J., Graham, D. L. R., Hartman, J., Lippen, V., Allen, G., and Sutherland, J. 2000. *Factors Related to Domestic Violence Court Dispositions in a Large Urban Area: The Role of Victim/Witness Reluctance and Other Variables.* Washington, D.C.: National Institute of Justice.

Berman, G. 2000. "What is a Traditional Judge Anyway?" *Judicature* 84: 78-85.

Berman, G. and Feinblatt, J. 2001. "Problem-Solving Courts: A Brief Primer." *Law and Policy* 23, 125-140.

Berman, G. and Feinblatt J. 2005. *Good Courts: The Case for Problem-Solving Justice.* New York, NY: The New Press.

Bies, R. J. and Shapiro, D. L. 1988. "Voice and Justification: Their Influence on Procedural Fairness Judgments." *Academy of Management Journal* 31: 676-685.

Brockner, J., Siegel, P. A., Daly, J. P., Tyler, T., and Martin, C. 1997. "When Trust Matters: The Moderating Effect of Outcome Favorability." *Administrative Science Quarterly* 42: 558-583.

Brockner, J., Tyler, T. R., and Cooper-Schneider, R. 1992. "The Influence of Prior Commitment to an Institution on Reactions to Perceived Unfairness: The Higher They Are, the Harder They Fall." *Administrative Science Quarterly* 37: 241-261.

Carey, S. M., Crumpton, D., Finigan, M. W., and Waller, M. 2005. *California Drug Courts: A Methodology for Determining Costs and Benefits: Phase II: Testing the Methodology: Final Report.* Submitted to the Administrative Office of the Courts, Judicial Council of California. Portland, OR: NPC Research.

Cascardi, M., Poythress, N. G., and Hall, A. 2000. "Procedural Justice in the Context of Civil Commitment: An Analogy Study." *Behavioral Sciences and the Law* 18: 731-740.

Casper, J. D., Tyler, T., and Fisher, B. 1988. "Procedural Justice in Felony Cases." *Law & Society Review* 22: 483-507.

Casey, P. M. and Rottman, D.B. 2003. *Problem-Solving Courts: Models and Trends.* Williamsburg, VA: National Center for State Courts.

Casper, J., Tyler, T., and Fisher, B. 1988. "Procedural Justice in Felony Cases." *Law and Society Review* 22: 483-508.

Cissner, A. and Puffett, N. 2006. *Do Batterer Program Length or Approach Affect Completion or Re-Arrest Rates? A Comparison of Outcomes between Defendants Sentenced to Two Batterer Programs in Brooklyn.* New York, NY: Center for Court Innovation.

The City of New York. 1998. Teen Relationship Abuse Fact Sheet.

Commission to Combat Family Violence. 1999. *Blueprint: The Adopt-a-School Initiative: A School-Based Teen Relationship Abuse Prevention Program.* New York, NY.

Condelli, W. S. and DeLeon, G. 1993. "Fixed and Dynamic Predictors of Client Retention in Therapeutic Communities." *Journal of Substance Abuse Treatment* 10(1): 11-16.

Conference of Chief Justices and Conference of State Court Administrators Resolution 22: In Support of Problem Solving Principles and Methods (available at http://cosca.ncsc.dni.us/-WhitePapers/ResolutionNatl%20Agenda-Final-Aug-04.pdf).

Cooper, C. 2002. "The Characteristics of American Drug Court Programs." *Offender Programs Report* 6: 1 (May/June): 1-2, 8-11.

Cosden M., Ellens, J., Schneell J., and Yamini-Diouf Y. 2005. "Efficacy of a Mental Health Treatment Court with Assertive Community Treatment." *Behavioral Sciences and the Law* 23: 199-214.

Council of State Governments, The Consensus Project. 2005. Fact Sheet on Criminal Victimization of People with Mental Illness (retrieved December 10, 2005 from http://consensusproject.org/infocenter/factsheets/fact_crime_victims).

Davis, R. C., Smith, B. E., and Rabbitt, C. R. 2001. "Increasing Convictions in Domestic Violence Cases: A Field Test in Milwaukee." *Justice System Journal* 22: 62-72.

Davis, R. C., Taylor, B. G., and Maxwell, C. M. 2000. *Does Batterer Treatment Reduce Violence: A Randomized Experiment in Brooklyn.*

Final report to the National Institute of Justice. New York, NY: Victim Services (now Safe Horizon).

DeLeon, G. 1988. "Legal Pressure in Therapeutic Communities." *Journal of Drug Issues* 18: 625-640.

Denckla, D. and Berman, G. 2001. *Rethinking the Revolving Door: A Look at Mental Illness in the Courts.* New York, NY: Center for Court Innovation.

Deschenes, E., Turner, S., and Greenwood, P. W. 1995. "Drug Court or Probation? An Experimental Evaluation of Maricopa County's Drug Court." *Justice System Journal* 18: 55-73.

Ditton, P. 1999. *Mental Health Treatment of Inmates and Probationers.* Washington D.C.: U.S. Department of Justice, Office of Justice Programs, Bureau of Justice Statistics.

Dunford, F. W. 2000. "The San Diego Navy Experiment: An Assessment of Interventions for Men who Assault their Wives." *Journal of Consulting and Clinical Psychology* 68 (3): 468-476.

Eckberg, D. 2001. *Hennepin County Community Justice Project: Summary Report of Short-Term Evaluation.* Hennepin County, Minnesota: Hennepin County District Court Research Department.

Eckberg, D. A. and Podkopacz, M. R. 2002. "Domestic Violence Court in Minneapolis: Three Levels of Analysis." Presented at the Annual Conference of the American Society of Criminology, Chicago, IL.

Farole, D. J. and Cissner, A. B. 2005. *Seeing Eye to Eye: Participant and Staff Perspectives on Drug Treatment Courts.* New York, NY: Center for Court Innovation.

Farole, D. J., Puffett, N. K., and Rempel, M. 2005. *Collaborative Justice in Conventional Courts: Stakeholder Perspectives in California.* Phase Two report submitted to the California Administrative Office of the Courts (AOC), Center for Court Innovation and California AOC.

Farole, D. J., Puffett, N. K., Rempel, M., and Byrne, F. 2004. *Collaborative Justice in Conventional Courts: Opportunities and Barriers.* Report submitted to the California Administrative Office of the Courts (AOC), Center for Court Innovation and California AOC.

Farole, D. J., Puffett, N. K., Rempel, M., and Byrne, F. 2005. "Applying Problem-Solving Principles in Mainstream Courts: Lessons for State Courts." *Justice System Journal* 26: 57-75.

Feder, L. R. and Dugan, L. 2002. "A Test of the Efficacy of Court-Mandated Counseling for Domestic Violence Offenders: The Broward County Experiment." *Justice Quarterly* 19(2): 343-375.

Feder, L. and Wilson, D. B. 2005. "A Meta-Analytic Review of Court-Mandated Batterer Intervention Programs: Can Courts Affect Abusers' Behavior?" *Journal of Experimental Criminology* 1: 239-262.

Feeley, M. M. 1992. *The Process is the Punishment.* New York, NY: Russell Sage Foundation.

Feinblatt, J. and Berman, G. 1997. *Responding to the Community: Principles for Planning and Creating a Community Court.* Washington, DC: Bureau of Justice Assistance.

Field, G. 1992. "Oregon Prison Drug Treatment Programs." In *Drug Abuse Treatment in Prisons and Jails,* eds. C.G. Leukefeld and F.M. Tims. Rockville, MD: National Institute on Drug Abuse.

Fielding, J. E., Tye, G., Ogawa, P., Imam, I. J., and Long, A. M. 2002. "Los Angeles County Drug Court Programs: Initial Results." *Journal of Substance Abuse Treatment* 23: 217-224.

Fisler, C. 2005. "Building Trust and Managing Risk: A Look at a Felony Mental Health Court." *Psychology, Public Policy, and Law* 11(4): 587-604.

Fox, A. 2004. *Bridging the Gap: Researchers, Practitioners, and the Future of Drug Courts.* New York, NY: Center for Court Innovation.

Fox, A. and Wolf, R. V. 2004. *The Future of Drug Courts: How States are Mainstreaming the Drug Court Model.* New York, NY: Center for Court Innovation.

Frazer, M. S. 2005. *Op Data, 2004: Red Hook, Brooklyn.* New York, NY: Center for Court Innovation.

Gardner, W., Hoge, S. K., Bennett, N. S., Roth, L. H., Lidz, C. W., and Monahan, J. 1993. "Two Scales for Measuring Patients' Perceptions of Coercion During Mental Hospital Admission." *Behavioral Science and the Law* 11: 307-21.

Garland., D. 2001. *The Culture of Control.* Chicago, IL: University of Chicago Press.

Gary Bess Associates. 2004. Butte County Forensic Resource Team (FOREST) Mentally Ill Offender Crime Reduction (MICOR) Grant Program (Retrieved July 20, 2006 from http://www.garybess.com/samples/Applied_Research_2.pdf).

Gavin, C. and Puffett, N. K. 2005. *Criminal Domestic Violence Case Processing: A Case Study of the Five Boroughs of New York City*. Final research report submitted to the New York State Division of Criminal Justice Services and the Office on Violence Against Women of the U.S. Department of Justice. New York, NY: Center for Court Innovation.

Goldkamp, J. 2003. "The Impact of Drug Courts." *Criminology and Public Policy* 2: 2: 197-206.

Goldkamp, J. and Irons-Guynn, S. 2000. *Judicial Strategies for the Mentally Ill in the Criminal Caseload: Mental Health Courts in Fort Lauderdale, Seattle, San Bernardino, and Anchorage*. Washington, D.C.: U.S. Department of Justice, Office of Justice Programs, Drug Courts Program Office.

Goldkamp, J. S., Weiland, D., Collins, M., and White, M. 1996. *The Role of Drug and Alcohol Abuse in Domestic Violence and its Treatment: Dade County's Domestic Violence Court Experiment*. Final Report. Philadelphia, PA: Crime and Justice Research Institute.

Goldkamp, J., Weiland, D., and Irons-Guynn, C. 2000. *Developing an Evaluation Plan for Community Courts: Assessing the Hartford Community Court Model*. Philadelphia, PA: Crime and Justice Research Institute.

Goldkamp, J. S., White, M. D., and Robinson, J. D. 2001. *From Whether to How Drug Courts Work: Retrospective Evaluation of Drug Courts in Clark County (Las Vegas) and Multnomah County (Portland)*. Final Project Report. Philadelphia, PA: Crime and Justice Research Institute.

Goldkamp, J., White, M. D., and Robinson, J. B. 2002. *An Honest Chance Perspective on Drug Courts: Findings from Drug Court Participant Focus Groups in Brooklyn, Las Vegas, Miami, Portland, San Bernadino, and Seattle.* Philadelphia, PA: Crime and Justice Research Institute.

Gottfredson, D., Najaka, S. S., and Kearley, B. 2003. "Effectiveness of Drug Treatment Courts: Evidence from a Randomized Trial." *Criminology and Public Policy* 2 (2): 171-196.

Gottfredson, D. C., Kearley, B., Najaka, S. S., and Rocha, C. 2003. *Baltimore City Drug Treatment Court: Evaluation of Client Self-Reports at Three-Year Follow-Up*. Baltimore, MD: University of Maryland.

Gover, A. R., MacDonald, J. M., and Alpert, G. P. 2003. "Combating Domestic Violence: Findings from an Evaluation of a Local Domestic Violence Court." *Criminology and Public Policy* 3 (1): 109-132.

Government Accountability Office. 2005. *Adult Drug Courts: Evidence Indicates Recidivism Reductions and Mixed Results for Other Outcomes*. GAO-05-219, February.

Griffin, P. A., Steadman, H. J., and Petrila, J. 2002. "The Use of Criminal Charges and Sanctions in Mental Health Courts." *Psychiatric Services* 53: 1285-1289.

Hakuta, J. 2006. Impact of the Midtown Community Court on Case Processing and Case Outcomes. Unpublished memo.

Harrell, A. 2003. "Judging Drug Courts: Balancing the Evidence." *Criminology and Public Policy* 2: 2: 207-212.

Harrell, A., Cavanagh, S., and Roman, J. 1998. *Findings from the Evaluation of the D.C. Superior Court Drug Intervention Program.* The Urban Institute. Washington, D.C.

Harrell, A., Roman, J., Mitchell, O., and Marlowe, D. 2000. "The Use and Impact of Sanctions in Drug Intervention Programs for Offenders." Paper presented at the Annual Meetings of the American Society of Criminology, San Francisco, CA, November.

Harrell, A., Roman, J., and Sack, E. 2001. *Drug Court Services for Female Offenders,* 1996-1999: Evaluation of the Brooklyn Treatment Court. Washington, D.C.: The Urban Institute.

Harrell, A., Schaffer, M., DeStefano, C., and Castro, C. 2006. *The Evaluation of Milwaukee's Judicial Oversight Demonstration.* Washington, D.C.: The Urban Institute.

Healey, K., Smith, C., and O'Sullivan, C. 1998. *Batterer Intervention: Program Approaches and Criminal Justice Strategies.* Washington, D.C.: United States Department of Justice.

Henning, K. and Klesges, L. M. 1999. *Evaluation of the Shelby County Domestic Violence Court.* Final report. Shelby County, TN.

Herinckx, H., Swart S. C., Ama S. M., Dolezal C. D., and King, S. 2005. "Rearrest and Linkage to Mental health Services Among

Clients of the Clark County Mental Health Program. *Psychiatric Services* 56(7): 853-857.

Hickman, L., Jaycox, L., and Aronoff, J. 2004. "Dating Violence Among Adolescents: Prevalence, Gender Distribution, and Prevention Program Effectiveness." *Trauma, Violence, and Abuse* 5(2), 123-142.

Hiller, M., Knight, K., and Simpson, D. D. 1998. "Legal Pressure and Treatment Retention in a National Sample of Long-Term Residential Programs." *Criminal Justice and Behavior* 25: 463-481.

Hotaling, G. T. and Buzawa, E. S. 2003. *Victim Satisfaction with Criminal Justice Case Processing in a Model Court Setting.* Washington, D.C.: National Institute of Justice.

Hough, M. and Park, A. 2002. "How Malleable are Public Attitudes to Crime and Punishment?" in Roberts, J. and Hough, M. (eds) *Changing Attitudes to Punishment: Public Opinion around the Globe.* Cullompton, England: Willan Publishing.

The Justice Education Center. 2002. *Evaluation of the Hartford Community Court.* West Hartford, CT: The Justice Education Center, Inc.

Kearley, B. W. and Gottfredson, D. C. 2003. "Predicting Success in the Baltimore City Drug Treatment Court: The Influence of Personal Characteristics and Suspended Sentence Length." Presented at the Annual Conference of the American Society of Criminology, Denver, CO.

Keilitz, S. L. 2000. *Specialized Domestic Violence Case Management in the Courts: A National Survey.* Williamsburg, VA: National Center for State Courts.

Kleiman, M. A. R. 2001. "Controlling Drug Use and Crime with Testing, Sanctions, and Treatment." In *Drug Addiction and Drug Policy: The Struggle to Control Dependence,* eds. P. Heymann and W. Brownsberger. Cambridge, MA: Harvard University Press.

Korsgaard, A. and Roberson, L. 1995. "Procedural Justice in Performance Evaluation: The Role of Instrumental and Non-Instrumental Voice in Performance Appraisal Discussions." *Journal of Management* 21: 657-669.

Kralstein, D. 2005. *Community Court Research: A Literature Review.* New York, NY: Center for Court Innovation.

Labriola, M., Rempel, M., and Davis, R. C. 2005. *Testing the Effectiveness of Batterer Programs and Pudicial monitoring: Results from a Randomized trial at the Bronx Misdemeanor Domestic Violence Court.* Final report submitted to the National Institute of Justice. New York, NY: Center for Court Innovation.

Leigh, G., Ogborne, A. C., and Cleland, P. 1984. "Factors Associated with Patient Dropout from an Outpatient Alcoholism Treatment Service." *Journal of Studies on Alcohol* 45 (4): 359-362.

Lewis, B. F. and Ross, R. 1994. "Retention in Therapeutic Communities: Challenges for the Nineties." In F. M. Tims, G. DeLeon, and N Jainchill (Eds.), *Therapeutic Community: Advances in Research and Application.* Rockville, MD: National Institute of Drug Abuse.

Lind, A. E., Kulik, C. T., Ambrose, M., and de Vera Park, M. V. 1993. "Individual and Corporate Dispute Resolution: Using Procedural Justice as a Decision Heuristic." *Administrative Science Quarterly* 38: 224-251.

Lind, A. E., Kurtz, S., Musante, S. L., Walker, L., and Thibaut, J. 1980. "Procedural and Outcome Effects on Reactions to Adjudicated Resolution of Conflicts of Interest." *Journal of Personality and Social Psychology* 39: 643-653.

Longshore, D., Ettner, S., Evans, E., Hardy, M., Hser, Y. I., Prendergast, M., Teruya, C., and Urada, D. 2003. *Evaluation of the Substance Abuse and Crime Prevention Act of 2002 Report: Implementation: July 1, 2001 to June 30, 2002.* Report prepared for the Department of Alcohol and Drug Programs California Health and Human Services Agency, Los Angeles, CA: UCLA.

Maddux, J. F. 1983. "Improving Retention on Methadone Maintenance." In J. Inciardi, F. Tims, and B. Fletcher (Eds.), *Innovative Approaches in the Treatment of XQ Abuse: Program Models and Strategies.* Westport, CT: Greenwood Press. Pp. 21-33.

Malkin, V. 2003. "Community Courts and the Process of Accountability: Consensus and Conflict at the Red Hook Community Justice Center." *American Criminal Law Review* 40: (4).

Malkin, V. 2005. "The End of Welfare As We Know It: What Happens When the Judge is in Charge." *Critique of Anthropology* 25: 361-388.

Marlowe, D. 2003. "A Sober Assessment of Drug Courts." *Federal Sentencing Reporter* 16: 1-3.

Marlowe, D. 2004. "Cutting Edge Drug Court Research." Presented at the Annual Meetings of the New England Association of Drug Court Treatment Professionals, Boston, MA.

Marlowe, D. B., Festinger, D. S., and Lee, P. A. 2004. "The Judge is a Key Component of Drug Court." *National Drug Court Institute Review* IV (2): 1-34.

Mastrofski, S. D., Snipes, J. B., and Supina, A. E. 1996. "Compliance on Demand: The Public's Response to Specific Police Requests." *Journal of Research in Crime and Delinquency* 33: 269-305.

Mazur, R. and Aldrich, L. 2003. *What Makes a Domestic Violence Court Work? Lessons from New York.* New York, NY: Center for Court Innovation.

McCoy, C. 2003. "The Politics of Problem-Solving: An Overview of the Origins and Development of Therapeutic Courts." *American Criminal Law Review* 40 (4): 1513-1544.

The Mental Health Court Survey (Retrieved January 10, 2006 from http://www.mentalhealthcourtsurvey.com).

Miethe, T. D., Lu, H., and Reese, E. 2000. "Reintegrative Shaming and Recidivism Risks in Drug Court: Explanations for Some Unexpected Findings." *Crime and Delinquency* 46: (4): 522-541.

Moore, K. 2004. *Op Data, 2001: Red Hook, Brooklyn.* New York, NY: Center for Court Innovation.

Mueller, C. and M. Landsman. 2004. "Legitimacy and Justice Perceptions." *Social Psychology Quarterly* 67: 189-202.

Newmark, L., Rempel, M., Diffily, K. and Kane, K.M. 2001. *Specialized Felony Domestic Violence Courts: Lessons on Implementation and Impact from the Kings County Experience.* Washington, D.C.: Urban Institute.

Nisbett, R. E. and Wilson, T. D. 1977. "The Halo Effect: Evidence for the Unconscious Alteration of Judgments." *Journal of Personality and Social Psychology* 35: 450-456.

Nolan, J. L. 2001. *Reinventing Justice: The American Drug Court Movement.* Princeton, NJ: Princeton University Press.

Northeastern University's Center for the Study of Sport in Society. 2001. 2000-2001 MVP Evaluation Report. (Retrieved on July 10, 2006 from http://www.northeastern.edu/csss/mvp /mvp-evaluation2.htm).

O'Keefe, K. 2003. *The Staten Island Treatment Court Preliminary Evaluation.* Report submitted to the Staten Island Treatment Court and the New York State Unified Court System. New York, NY: Center for Court Innovation.

Paternoster, R., Brame, R., Bachman, R., and Sherman, L. 1997. "Do Fair Procedures Matter? The Effect of Procedural Justice on Spouse Assault." *Law and Society Review* 31: 163-204.

Peters, R., Haas, A., and Murrin, M. 1999. "Predictors of Retention and Arrest in Drug Courts." *National Drug Court Institute Review* 2: 33-60.

Peters, R. and Murrin, M. 1998. *Evaluation of Treatment-Based Drug Courts in Florida's First Judicial Circuit.* Tampa, FL: Department of Mental Health Law and Policy, Louis de la Parte Florida Mental Health Institute, University of South Florida.

Peterson, R. R. 2002. *Cross-Borough Differences in the Processing of Domestic Violence Cases in New York City Criminal Courts.* New York, NY: New York City Criminal Justice Agency.

Podkopacz, M. R., D.A. Eckberg and Zehm, K. 2004. *Drug Court Defendant Experience and Fairness Study.* Minneapolis, MN: unpublished manuscript. Fourth Judicial District Court of Minnesota.

Porter, R. 2000. *Implementing a Drug Court in Queens County: A Process Evaluation.* New York, NY: Vera Institute of Justice.

Porter, R. 2001. *Treatment Alternatives in the Criminal Court: A Process Evaluation of the Bronx County Drug Court.* New York, NY: Vera Institute of Justice.

Poythress, N. G., Petrila, J., McGaha, A., and Boothroyd, R. 2002. "Perceived Coercion and Procedural Justice in the Broward Mental Health Court." *International Journal of Law and Psychiatry* 25: 517-533.

Price, K., Lavelle, J., Henley, A.H., Cocchiara, F.K., and Buchanan, R. 2004. "The Effects of Voice-Based Participation Across Multiple and Interrelated Stages of Decision-Making." *Academy of Management Proceedings.* 2004: 1-6.

Pruitt, D.G., Peirce, R.S., McGillicuddy, N.B., Welton, G.L., and Castrianno, L.M. 1993. "Long-Term Success in Mediation." *Law and Human Behavior* 17: 313-330.

Puffett, N. K. and Gavin, C. 2004. *Program Outcome and Recidivism at the Bronx Misdemeanor Domestic Violence Court.* New York, NY: Center for Court Innovation.

Rain, S. D., Williams, V. F., Clark Robbins., P., Monahan, J., Steadman, H. J., and Vesselinov, R. 2003. "Perceived Coercion at Hospital Admission and Adherence to Mental Health Treatment After Discharge." *Psychiatric Services* 54 (1): 103-105.

Redlich, A.D., Steadman, H. J., Monahan, J., Petrila, J., and Griffin, P.A. 2005. "The Second Generation of Mental Health Courts." *Psychology, Public Policy, and Law* 11 (4) 527-538.

Rempel, M. 2002. *Five Years of the Brooklyn Treatment Court: Final Research Report on Participants Entering June 1996-September 2001.* Report submitted to Center for Substance Abuse Treatment. New York, NY: Center for Court Innovation.

Rempel, M. and DeStefano, C. 2001. "Predictors of Engagement in Court-Mandated Treatment: Findings at the Brooklyn Treatment Court, 1996-2000." *Journal of Offender Rehabilitation* 33: 87-124.

Rempel, M., Kralstein, D., Cissner, A., Cohen, R., Labriola, M., Farole, D., Bader, A., and Magnani, M. 2003. *The New York State Adult Drug Court Evaluation: Policies, Participants, and Impacts.* Report submitted to the New York State Unified Court System and the Bureau of Justice Assistance. New York, NY: Center for Court Innovation.

Rempel, M. 2006. "Recidivism 101: Evaluating the Impact of Your Drug Court." *National Drug Court Institute Review* V (2): 83-112.

Rennison, C. M. 2001. *Intimate Partner Violence and Age of Victim, 1993-99*. U. S. Department of Justice, Office of Justice Programs, Bureau of Justice Statistics, Special Report.

Roman, J. and DeStefano, C. 2004. "Drug Court Effects and the Quality of Existing Evidence." In J. Butts and J. Roman (Eds.), *Juvenile Drug Courts and Teen Substance Abuse*. Washington, D.C.: Urban Institute Press.

Rottman, D. 2000. "Public Perception of State Courts: A Primer." Paper presented at the Third National Symposium on Court Management. (Retrived April 25, 2006 from http://www.ncsconline.org/WC/Publications/Res_AmtPTC_PublicPerceptions_PrimerPub.pdf).

Rottman, D., Hansen, R., Mott, N., and Grimes, L. 2003. *Perceptions of the Courts in Your Community: The Influence of Experience, Race and Ethnicity*. Williamsburg, VA: National Center for State Courts.

Royal College of Psychiatrists' Research Unit, Health of the Nation Outcomes Scale (Retrieved January 10, 2002 from http://www.rcpsych.ac.uk/cru/honoscales/index.htm).

Rubin, D. B. 1973. "Matching to Remove Bias in Observational Studies." *Biometrics* 29: 159-183.

Sack, E. 2002. *Creating a Domestic Violence Court: Guidelines and Best Practices.* San Francisco, CA: Family Violence Prevention Fund.

Sagatun-Edwards, I., Hyman, E. M., LaFontaine, T., and Nelson-Serrano, E. 2003. "The Santa Clara County Juvenile Domestic and Family Violence Court." *Journal of the Center for Families, Children, and the Courts* 4: 91-114.

San Diego Superior Court. 2000. *Evaluation Report for the San Diego County Domestic Violence Courts.* San Diego, CA: San Diego Superior Court.

Schafer, C. and Zweig, J. 2004. "National Portrait of Adult Drug Courts: Findings from the 2004 Drug Court Survey." Paper presented at the Annual Conference of the American Society of Criminology, Denver, CO.

Schaubroeck, J., May, D. R., and Brown, F. W. 1994. "Procedural Justice Explanations and Employee Reactions to Economic Hardship: A Field Experiment." *Journal of Applied Psychology* 79 (3): 455-460.

Sherman, L. W. 2001. *Trust and Confidence in Criminal Justice.* Philadelphia, PA: Fels Center of Government.

Smith, A. 2001. "Domestic Violence Laws: The Voices of Battered Women." *Violence and Victims* 16 (1): 91.

Steadman, H. J., Davidson, S., and Brown, C. 2001. "Mental Health Courts: Their Promise and Unanswered Questions." *Psychiatric Services* 52: 457-458.

Steketee, M. W., Levey, L. S. and Keilitz, S. 2000. *Implementing an Integrated Domestic Violence Court: Systemic Change in the District of Columbia*. Williamsburg, VA: National Center for State Courts.

Sunshine, J. and Tyler, T. R. 2003. "The Role of Procedural Justice and Legitimacy in Shaping Public Support for Policing." *Law & Society Review* 37: 513-547.

Sviridoff, M., Rottman, D., Ostrom, B., and Curtis, R. 2000. *Dispensing Justice Locally: The Implementation and Effects of the Midtown Community Court*. Amsterdam: Harwood Academic Publishers.

Sviridoff, M., Rottman, D., and Weidner, R. 2002. *Dispensing Justice Locally (Part II): The Impacts, Cost and Benefits of the Midtown Community Court*. New York, NY: Center for Court Innovation.

Sydeman, S. J., Cascardi, M., Poythress, N. G., and Rittenband, L. M. 1997. "Procedural Justice in The Context Of Civil Commitment: A Critique of Tyler's Analysis." *Psychology, Public Policy, & Law* 3: 207-221.

Taxman, F. 1999. "Unraveling 'What Works' for Offenders in Substance Abuse Treatment Services." *National Drug Court Institute Review* 2: 93-134.

Thibault, J. W. and Walker, L. 1975. *Procedural Justice: A Psychological Perspective*. Hillsdale, NJ: Lawrence Erlbaum.

Tyler, T. 1990. *Why People Obey the Law*. New Haven, CT: Yale University Press.

Tyler, T. 1997. "The Psychology of Legitimacy: A Relational Perspective on Voluntary Deference to Authorities." *Personality and Social Psychology Review* 1: 323-345.

Tyler, T. R. 1997. "Citizen Discontent with Legal Procedures: A Social Science Perspective on Civil Procedure Reform." *American Journal of Comparative Law* 45: 871-904.

Tyler, T. R. and Huo, Y. J. 2002. *Trust in the Law*. New York, NY: Russell Sage Foundation.

Tyler, T. R. and Wakslak, C. J. 2004. "Profiling and Police Legitimacy: Procedural Justice, Attributions of Motive, and Acceptance of Police Authority." *Criminology* 42: 253-279.

Ursel, J. E. and Brickey, S. 1996. "The Potential of Legal Reform Reconsidered: An Examination of Manitoba's Zero-Tolerance Policy on Family Violence." In T. O'Reilly-Fleming (Ed.), *Post-Critical Criminology*, p. 56-77. Scarborough, Ontario: Prentice-Hall.

U.S. Census Bureau. 2000. "American Fact Finder." Washington, D.C.: U.S. Census Bureau (http://factfinder.census.gov/servlet /BasicFactsServlet).

Van Stelle, K., Mauser, E., and Moberg, D. 1994. "Recidivism to the Criminal Justice System of Substance-Abusing Offenders Diverted into Treatment." *Crime and Delinquency* 40: 175-196.

Weber, J. 2000. "Domestic Violence Courts: Components and Considerations." *Journal of the Center for Families, Children & the Courts* 2: 23.

Weidner, R. and Davis, C. 2000. *Benefits and Costs of the Hennepin County Community Court—A Preliminary Analysis*. Minneapolis, MN: Institute on Criminal Justice, University of Minnesota Law School.

Wexler, D. B. and Winick, B. J. (Eds.) 1996. *Law in a Therapeutic Key*. Durham, N.C.: Carolina Academic Press.

Wexler, H., Falkin, G., Lipton, D., and Rosenblum, A. 1992. "Outcome Evaluation of a Prison Therapeutic Community for Substance Abuse Treatment." In C. Leukefeld and F. Tims (Eds.), *Drug Abuse Treatment in Prisons and Jails*. Rockville, MD: National Institute on Drug Abuse.

Wilson, D., Mitchell, O., and MacKenzie, D. L. 2002. "A Systematic Review of Drug Court Effects on Recidivism." Paper presented at the Annual Meetings of the American Society of Criminology, Chicago, IL.

Wolf, R. V., Aldrich, L., and Moore, S. 2004. *Planning a Domestic Violence Court: The New York State Experience*. New York, NY: Center for Court Innovation.

Wolfe, D. A., Scott, K., Wekerle, C., and Pittman, A. L. 2001. "Child Maltreatment: Risk of Adjustment Problems and Dating Violence in Adolescence." *Journal of the American Academy of Child and Adolescent Psychiatry* 40 (3): 282-289.

Young, D. and Belenko, S. 2002. "Program Retention and Perceived Coercion in Three Models of Mandatory Drug Treatment." *Journal of Drug Issues* 32 (1): 297-328.